Human Rights and Foreign Aid

By trying to alleviate poverty abroad, foreign development assistance tries to meet, among other things, basic human needs, which some schools of thought classify as basic human rights. However, because development abroad has often been treated as a tool for the pursuit of donor interests, rather than as an end in itself, it often ends up not only neglecting basic human rights, but making the situation worse.

Bethany Barratt develops this argument by presenting a systematic external examination of the internal documentation of aid rationale in three major donor countries (Britain, Canada and Australia). The book sets the discussion of these documents in the context of the foreign policy process and structure of each donor, and contrasts it with the results of statistical analyses of key factors in aid. It shows that different criteria are applied to the various categories of recipient states, resulting in an inconsistent treatment of recipient rights as an aid criterion.

While the book demonstrates important gulfs between rhetoric and reality, between elected policy-makers and aid-implementing agencies, and between the donors themselves, it comes to relatively optimistic conclusions about the general direction of foreign assistance and its increasingly pure focus on poverty alleviation.

This substantive and important book will be invaluable to students, researchers and policy-makers in the fields of politics, economics and development.

Bethany Barratt is an Assistant Professor of Political Science at Roosevelt University, Chicago, Illinois.

Routledge research in human rights

Human Rights and Foreign Aid

For love or money?

Bethany Barratt

 Routledge
Taylor & Francis Group

LONDON AND NEW YORK

First published 2008
by Routledge
2 Park Square, Milton Park, Abingdon, Oxon OX14 4RN

Simultaneously published in the USA and Canada
by Routledge
270 Madison Ave, New York, NY 10016

Routledge is an imprint of the Taylor & Francis Group, an informa business

© 2008 Bethany Barratt

Typeset in Times by Wearset Ltd, Boldon, Tyne and Wear
Printed and bound in Great Britain by TJI Digital, Padstow, Cornwall

British Library Cataloguing in Publication Data
A catalogue record for this book is available from the British Library

Library of Congress Cataloging in Publication Data
A catalog record for this book has been requested

ISBN10: 0-415-77125-0 (hbk)
ISBN10: 0-203-93616-7 (ebk)

ISBN13: 978-0-415-77125-2 (hbk)
ISBN13: 978-0-203-93616-0 (ebk)

For Christian, my parents and my friends in development assistance

And in memory of Steven C. Poe

Contents

Acknowledgments

In the course of writing this book I have learned a lot about generosity. This book would not exist without the kindness and talent of countless people.

First, Heidi Bagtazo, Harriet Brinton and Amelia McLaurin at Routledge have been boundlessly supportive and patient.

My colleagues have been extremely generous with their time and expertise. My dissertation chair, Scott Gartner, who has done excellent work primarily in the field of conflict studies and the domestic determinants of international behavior, spent hours listening and thinking about issues of development and human rights during the course of my graduate work at the University of California, Davis. My work is incalculably the better for the close and critical reading of various components by David Black, Sabine Carey, Mark Gibney, Joanne Gowa, Rhoda Howard-Hassmann, Pat James, Leslie Johns, Brian Lai, Carol Lancaster, Todd Landman, David Morrison, Marc O'Reilly, Steve Poe, Richard Taylor, Jenifer Whitten-Woodring, and four anonymous reviewers for Routledge. Invaluable data assistance was provided by Doug Bond and Joe Bond of the PONSACS project.

Earlier versions of this work were presented at meetings of several professional associations, including the Journeys in World Politics Workshop at the University of Iowa, the American Political Science Association, the International Studies Association and the Midwest Political Science Association. Numerous discussants and audience members there afforded invaluable insights.

Excellent research assistance was provided by Wendy Bohan and Ron Friedman. My friend Therese Boling supplied similarly superlative research assistance at several stages, along with unflagging support and enthusiasm.

Tireless staff at DfID, CIDA and AusAID have been extremely generous toward a nosy and persistent researcher. Many have given boundlessly of their time, effort, good humor and tour-guiding skills. Richard Ball and Alex Carrasco, as well as the entire information management section of the Asia branch at CIDA, were very generous with their time and their scanners. Steve Taylor at AusAID went from being my email sparring partner to being my friend and fellow kangaroo-seeker in Canberra. Richard Sharp at DfID had the dubious distinction of being the first person at any of the agencies to answer my repeated requests for access to information. Without my friends David Barker and

Richard Taylor at DfID, my archival research would have been much more difficult, and infinitely less fun.

NGO staff have been tireless in answering questions and reaffirming the importance of this work, chief among them Andre Frankovitz at HRCA and Tim O'Connor at Aidwatch.

Despite the best efforts of these and many other fine people, the work which follows retains a host of imperfections, the responsibility for which is entirely my own.

My undergraduate advisor at Duke, Ole Holsti, has not read this work but has been an invaluable mentor in my career and my life for the past 15 years.

Final and most important thanks go to my colleague and ever-patient partner, Christian Erickson.

As this book was in production, one of the founders of quantitative human rights scholarship passed away suddenly. Steve Poe was not only at the forefront of research in the field, but was among the kindest and most intellectually generous colleagues I have ever met. He has left a great hole in our community, and is sorely missed.

Abbreviations and acronyms

ADAA	Australian Development Assistance Agency
ADAB	Australian Development Assistance Bureau
AI	Amnesty International
AIDAB	Australian International Development Assistance Bureau
AIPAC	American Israel Public Affairs Committee
ALP	Australian Labour Party
ANZUS	Australia New Zealand United States (mutual defence treaty)
ASEAN	Association of South East Asian Nations
ASSIST	Assistance to Support Stability with In-Service Training
ATP	Aid and Trade Provision
AusAID	Australian Agency for International Development
BTI	British Trade International
CAP	Country Assistance Plan
CAT	Convention Against Torture
CDPF	Country Development Programming Framework
CIA	Central Intelligence Agency
CIDA	Canadian International Development Agency
CIDA-INC	Canadian International Development Agency Industrial Cooperation Programme
CIRI	Cingranelli and Richards Human Rights Index
CIS	Commonwealth of Independent States
CSCE	Commission for Security and Cooperation in Europe
CSP	Country Strategy Paper
DAC	Development Assistance Committee
DCP	Development Cooperation Paper
DCS	Development Cooperation Strategy
DFAIT	Department of Foreign Affairs and International Trade
DFAT	Department of Foreign Affairs and Trade
DfID	Department for International Development
DIFF	Development Import Finance Facility
DoD	Department of Development
DPRK	Democratic People's Republic of Korea
DTI	Department of Trade and Industry

EAO	External Aid Office
ECHR	European Convention on Human Rights
EDC	Economically Developed Country
EPA	Economic Planning Agency
EU	European Union
FAC	Foreign Affairs Committee
FCO	Foreign and Commonwealth Office
FOI	Freedom of Information
FTAA	Free Trade Area of the Americas
GDP	Gross Domestic Product
GG	good governance
GIC	Good International Citizenship
GNI	Gross National Income
GOF	Global Opportunities Fund
HIPC	Heavily Indebted Poor Countries
HR	human rights
HRCA	Human Rights Council of Australia
HRDGG	Human Rights, Democracy and Good Governance
HRPF	Human Rights Project Fund
HRW	Human Rights Watch
ICC	International Criminal Court
ICCPR	International Covenant on Civil and Political Rights
ICESCR	International Covenant on Economic, Social and Cultural Rights
ICPSR	Interuniversity Consortium on Political and Social Research
IDA	International Development Act
IDEA	Integrated Data for Events Analysis
IGO	intergovernmental organization
ILO	International Labour Organization
JIBC	Japanese International Bank for Cooperation
JICA	Japanese International Cooperation Agency
KEDS	Kansas Events Data Set
LDC	Less Developed Country
LLDC	Least Developed Country
MCF	Millennium Challenge Fund
MDG	Millennium Development Goals
MFN	Most Favored Nation
MNC	multinational corporation
MoF	Ministry of Finance
MoFA	Ministry of Foreign Affairs
NAA	National Archives of Australia
NAFTA	North American Free Trade Agreement
NAP	National Action Plan
NATO	North Atlantic Treaty Organization
NIEO	New International Economic Order
NGI	non-governmental institution

NGO	non-governmental organization
NIC	Newly Industrialized Country
NORAD	Norwegian Agency for Development Cooperation
ODA	Overseas Development Assistance
ODM	Overseas Development Ministry
OECD	Organization for Economic Cooperation and Development
OECF	Overseas Economic Cooperation Fund
OOF	Other Official Flows
PANDA	Protocol for the Assessment of Nonviolent Direct Action
PM	Prime Minister
PNG	Papua New Guinea
PONSACS	Program on Nonviolent Sanctions and Cultural Survival
PPC	Percent Predicted Correctly
PRE	Proportional Reduction in Error
PUS	Permanent Undersecretary of State
SAP	Structural Adjustment Programme
SCFAIT	Standing Committee on Foreign Affairs and International Trade
SJCRCFP	Special Joint Committee Reviewing Canadian Foreign Policy
SSEA	Secretary of State for External Affairs (Canada)
UAE	United Arab Emirates
UDHR	Universal Declaration of Human Rights
UK	United Kingdom
UN	United Nations
US	United States
USAID	United States Agency for International Development
VN	Vietnam
WP	White Paper

1 Introduction

The 'rights way'[1] in foreign policy?

This book is fundamentally about justice and hope. It sprang from the conviction that, if more people knew what was really going on in foreign policy-making, and how the policies of democratic states can sometimes actually lead to bad practices elsewhere, they would demand better behavior from their governments. I had read the powerful arguments made by Chomsky and Hermann (1978) about the 'Washington connection' and human rights abuse abroad, and they rang true to me, but I wanted evidence. So, clearly, did others. The last three decades have seen increasingly sophisticated empirical work in the policy community and the academic literature addressing the question of how and when rights matter to policy-makers. Increasingly these investigators are asking a harder question: 'when do they *really* matter?' These have built on earlier rich descriptive work on the stances of policy-makers[2] and used the increasingly nuanced quantitative data on foreign policy outcomes to determine how much states' foreign policy-makers really support – in measurable ways – what their formal and informal policy statements *say* they support. Through the growing pastiche of nuanced case studies and statistical analyses, we are beginning to triangulate on real answers to these questions about the ethical meanings of foreign relations – perhaps the most important questions in international politics.

One of the things this pastiche has revealed is how very often the record looks quite different in the aggregate than it does in the particular. This is especially the case because we are most likely to hear about the most dramatic cases of rights abuses and how other states have – or so often have not – responded to them. These differences made me wonder: was it perhaps not that there was not a 'real' commitment to human rights in democracies' foreign policies, but rather that this commitment existed in the presence of other 'real' foreign policy goals? Was there perhaps a specific subset of cases that we could identify where issues of rights were more likely to be taken into account? The normative punch line, of course, was that, if this was the case, finding that subset of cases where human rights mattered should tell us what would have to happen to make human rights matter all the time.

I was interested in wealthy, relatively powerful states, because it is these states that can effect positive change in the international system. And I was interested in democracies because they are the ones who we might most expect to have the will to effect such changes.

Given the current historical moment, I want to be very clear about what I mean by effecting positive change. I try very hard in the pages that follow not to make claims about the moral superiority of particular regime types. By positive political change I do not mean unilateral interventions aimed at changing specific political arrangements that have been established through a truly participatory process of consensus. By positive change I mean making the poorest people less poor and more empowered, making people who cannot express themselves free to do so, and making governments that would abuse the people to whom they are responsible unable to do so.

So why expect leaders of states with regimes that can broadly be defined as democratic to be more likely to have the political will to act for positive change? Instances of course abound in which leaders of democratic states act in ways that allow or compel behavior that clearly violates fundamental human rights. One of the most dramatic examples would be the slowness of Franklin Roosevelt, Winston Churchill and others to react to the Holocaust, but leaders every day choose not to take stronger action against violator regimes like Burma, China and Sudan. As the Irish politician and philosopher Edmunde Burke said, 'the only thing necessary for the triumph of evil is that good men do nothing'.

However, leaders in democracies do as a whole protect human rights domestically better than do leaders of nondemocratic states. Because of this protection, and because of the laws compelling it and the philosophical commitments underpinning these laws, most members of the public in democracies support at least a minimal role for human rights in foreign policy. They believe that *in extremis* it is appropriate to deploy foreign policy tools to intervene in the cause of human rights in another state. Sovereignty no longer serves as a fig leaf for gross human rights violations, especially those such as personal integrity, the violation of which has no widely accepted logical or moral defense in any cultural tradition. This general consensus has led all advanced democracies to ratify at least some of the manifold UN human rights treaties and covenants, and more importantly (*de facto*, though not *de jure*) to the passage of domestic laws that ensure at least a minimal basic respect for human rights in foreign policy decisions.

I became interested in looking beyond United States foreign policy because a wealth of evidence was accumulating on these very questions from a number of excellent studies done in the US setting. Yet the US is an outlier in so many ways that it becomes dangerous to generalize from these studies. So I decided to turn to other donor states that were like the US in some ways, but much more like each other, and much more typical of the overall donor community. The result is a nested research design that begins with cross-donor, aggregate statistical analyses of different kinds of aid decisions. The heart of the book is the focused donor-special case chapters, which wed statistical analysis to new archival research in a way that offers a novel approach to the study of foreign aid.

In the course of this research, I have spent hundreds of hours in the official development assistance agencies of the UK, Canadian and Australian governments. Through the generosity of these agencies I have had access to much internal documentation that is here being systematically shared with an academic audience for the first time. And I have become convinced that there really is no 'typical' aid agency, nor 'typical' approach to aid. There are tendencies, but that is all.

I refer above to 'leaders in democratic states'. In the following chapters I frequently use the common semantic shortcut of anthropomorphizing states and referring to them as unitary actors. Thus I will make reference, for instance, to the actions of Australia. But it is crucial to my approach to bear in mind that decisions are always taken by people, not states. While states may have interests, only people can decide how to pursue those interests. And only people can go further to redefine the relevant interests to be pursued as encompassing more than just the welfare of a particular state. For if a leader can think in terms of, and fight for, the interests of the whole of the state, she can also potentially think in terms of the interests of a broader human community.

The plan of the book

Chapter 2 entails a more detailed consideration of the potential role for human rights in foreign policy. I briefly review the assumptions of several of the most important perspectives on international relations and foreign policy about the likelihood of states taking rights into account. I consider the dilemma that democracies face when deciding how to balance competing imperatives in the international system: self-interest (measured by economic standards but also by security), stability and justice. These competing imperatives result in mixed motives for states. I anticipate that certain kinds of domestic and external contextual factors will condition the extent to which states' foreign policies take human rights into account.

I discuss the focus on aid in Chapter 3. Originally I conceived of this project as simply the first in a series that would look at human rights' role in foreign policy decisions over various types of tools — here foreign aid, next military assistance, then trade and so on. In the course of researching and writing this book, however, I became acutely aware of the magnitude of global poverty, and of the woeful inadequacies of the resources devoted to addressing it. I also became deeply impressed with the moral and political commitments of not only the members of the aid community I met, but also with the convictions that often underlie the very concept of development assistance. While aid often simply serves as a tool, an international consensus has emerged over the last five or six decades that extreme global poverty, when some of us have so much, is simply unacceptable. This consensus has been such that development assistance has gone from a short-term and ad hoc tool to be applied only in special circumstances and relationships (e.g. the Marshall Plan, 1947–51, for rebuilding after World War II; or the Colombo Plan, from 1950, for Asian members of the

Commonwealth), to being a foreign policy goal unto itself. I discuss this further in the concluding chapter.

Chapter 4 addresses the qualitative and quantitative approach taken in the substantive case-study chapters. Some readers may wish to focus on the description of the qualitative research strategy and variable operationalization, and skim the latter part of the chapter as it deals in more detail with statistical methods and diagnostics than some readers may want. Chapter 5 then presents some evidence on overall aid trends in the donor community, to provide a context for the specific donor case discussions that follow in Chapters 6, 7 and 8.

The longest of these is Chapter 6, which focuses on the United Kingdom, because in it I describe some of the methodology and variable operationalization common to the donor case chapters that go beyond those covered in Chapter 4. These include definitions and measurements likely to be of interest to all readers, even those not as interested in statistical detail.

Each donor chapter starts with a history of the role of human rights in foreign policy, after which I describe the evolution of the donor's development assistance programme and some of its unique features. In all chapters I consider the role of international context and key internal players.

I mentioned above that various methods have been applied in extant investigations of related questions. I borrow – how successfully the reader will be left to judge – several sets of analytic tools, because I believe they tell us different things that together provide both wide angles and finer foci on aid decisions. The most important new contribution I present is the discussion and analysis of whole sets of development policy documents that have not been released to the public before. These are laid side by side with multivariate analyses of the actual recipient characteristics that are rewarded in aid-giving. I also discuss major whole-of-government policy documents that should be driving specific bilateral decisions. This allows for a threefold comparison between 1) the concepts conveyed in central government directives; 2) the way these are explicitly reflected in specific bilateral decisions; and 3) the statistical record on which conditions are actually associated with higher aid levels for recipients. This gives us a sense of the way that central policy is applied in particular cases, as well as an idea of the way that changes in policy language are matched by changes in policy outcome.

For each donor I describe the archival research conducted at each of the donor's official development assistance organ, and summarize some of my findings in the documentary evidence: how different kinds of considerations stack up in internal discussion of aid decisions, and what sorts of factors change the very calculus that is applied to states. I then discuss the results of statistical analyses designed to test the hypotheses presented in Chapter 3. These will be seen to be a rather mixed bag and display a good deal of disparity between the three donors, as well as a woefully small role for human rights when we look for their overall impact in the aggregate aid fortunes of recipient states.

This is one of the big stories of the book: while the discourse of human rights has made important normative changes in the way foreign policy-makers and activists think and talk about development, it has yet to be incorporated in any consistently robust way across the donor community, even through the appealing but sometimes fatally vague rubric of 'good governance'.

I then go on to suggest for each donor some reasons why rights may play a more subtle role, and propose ways to test more specifically the nature of this role. I perform some of these tests, but many will be the purview, I hope, of future research in this field. I end each chapter with a consideration of some specific recipient cases that furnish anecdotal evidence on the conditions under which aid policy responds to rights violations in the recipient, and the ways it does so.

Because there are several commonalities shared by the three donors on which I focus, Chapter 9 presents some evidence on my hypotheses from extant studies on three other donors: – Norway, Japan and the US – that afford a broader context for considering the role of different domestic and international imperatives in states' incorporation of human rights into their foreign policy perspectives.

While there is no way to definitively establish this using the evidence presented here, and regardless of some rather pessimistic findings, after completing this research my impression is that for every aid decision that is made on the clear basis of donor self-interest, there is another that is firmly grounded in a desire to help recipients. That aid often does not end up doing this is partly the result of mixed motives, but also the result of myriad difficulties in implementing development strategies in parts of the world that have stubbornly, for any of a number of reasons, remained underdeveloped.

My dependent variable, aid policy, and my key independent variable, human rights, share an important characteristic. Both require policy-makers to ground definitions of interest in not merely a sense of national community but a sense of global society. To what extent can leaders make the shift from the former to the latter? Their ability to do so will be determined by many individual, social, national and systemic characteristics. In the following chapter I present an approach which emphasizes the role of domestic political processes, norms and institutional structures; the nature of the international system; the role of the media; and sometimes, the leadership of important personalities. I choose – as one always must – to leave aside other undoubtedly important parts of the calculus. The news is sometimes not particularly good. But in trying to get at the 'real motivations' of policy-makers, I inadvertently discovered that for many of them, and especially for those charged with implementation – the key source of interests truly is the larger global community. This suggests that an important avenue for future research might start with the question of why policy-makers and implementers who start with the narrower definition of interests choose to adopt the broader one.

In reading the descriptions of the results in the following chapters, particularly the statistical results, I hope that readers will not entirely forget the realities behind the numbers: that the statistical regularities described often represent indescribable suffering on the part of hundreds of millions of individuals – not only torture, disappearance or other violations of personal integrity, but severe deprivation, malnutrition, starvation, homelessness and hopelessness. Global poverty, when so many are so rich, is a violation of rights as well.

Is the enforcement of human rights, ostensibly at the heart of the democratic form of government, something for which donors are willing to sacrifice gains in other arenas, or is it only pursued when it is not costly to do so? This is a critical question in a world where policy-makers claim to fight to spread democracy – because when terms like 'human rights' become hollow, so does one of the organizing principles that defines democracy.

2 The role of human rights in foreign policy

It is the purpose of this chapter not to briefly review the major theories of international relations *in toto* but rather to examine, broadly, the major schools of thought to see what role they allow for human rights in foreign policy-making. Some initial comments about the purview of this research are first in order.

I adopt a comparative perspective on the bilateral aid decisions of Organization for Economic Cooperation and Development (OECD) member donor states with a focus on the policies of the three big Commonwealth donor states: Australia, Canada and the United Kingdom. Similar questions have been ably addressed in the context of the US by a number of scholars (e.g. Apodaca and Stohl 1999; Cingranelli and Pasquarello 1985; Hofrenning 1990; Lumsdaine 1993, Mertus 2004; McCormick and Mitchell 1988; Milner *et al.* 1999; Poe 1990, 1991, 1992; Poe *et al.* 1999), and in this work I explore some of their contentions and findings in the context of the broader donor community.

What does 'human rights' mean?

We next consider rights as one of the sets of goals that states may choose to pursue in their foreign policy.

Human rights is a concept that is notoriously prone to selective interpretation that varies dramatically in different times and places. The famous ideological and political battles that led to the creation of the International Covenant on Civil and Political Rights (ICCPR) and International Covenant on Economic, Social and Cultural Rights (ICESCR) out of the extraordinarily comprehensive Universal Declaration of Human Rights (UDHR), took place across not only the political gulf of the Cold War but across ancient differences in commitments and understandings of what it is that makes for a life of dignity and worth. I will not here review the pantheon of different conceptions of rights and obligations, spanning the length of dimensions tracing the tension between individual and collective rights; between economic, social, cultural, political and civil rights; and between dramatically differing beliefs about the sources of these rights and the appropriate role of government in their assurance. This task has been done ably elsewhere (e.g. Donnelly 2004; Shue 1996). It is worthwhile to note, though, that even further definitional complication has occurred in recent years with the conflation both rhetorically and in practice of democracy with rights, something that is discussed in detail by Tomasevski (1993) and more recently, by Mertus (2004) and Neumeyer (2004). This particular conflation will be very evident in the case studies which follow in later chapters.

I do not, then, argue here for a particular definition of human rights. However, I do attempt to determine what human rights have meant in the foreign policies of major donor states. As human rights have become more fashionable as a foreign policy goal it has been tempting to interpret the term more and more broadly, cloaking a broad range of goals, including self-interested ones, in the rhetoric of rights, a tactic which has been employed perhaps most frequently by the US (for an excellent recent discussion see Mertus (2004)). While the quantitative component of the research that follows does focus on one of the most basic sets of rights – personal integrity rights[1] – in each of the country case studies that follows I trace the evolution of the concept of human rights in the policies of each donor state through official documents and revealed policy preferences.

Policy processes rarely allow for application of strict definitions of human rights. Instead, as Tomasevski puts it, bilateral relations

> emerge as the outcome of intergovernmental negotiations; hence they represent a political compromise and not the result of the application of any theory. Theories of human rights and interpretations of specific standards appear later, with the unenviable task of clarifying what governments meant when committing themselves to certain conduct and ... how to use ... governmental promises to protect people against abuses of power.
>
> (Tomasevski 1993: xv)

However, an attempt to understand what leaders mean when they refer to rights is crucial for understanding when rights will be prioritized. This is so for two main reasons. First, the way that human rights are defined determines their relationship to other foreign policy goals. Second, the only way to definitively test whether and when leaders prioritize rights is to examine cases where pursuing rights negatively affects a government's pursuit of another foreign policy goal.

Human rights in the panoply of foreign policy goals

There is no need to belabour the point that all states have a variety of goals in foreign policy – national security, territorial gain, economic competitiveness and so forth – and that choices must be made among them. Donnelly argues, and few would take issue with his assertion, that for most states international human rights fall near the bottom of the list.

Is this surprising? To ask a state to prioritize human rights abroad over other goals is to ask it to be an altruist twice over. First, we are asking it to use foreign policy resources to pursue the good of those in other states rather than that of their own citizens. Second, we are asking it to help the very people in other states who are least likely to be able to help it in return, often against the objections of those in power – those who *can* help in return.

In which kinds of cases is the pursuit of international human rights most clearly in conflict with other foreign policy goals? Though governments seldom admit of it in foreign policy statements, certainly many observers have implied that rights are more often than not in conflict rather than concert with other goals of foreign policy. During the Cold War the US had its 'ABC democrats', and in the age of globalization many critics cite the need for rights protections as a 'corrective' to the free market (see for instance Tomasevski 1993: xiii). While government rhetoric is often chary to admit incommensurability between policy goals, clearly there are costs in other arenas for pursuing human rights.

Donnelly (2004) suggests that, if we think very broadly about foreign policy goals as falling into the categories of security, economy, human rights and other, it is essentially impossible to think of an example of when a state has put the pursuit of human rights abroad above its own security interests. However, there have been notable cases (if they are still the exception) when human rights concerns have apparently outweighed economic ones. These include Dutch aid sanctions against key trade partner Indonesia during the worst abuses of the Suharto regime, and many states' sanctions of China after Tiananmen. Notably, Donnelly cites the US as a key sanctioner despite the granting of Most Favored Nation (MFN) status the following year, calling sanctions 'the central issue' in US–China relations until 1994 as a result (Donnelly 2004: 163). But most states that shared the closest geographic (Russia) or trade (Japan, India) interests with China were deafeningly – intentionally – silent on the issue. The disturbing implication of this, of course, especially in light of China's meteoric economic rise, is that the more economically dominant a state becomes, the less likely it is to suffer reprimand for internal repression.

From Woodrow Wilson's (1917) exhortation that the US 'make the world safe for democracy', to NATO's professed commitment to halting genocide through intervention in the Balkans in the 1990s, democracies have a long record of committing blood and treasure to the cause of international political and civil rights. The rhetoric of human rights is clearly visible in the norms and legal structure of foreign policy in most democracies. Every major developed democracy's foreign policy guidelines include explicit mention of human rights as a guiding principle.

I will suggest that low-level tools are generally employed to pursue rights because higher-level ones are deemed too costly. I believe that the effect of recipient country human rights abuses on donor country contribution is mitigated by three sets of characteristics, one pertaining to the recipient country's value to the donor government, another to the donor country's government itself, and another to the type of situation, *ceteris paribus*. This cross-national research design explicitly tests the different weights of the sets of payoffs donors face when deciding to aid a repressive recipient.

I focus on bilateral state-to-state relations. Much literature about human rights in international relations focuses on the role of international law and organizations and civil society. This is appropriate given that human rights by definition are couched as universal goals. Many of the theoretical propositions I consider below either assume or predict that the importance of the state as an actor in international relations is on the wane, especially those that are more optimistic about the potential for process (such as the rule of international law) or for principles (such as universal human rights) to have an effect, such as adherents to the English School (e.g. Chandler 2004).

Given this, it is important to stress that the key actor for this project is unambiguously the state. This may be seen as ironic in two senses: because I am interested in the rise of principles which claim to be universal, and because I am interested in how states incorporate goals into their overall foreign policy agendas that may appear to go against conventional definitions of the national interest. So we may assume that states, of all actors, are unlikely to take an interest in, and to deploy their foreign policy tools to pursue human rights in other states. But it is still states who are the central actors on the global stage and it is still, therefore, actors rather than egos or international law, that are most likely to have an effect on the behaviours of other states.

Within states there are two separate levels of choices that foreign policy-makers have to make: those over goals and those over tools. While this book focuses on human rights as a goal in the context of other, often competing foreign policy choices, of course it can be pursued using a variety of tools. Though these have been amply covered elsewhere, particularly as they pertain to human rights (see for instance Baehr and Castermans-Holleman 2004; Donnelly 2004; Luard 1981), it is helpful to remember their full range, which includes, in approximate ascending order of costliness:

> confidential representations, joint representations with other governments, public statements, support for calls for international investigation, initiation of calls for investigation, cancellation or postponement of ministerial visit, restrictions on cultural and sporting contacts, arms embargoes, aid reduction, withdrawal of ambassadors, cessation of aid, breaking diplomatic relations, and trade sanctions.
>
> (Luard 1981: 26–7, cited in Donnelly 2004: 165)[2]

Donnelly also adds support for civil society groups, aiding legal opposition groups, aiding illegal nonviolent opposition movements, aiding armed opposition movements, and invasion. This order is important because, as Donnelly reminds us, the more important the goal, the more costly a tool a state will be willing to engage to pursue it. Therefore, one way that we can determine the importance states place on human rights is to look at the tools that have been employed to pursue it. I describe the choices about these tools that have been made in the three major donors in the following chapters. For now it is enough to note that a major industrialized nation has never resorted to the costliest sort of tool – military intervention – to pursue a human rights goal when it was in conflict with other foreign policy goals. The most recent example of intervention for apparently humanitarian purposes – the NATO interventions in Kosovo – was driven by a host of concerns other than humanitarian ones, such as regional stability and sending a signal about the relevance of the US-led NATO alliance (Bisset 2000; Mertus 2004).

Does a role for ethical considerations exist in practice or is this just an attractive semantic stance? What is indicated by the fact that democracies only sometimes react to antidemocratic domestic actions in other states? Under what conditions does the human rights situation in a particular recipient start to matter to donors? Is it only when they think the rest of the world is watching? Is it less likely to matter when they want to maintain good relations with the recipient for other reasons? For instance, 20 years of fundamental abrogation of political and civil rights in East Timor by Indonesia led to cuts in aid from Canada, the US and Australia only after the widely publicized 1992 Santa Cruz Massacre and the 1997 riots. These questions are taken up in the donor chapters.

Let us now consider some of the most pervasive theories of international relations, in terms of whether rights are allowed a role in foreign policy; which kinds of rights these would be, the role that would be predicted for these rights in the overall array of foreign policy goals, and any predictions they might make about the best tools to use to pursue these rights – when these rights are in fact a priority. Different theories of international relations predict different answers to these questions. The theoretical sketches below are not, again, meant to cover all key components of each theory's approach to foreign policy – only its treatment of rights. In all cases there are important exceptions to my generalizations as well, but I aim to highlight some of the most important implications for rights that are either explicit or implicit in the central assumptions of these schools of thought.

Realism

Realists at least since Macchiavelli have argued that ethical concerns were irrelevant to understanding the decisions states make in international relations.[3] For Machiavelli, the ethical guidelines that might be applied to the private sphere were not merely inapplicable to the conduct of international politics, but, if adhered to, would probably be detrimental to a state's position in the international arena. This assertion has been made over and over in the development of realist thought (i.e. Waltz 1979). For realists, all politics is, as Clausewitz said, war by other means, and individual ethical considerations do not – and should not – apply. International politics' sole goal is to reach necessary objectives in the most efficient way, and there is no room in the calculus of efficiency for moral or ethical considerations. In the language of rational choice, relevant information for the self-interested state actor includes the power and capability of other states. Seldom, if ever, is it relevant to know the status of individual rights in that country unless it affects state power.

Realists, then, predict three things. First, that the single most important kind of consideration in any area of foreign policy-making is the maintenance of state security. In the realm of aid policy, this means that potential recipients that support donor interests will be most likely to receive aid, and those security goals will trump other factors in aid decisions. Second, many realists (Gurr 1994; Mearsheimer 1990) predict that preoccupation with anarchy and uncertainty should in fact be more pronounced since the end of the Cold War, in the absence of a stabilizing balance of power/terror.

But many proponents of such arguments have focused on the case of the United States. Would an examination of non-superpower states support such arguments? I suggest that the calculus of non-superpower states differs in important ways from that of superpowers. For one thing, strategic concerns may take a backseat to economic ones.

A third realist prediction is that external pressures have primacy and there are few meaningful roles for substate actors in the foreign policy process. But, as the very fruitful debate on democratic peace demonstrates, domestic considerations can sometimes be decisive in foreign policy decisions such as conflict initiation (Reiter and Stam 1998; Russett 1996), prosecution (Bueno de Mesquita and Lalman 1990; Gartner 1997; Reiter and Stam 1998; Russett 1996), and termination. Holsti (1992, 2004) has found that public opinion can have a significant effect on the foreign policy-making process, at least in the United States.

Domestic sources of foreign policy I: the electoral connection

Arguments about the constraints placed on democratic governments by electoral accountability generate further predictions about whether and when ethical concerns should affect foreign policy decisions. I assume that leaders generally prefer to retain office above all else (Bueno de Mesquita and Siverson 1995), and that they anticipate that the economic well-being of the country is the single most consistently important cue to which voters look when evaluating a leader's performance (see for instance Brooks and Brady 1999; Holsti 2004).

Democratic governments that see their control of government as being at risk are more likely to be preoccupied with economic concerns than are those less at risk. This is because constituents are even more likely to judge leaders' performance on the overall strength of the economy than on their own personal well-being, let alone the government's stances on foreign human rights concerns (Dalager 1996; Pomper 1993).

There are two primary dimensions upon which a government may be at risk. First, leaders are more sensitive to risk when elections are more temporally proximate. Second, they are more vulnerable when a government rules by coalition or by a small minority, rather than a large one. Other risk sensitization factors include low approval ratings and costly foreign conflicts.

As both temporal proximity to an election and size of the ruling party's majority decreases, sensitivity to economic considerations should increase. There is a good deal of evidence now that leaders enjoy decreasing freedom of action as they become more vulnerable. For instance, Bueno de Mesquita and

Siverson (1995) find that democratic governments are more risk-averse in war involvement decisions than are authoritarian ones, because of the greater threat war costs pose to their tenure than to the tenure of autocratic leaders. Prins and Sprecher (1999) find that majority governments are more likely to reciprocate militarily (exhibiting greater risk acceptance) than are other kinds of governments. Ireland and Gartner (2001) find that minority governments are less dispute-prone because they have less room to maneuver politically than do governments with a more secure grip on the reins of power. Furthermore, legislative composition that is unfavorable to the ruling government can hinder decision-makers' ability to both become involved in and perform in disputes (Gaubatz 1991; Zaller 1992).

These arguments would predict that the economic gains from international interactions will be particularly important to a donor when the donor government perceives itself to be at risk of losing office.

Domestic sources of foreign policy II: the civil society connection

Civil society can have substantial impact on political outcomes in democratic states (e.g. Dahl 1958; Olson 1965). Constituencies that value human rights in foreign policy tend to be numerically smaller than those who will be most aware of – and most concerned with – overall economic performance. On one hand, both national human rights interest groups and chapters of international human rights NGOs such as Human Rights Watch and Amnesty International exist in every democratic state. But while these groups have access to lobbying resources, public forums and media outlets for exposing failure of donor governments to act, such resources pale in comparison to the economic and strategic incentives that exist for donor governments to pursue economic gain and trade relationships.

Those who take interest groups seriously would predict that these interest groups may be able to make human rights a priority to the public, and therefore to policy-makers, in cases of extreme violations, but that generally they lack the resources to have an ongoing effect on the policy process.

Neoliberalism

In terms of a role for rights, or a role for altruism more generally, neoliberals have not dramatically parted ways with the neorealist arguments that they have challenged. For most neoliberals, states' self-interest is still the central issue – though it need not always conflict with the interests of other states. Trans-national institutions and regimes can help to create 'cooperation under anarchy' (Axelrod and Keohane 1993; Keohane 1993; Lipson 1993) and even shape interests and incentive structures so that anarchy need not be a source of threat. Mutual benefit is possible, particularly in the field of economic cooperation. More specifically, 'the more you let market forces rule and the more you open your economy to free trade and competition, the more efficient and flourishing your economy will be' (Friedman 1999). States are most likely, therefore, to use foreign policy to pursue these goals, rather than rights, unless of course rights constitute a means to these more basic goals.

Constructivism

Because of the role it accords identity and ideas, constructivism may at first blush appear to allow for the potential for states to reconceptualize their foreign policy goals based not on traditional state interests but rather on a postWestphalian agenda that gives higher precedence to international norms and institutions (see e.g. Chandler 2004; Keck and Sikkink 1998; Sikkink 1991, 2004). Constructivists often point to the increased legitimacy and enhanced enforcement mechanisms of international law, as well as government's attempts to pay at least rhetorical attention to human rights, as evidence of these trends. For many constructivists the end of the Cold War meant that states were now free to consider priorities other than the East–West strategic standoff. While constructivist scholars might not predict which *kinds* of rights states would espouse in their foreign policies (it would, presumably, depend on their identity), they might predict a potential elevation of those rights on foreign policy agendas, especially with the spread of transnational activist networks and a more truly global civil society (Chandler 2004).

English School

The English School's normative cosmopolitanism can be understood as another response to the amoralism of realism and the abstraction of its behavioralist epistemological turn. To a greater degree than neoliberalism, it has maintained the importance of ethics, but like realism it has warned against presumptions of *universal* morality (e.g. Chandler 2004) – a de facto challenge to the idea of universal human rights of any sort. English School adherents generally see the way forward for an ethical tolerant international society and in the procedures and rules of international law. (This was in its earliest conceptions often a response to the universalizing nature of fascism and communism).

Respect for at least personal integrity, civil and political rights is prima facie at the heart of democratic governance, is explicitly protected in the constitutions of most democracies, and has long enjoyed a privileged place in the foreign policy rhetoric of most democratic states. Democratic countries have normative, and frequently legal, incentives to take human rights into account when making international aid decisions. Legal incentives exist in the form of international instruments such as the Geneva Conventions and the European Convention on Human Rights, as well as in the constitutions of donor states.[4]

So scholars in this tradition are unlikely to espouse a particular sort of rights, but they generally predict and in fact champion strengthening international law, since this can shape states' foreign policy goals as well as prove an effective tool for pursuing those goals. The role for rights in the foreign policy of each state is determined by the state's laws and the extent to which it is a party to international legal agreements regarding human rights.

Certainly these are not the only schools of political thought that have considered the role of human rights in international relations. For instance, critical political theory (especially drawing on Habermas) has had valuable contributions to make to the theoretical conversation. Eva Erman has made valuable contributions in her analysis of the impact of changing discourse around human rights at the UN. But these constitute the basic expectations of the mainstream of some of the most dominant schools of thought within the discipline.

The argument of the book

While, for superpowers, geopolitical strategic interests are the pole star of foreign policy, middle-power donors are more likely to use their economic relationship with recipients as their primary sorting criterion. To take the example of aid policy, discussed further in the next chapter, some recipients may appear to the donor to be so valuable that the donor would rather continue to generate goodwill through aid than jeopardize access to the recipient by cutting it off, even if there appears good reason to do so. These are countries that offer significant trade potential to the donor country (especially through mechanisms such as 'tied aid'), have fertile export markets, and large or expanding economies.[5] These countries are less likely to be punished and, if they are, are likely to be punished less severely, than are other recipients for commensurate human rights abuses, all else being equal (Gillies and Brecher 1989; Scharfe 1996). In fact, the more economic benefit a donor derives from a recipient, the less significant the role of factors such as good governance and domestic repression in aid decisions regarding that recipient.

The link between aid and trade is explicitly evident in the mechanism of 'tied aid' which was for decades a key tool employed by donor states to ensure that they got a return on their aid 'investment'. Tied aid is that which can be spent only on certain items or on certain markets – usually, the donor's export markets – generally with little consideration as to whether this is the most efficient use of the aid, or the most appropriate, given the recipient's needs.

In addition, drawing on arguments about the domestic sources of foreign policy, I predict that the effect of economic importance on the human rights–aid relationship is conditioned by vulnerability. (Vulnerability, in essence, conditions the conditioning effect of economic considerations.) It is also conditioned by visibility, and states (especially democracies, who explicitly identify as champions of rights at home) will become especially sensitive to their obligations to protect these rights elsewhere when violations are widely publicized.

Of course not all economic relationships are equal. Trade with any one partner is unlikely to account for more than a small fraction of an industrialized state's total trade (and in most cases, it only comprises a fraction of a percent of overall revenues). It is not certain that the general electorate would even notice the loss or gain of a single export market (or, alternatively, import source). But relations with the fastest-growing markets are generally highly publicized (one need only consider the frequency with which trade with China merits head-lines), and any dramatic change in an important relationship may be enough to convey to the public the impression of a lost opportunity.[6] The most important of these bilateral relationships involve key sources of important non-substitutable goods.

3 Development assistance

From means to end

The motives for granting aid are a constant subject of inquiry and speculation. The actual purpose of aid and its impact cannot be assessed for all aid by all donors. They are praised by some for their noble goals of eradicating world poverty, accused by others of perpetuating and increasing poverty rather than eliminating it.

(Tomasevski 1993: 29)

Why aid?

I focus on the economic assistance dimension of foreign policy for two reasons. First, economic resources are by far the most fungible, and aid potentially affects nearly every other aspect of a recipient's fortunes. Second, the global economy is increasingly the terrain upon which states' strategies of cooperation and competition are carried out.

Aid is a unique tool of foreign policy in that its very name defines not only a tool but a goal – the more so since the term 'development assistance' has come into favor in most of the donor community. Aid or development assistance literally means that the target of the assistance is supposed to be benefiting – being aided, explicitly in its 'development'. (The content of this development is the subject of increasing debate, as we will see.)

But why give? The theoretical and practical answers to this question have varied widely.

History and goals of aid – theory

Modern aid began with colonialism and the sense of responsibility (whether self-interested or altruistic) that grew out of it. The 1929 Colonial Development Act (UK), often cited as the first modern example of legislated development assistance, clearly focuses on Britain's responsibilities to its overseas dominions. But mixed messages existed even then, as the Act also aimed to encourage trade between Britain and her overseas territories. The post-World War II success of the Marshall Plan and Point IV of the Truman doctrine demonstrated that aid could be successfully deployed for political purpose, and for many this instance of use in and of itself legitimized the use of aid in such a manner.

From then on, aid would reflect this holy trinity of aims:

1   Assisting strategic allies (which often included former colonies or co-members of the Commonwealth, whose 'strategic' value might be debated, but which were allies due to historical cultural, political and economic ties);
2   Trade benefits for the donor;
3   General global stability through development and economic growth; though there is often a failure to distinguish between the two in practice.

Original bases in moral obligation

Throughout the history of modern aid, 'appeals to morality have been used by governments and international agencies to justify their aid programmes' (Riddell 1987: 5), though it is rare to find governments appealing *solely* to morality.[1]

Moral justifications were not merely an early humanitarian impulse that then fell by the wayside, but were revisited time and again to provide justification for aid flows when other justifications fell short. For instance, in 1960 John Kennedy announced that aid which had been increasingly predicated on the anticommunist imperative should rather be driven by an underlying moral imperative (Riddell 1987: 6). In 1969, the Report of the Commission on International Development (the Pearson Report, chaired by former Canadian PM Lester Pearson), *Partners in Development*, illustrated the extent to which moral justifications had become *de rigueur* in the donor community. It answered the 'why aid?' question thus: 'the simplest answer is a moral one: that it is only right for those who have to share with those who have not' (cited in Riddell 1987: 7). Until the late 1970s, in fact this was understood as the default justification for aid (Riddell 1987: 3).

Yet morality is as fraught and culturally constrained a concept as that of human rights. Much of the debate about the moral bases of aid rests on assumptions about what aid actually achieves. While results-based evaluation has become more emphasized in the donor community in recent years, for much of the formative period of aid theory and aid policy alike, results were generally assumed rather than documented. Documentation is a notoriously sticky business (for a good discussion of this see Riddell 1987), and the fact that inequalities between North and South have by nearly every measure grown along with aid transfers has led many to wonder – in the words of a 1988 Canadian Parliamentary report *'For Whose Benefit?'* (Government of Canada 1988). That is, by helping the governments of poor countries, do we necessarily help the poorest people in those countries? And what are the effects for the donor?

Trade promotion and development

After the essentially altruistic, if rather paternalistic, early focus of aid, the other – only slightly less important – cited in early aid policy (such as the 1929 Colonial Development Act) was trade. This is a goal that, like altruism, has been relatively consistent, especially for middle-power states (see e.g. Stokke 1989). The 1980s saw a swing to using aid to push for greater market openness in developing countries, in the belief that this would not only open them further to the donors' markets (something also encouraged through tied aid discussed below), but would also lead to faster development for the recipient states. This set of arguments would be one of the most consistent justifications for aid competing with the ethical case (Riddell 1987: 4).

Colonies and decolonization/Commonwealth

As colonialism was the crucible in which early aid programmes and both ethical and commercial rationales evolved, so too did decolonization lead to major changes in the aid programme over time. While the colonial powers' sense of moral obligation would remain, the processes of decolonization had global effects that influenced all donors, not just the original colonial powers. Judith Hart, the influential Minister of Overseas Development in the UK during the late 1970s, noted that

> there are times when the moral responsibility of the British people – remembering that all the commonwealth developing countries were part of our history of imperialism, which was an unusual mix of exploitation and paternalism – towards a high proportion of the poor of the world must be exercised in Government so as to represent in its own actions and policies the essential morality of political philosophies in Britain.
>
> (Riddell 1987: 8)

Former colonial powers and even developed members of the Commonwealth and the Francophonie began to sense their obligations as members of the global North generally rather than in their specific bilateral colonial relationships.[2]

Evolution – Cold War and geopolitics

The Marshall Plan, as noted above, not only demonstrated the willingness of the US to exploit foreign aid to achieve geopolitical gains, but suggested that such a strategy could be extremely effective. The US's allies in the donor community followed similar approaches during the Cold War (the US has often played a lead role in agenda-setting in the donor community). The focus on states that were not allied with the Soviet Union was justified on the grounds of both strategic expediency and need. (The US and its allies argued that Soviet client states' basic assistance needs were met by the Soviets). Strategic concerns, especially during the Cold War, have been a top foreign policy priority for many Western donor states in part because of the leadership of the US and the role of military and ex-military personnel in the governments of most donors.

Post-Cold War: refocus on recipient-centered development and poverty reduction

That aid helps promote development is the most widely given reason for it, though notoriously difficult to test empirically. Two periods in the twentieth century shifted the discussion back toward a focus on the recipient – the overall greater emphasis on social justice that came to dominate the donor community during the mid-1960s to late-1970s[3] (coinciding with détente and a temporary lessening of strategic concerns), and then the lessened focus on geopolitics that characterized the immediate post-Cold War period. Throughout the 1970s and 1980s, though, development literature increasingly emphasized the needs of the poorest people, rather than just the poorest countries.[4] Of course the differences in standards of living between the developed and developing worlds only continue to increase, giving added weight to poverty-reduction goals but also calling into question past approaches aimed at poverty reduction.

Probably the most important component of this shift was a move from thinking about aid as help, to development as a general *process* that could not be effected by aid alone. The growing inequality between North and South even as aid was increasing seemed to indicate that current thinking about aid was not as effective as it needed to be, and that approaches to development needed to be more holistic, considering: approaches to aid in the context of what would actually work in specific recipients, ways aid could be made more effective, methods of coordination donors could adopt to ensure that aid did not work at cross-purposes (a frequent problem), and considerations of the appropriate role of aid in the context of the entire range of foreign policy tools.

This led to substantial semantic (but substantive) and institutional shifts, as 'aid' was referred to less and less in favor of 'development assistance' (and increasingly 'development cooperation') and donor-state aid agencies increasingly adopted titles that reflected a focus on development generally rather than aid or assistance specifically.

We can also see two impulses behind assistance here that may be at odds with each other. Is it best (as many analysts argued in the 1970s and 1980s), when takeoff is not occurring, to focus on direct poverty alleviation and helping the poorest (the moral impulse coming back in)? On the other hand, does not development entail more than just poverty alleviation? The end of the Cold War, by removing the ubiquitous imperatives of the geopolitical standoff, and some of the rationale for political conditionality in aid, seemed to open up the ideological and practical space to begin to think more holistically and creatively about what development really meant and how donors could have the greatest impact.

Social goals

Part of this switch from thinking about aid to thinking about development more generally has included a more expansive view of development and therefore an expansion of the mandate of aid agencies. Development has come to include a number of social goals that could, in fact, be thought of as basic human rights even when they are not referred to as such. These include health, education, social inclusion, democratization, gender equality and sustainability.

Neoliberalism and good governance

Immediately after the end of the Cold War, globalization appeared to be the dominant international trend and while of course opinion varied on whether its benefits outweighed its perils, it was impossible to ignore the fact of its existence and acceleration. Neoliberal governments in key donors like the US and UK were quick to attend to the opportunities for greater market openness afforded by the end of the Cold War and to link this to other forms of openness as well. Battling corruption and protectionism in recipient states became a key target of development strategies, reflecting in part a return to Rostovian faith in the chance that this might initiate self-sustained development, if only transparent and minimalist governments would allow greater freedom for both their markets and their people. Democratization and free-marketeering have often been combined in the parlance of 'good governance' (GG). The rise of good governance as a key target in donor-community policies is a victory for the role of certain *kinds* of human rights (see below) in development strategy, but also brings with it risks of further violations of basic economic rights and exacerbation of existing inequalities within recipient states as greater market openness leads to at least short-term displacement, and structural adjustment requirements of multilateral or bilateral donors lead to more minimalist government and cuts in key recipient-government-supplied safety nets that may have in fact provided for the poorest in society. At its narrowest interpretation, good governance often reduces to a technocratic set of efficiency guidelines. Even at its most expansive it tends to focus on civil and political rights to the exclusion of economic, social and cultural rights (HRCA 1995: 44). The fact that GG is increasingly conflated with human rights approaches to development is a troubling semantic turn.

War on terror

The status of security as a goal has become greater since 9/11 and some donors are explicitly incorporating counterterror training considerations in their assistance policies.

Human rights

To what extent can we find a role for rights in any of these periods? As discussed in the previous chapter, this depends largely on what one defines as rights.

Basic needs as rights

It is not too difficult to find a role for rights in these discussions if one assumes, as does the UDHR, that basic needs (including food, water, shelter, security) are indeed basic rights. For instance, aid policy leaders in many donors have explicitly made this link. Judith Hart claimed that fulfillment of basic needs, and its enshrinement in law, in fact creates a basic right, and implies other rights as well.

> When the peoples of the third world, for the first time, can meet their basic needs – and let me slightly re-formulate that familiar phrase by saying: 'when their basic human rights are met' then for the first time they will have the opportunity for full participation within their own societies ... [and to] determine for themselves how best to create a legal and political structure which protects and advances their rights.
>
> (Hart, cited in Riddell 1987: 12)

Political and civil rights and good governance

'The legitimacy of promoting human rights in other countries derives from their universality ... rights of people anywhere represent a legitimate concern for people anywhere' (Tomasevski 1993: 153). However, though civil and political rights have long been at the forefront of the rights agenda for most developed countries, the pursuit of good governance and democracy as rights in and of themselves have come to the table only relatively recently, as we will see in the cases of specific donor states. However, while the rhetoric of civil and political rights has been incorporated into aid policy statements, it is less clear whether it has been incorporated in practice.[5] And critics object that these so-called HRDGG (Human Rights, Democracy, Good Governance) goals are appropriate ones for aid. For instance, Tomasevski believes that, since the pursuit of these rights is further from the original mandate of aid than are subsistence goals, donors are less likely to be able to affect them (Tomasevski 1993: xiii).

It should be noted that there is some disagreement that aid is even an appropriate tool for pursuing human rights, and, if used, whether it should be as a 'carrot' or a 'stick' (i.e. as a reward or a punishment). Matthews and Pratt (1988: 12) consider this tradeoff:

> A final consideration involves the distinction between punishments (sanctions) and rewards (inducements). As sanctions may provoke a hardening of attitudes within the violating country and, if applied unilaterally, are likely to be ineffective, rewards may better encourage change. Instead of threatening to cancel aid to a country with an abysmal human rights record, one might offer aid (or increased aid) if its human rights performance improved.
>
> (Matthews and Pratt 1988: 12)

We will see that, at least in the field of aid, donors have in some cases shown a clear preference for positive inducements.

Tensions between goals

In many cases, tensions are simply not to be admitted of, and the various goals of aid are treated – rhetorically at least – as though they were either independent or mutually reaffirming. 'The blending of appeals to morality and long term interests of donors is a particular feature emerging in official pronouncements in the late 70s and 80s' (Riddell 1987: 9). This was both reflected in and further driven by the release of the Brandt report in the early 1980s under the rhetoric of 'mutual interest'. Hart, for example, argued on multiple occasions that there was a natural overlap between national interests and encouraging development abroad (Riddell 1987: 8) and that, though every government department should first and foremost further British national interest, 'there are times when the understanding of the economic and human situation of two thirds of the world's population is not only relevant but essential to the definition of the long-term interest' (Riddell 1987: 8).

The domestic process: who and what matters

The elected

Within donor states, we can expect changes in development policy on the basis of the party in power and the policy proclivities of particular elected officials. It is important to remember of course that few donors allow for the sort of independent policy role played in the US's presidential system.

Civil service

The bureaucratic and political structures charged with foreign policy generally, and aid and human rights policies specifically, vary rather substantially between donor states. The strength of the independent civil service in many donors is the stuff of *Yes Minister* legend, but the institutional arrangements for addressing aid and development policy vary dramatically across time and across donors. First, in many cases aid policy is not the purview of a separate cabinet-level department with its own minister, but rather within the main foreign policy department (as was the case for many years in Britain, and is currently the case in Australia). This virtually guarantees that within the aid agency, the primacy of development as a goal will have to compete with more general foreign policy priorities of the moment. In some cases the aid agency is housed in a department that is also formally charged with trade promotion, which is likely to result in an even greater dilution of development priorities, particularly when trade and development goals conflict. However, even in institutional arrangements where development has its own cabinet-level department, foreign and trade offices as well as treasuries will both take an interest in, and attempt to influence, aid policy. Finally, where there is more extensive and coherent institutionalization of human rights in the foreign policy-making framework, human rights should be more systematically taken into account, both in rhetoric and in practice.

Outside interests

Aid policy considerations are rarely likely to be decisive in the voting booth. However, certain subsets of the public certainly do take a more sustained interest in development policy. This includes immigrants from recipient states and organized lobbies.

The business community is among the largest, best organized and most well-funded lobby sector in most donors and is interested in foreign policy to the extent that it promotes or inhibits commercial opportunities. Trade advantages are promoted by the government through strategies like 'tied aid' and special aid-for-trade deals or legislation such as the former Aid and Trade Provision (ATP) in Britain. But such tactics generally benefit a small proportion of the most well-connected companies in the donor state and have little general economic benefit, especially when tied aid serves primarily as an export subsidy for businesses that are not otherwise optimally efficient (for an extremely thorough discussion see Gounder 1995; Morrissey *et al.* 1992). An important side-effect of this characteristic is that it biases aid towards helping richer developing countries, as several of the analyses presented later demonstrate.

Interest groups and NGOs that are oriented around developmental and rights concerns are generally not as well funded or well connected as the business lobby. This contributes to the difficulty that morally grounded developmental or rights goals have in competing against commercial ones.

Because policy results often turn on how the national interest is defined in a given situation, one of the primary goals of development and human rights NGOs is to make human rights aspects of a particular aid decision appear to be of higher salience than other kinds of considerations. They have become increasingly successful at doing this as new technologies and transnational activist networks have facilitated global communication and mobilization, as dramatically demonstrated by the successes of Make Poverty History, Jubilee 2000 and Drop the Debt in setting the donor-community agenda and especially evincing promises from the G8 at the 2005 Gleneagles summit.

Donor economy

The healthier the donor's economy (in terms of its size, growth rate and trade balances), the more likely it is to be generous with aid.

Recipients

Recipient governments and members of civil society are widely consulted by most donors in the aid-allocation process; part of increasing moves towards inclusiveness in devising development strategies in recent years.

The external environment

Certain aspects of the global environment such as the Cold War, globalization and the war on terror have already been mentioned. It is worth noting, however, that in the case of many donors, particular attention must also be paid to the lead of powerful allies such as the EU, which is moving toward increasingly coordinated approaches to foreign policy, or the US (in the case of Australia or Canada).

There are at least two additional characteristics of the aid decision that are relevant to predicting the relative importance of the political, economic and strategic factors described above and in Chapter 1. These are the stage in the decision-making process (gatekeeping or allocation) and the type of aid.

Types of aid

Tied or untied

The OECD identifies four major 'tying' categories of aid: Tied aid, untied aid, partially tied aid, and technical assistance. Tied aid comes with 'strings attached' – the donor specifies where it is spent – often in the donor's markets.[6] Untied aid, in contrast, may be used in whichever way the recipient government sees fit. It covers 'aid which includes loans or grants whose proceeds are fully and freely available to finance procurement from substantially all developing countries and from OECD countries'. A third type of aid identified by the OECD is a mix of these two – 'partially tied'. Partially tied aid is not as limited as tied aid, but does specify a particular percentage be spent in donor-country markets (OECD, www.oecd.org//dac/pdf/DAC7B.PDF, last accessed 23 March 2006).

The final category is technical assistance. It is more difficult to locate a formal definition of technical assistance, though examples include helping 'establish proper procurement and contracting procedures for construction', contributing to 'the planning, coordinating, and monitoring of external assistance', and helping 'increase the efficiency and accountability of the ... government' (OECD, www.oecd.org//daf/ASIAcom/assistance/uz.htm, last accessed 26 March 2006).

It is imperative to identify tying status when examining factors in aid decisions, because different types of aid are often allocated differently. Tied aid is, for instance, explicitly designated for use in the donor's export markets (and will by definition, therefore, inflate the level of trade between donor and recipient). I predict that both economic and human rights concerns will have less of an effect on tied aid than on untied aid, where donors are likely to be much more selective. By extrapolation, one would expect disbursement of partially tied aid to be influenced by economic and ethical interests less than is the case with untied aid, but more than is the case with tied aid. The core analyses in this study focus on overall aid, but in the following chapter I examine empirical differences in the factors associated with disbursements of each kind of aid.

Budget support, program or project aid

Different options in aid disbursement allow the donor more or less control over the aid decision. While the specific terminologies vary a bit from donor to donor, general budget support goes straight to the recipient government with only the broadest controls over how it is deployed. Program aid goes to particular sectors, project aid goes to individual projects within those sectors. While more specifically allocated forms of aid give the donor more control, they also necessitate more administrative efforts and costs.

In some cases when a donor wishes to respond to undesirable performance in the recipient, they will shift from budget support to a form of aid over which they can exercise more control. This means that examining aggregate aid amounts will only tell part of the story of aid's responsiveness to recipient performance.

Other key aspects of aid

Of course this is only the tip of the iceberg in terms of delineating some of the most important aspects of aid. Aid varies widely by sector, and of course substantial aid is funneled through NGOs (especially in the presence of poor performance by the recipient government) and multilaterals. This study examines bilateral Overseas Development Assistance (ODA), but this is only one important facet of development assistance.

Types of decisions

Gatekeeping or allocation

Two decisions are examined for each donor–recipient dyad year, through which I evaluate the relative role of humanitarian, economic, strategic and other criteria. The first is the donor's decision to give the recipient aid, the second is its decision about the amount to allocate. While the answer to the second question is obviously contingent on the first, there are solid theoretical and epistemological reasons for modeling disbursement in two stages.

Theoretically, the two decisions need to be modeled separately because in the case of most donors, a slightly different set of actors interacts – in a slightly different process – for each decision. Most studies of the aid–human rights relationship have been based on the case of the US. In this case, the members of congressional committees, committee staffs and key decision-makers at the Department of State and the Agency for International Development describe the first decision as a 'gatekeeping' one in which certain countries were systematically excluded and others systematically included. The second decision is much more complex, with a higher level of give-and-take among actors. There is thus good reason to believe that different criteria may be at work at each stage in the decision-making process, and in fact this has been supported by many studies of the process in the US (e.g. Cingranelli and Pasquarello 1985).[7]

At the gatekeeping stage, the pool of potential recipients is comprised of the entire universe of states that are poorer than the donor. Therefore, more of these will be likely to be of little import to the donor than should be the case for those who have made it to the second stage. If the donor does not have strategic or economic stake in a country, it should be more willing to punish it for human rights violations. So the effect of the human rights variable might be greater at this stage than at the second, allocational, stage. In at least some donors there are also legal constraints that would lead to the human rights issue having a potentially greater impact at the gatekeeping decision stage than at the allocation stage. In the US, the 1975 Harkin Amendment to section 116 of the Foreign Assistance Act explicitly made 'the observance of certain basic human rights within the recipient countries a condition for the receipt of bilateral US economic aid' (Harkin *et al.* 1979: 17). While this linkage stipulates that the decision to give aid must take human rights into account, it does not make the same stipulation for aid amounts.

At the second stage, the universe of states consists only of countries already receiving aid from the donor. These recipients should on average score highly (relative to the universe of potential recipients) on at least one of the dimensions described in Table 3.1. For instance, the donor may have longer-standing ties with the recipient, or the recipient may possess an important natural resource. Hence, at the second stage, I would expect less variation in the independent variables. Recipients that make it to the allocation stage are already important to the donor for some reason.

In addition to the theoretical reasons for approaching the process in two stages, such a strategy allows maximum comparability with previous studies (see, for instance, Cingranelli and Pasquarello 1985; Poe 1990, 1992; Poe *et al.* 1999).

Finally, not only is it theoretically, empirically and epistemologically appropriate to model the disbursement process as having two stages, but doing so allows me to determine the extent to which selection effects are operating in the allocation process. Including all possible recipients of aid[8] in analyses of the first decision, but including only those chosen to receive aid in analyses of the second, endogenizes potential selection effects.[9]

Table 3.1 Extremely basic typology of aid decisions

Gatekeeping decision	Likely factors mitigating for or against this decision	Signal sent	Allocation decision	Likely factors mitigating for or against this decision	Signal sent
Cease aid	− institutional inertia − risk of relationship with recipient + shrinking aid budget + punish negative recipient behavior	Strongly negative unless done because recipient no longer needs it; i.e. 'graduation'	Decrease aid	− institutional inertia − risk of relationship with recipient + shrinking aid budget + punish negative recipient behavior	Mildly negative
Continue to not give aid	+ institutional inertia + shrinking aid budget	Mildly negative	Keep aid same	− shrinking aid budget + institutional inertia + maintain relationship with recipient + implicit approval of recipient policies	Neutral
Continue to give aid	− shrinking aid budget + institutional inertia + maintain relationship	Mildly positive	Increase aid	− shrinking aid budget − institutional inertia + improve relations with recipient + reward positive recipient behavior	Mildly positive
Begin aid	− shrinking aid budget − institutional inertia + improve relations with recipient + reward positive recipient behavior	Strongly positive			

Asymmetry

Even at those stages, there are different decisions to be made. A decision to not grant aid to a state that has received it before is not simply the reverse of the decision to grant aid to a state for the first time. A great deal of inertia is built into aid relationships and, once such a relationship has been established, strong institutional and political factors mitigate against ending it.

These differences have implications for the ways that I expect economic value to condition the role of human rights in these decisions. While economically valuable recipients should be *less* likely to be punished for human rights abuses, they should be *more* likely to be rewarded for good human rights performance. In the appendices to the next chapter, I explore the empirical differences between factors associated with the decision to reward versus the decision to punish.

Therefore, there are at least three key characteristics of an aid decision that need to be identified before one can predict the relative impact of economic versus humanitarian considerations, and interpret the results of analyses testing these impacts: what type of aid is being disbursed, whether the decision at hand is the gatekeeping or allocational one, and what the past aid history to that recipient is, because it is usually easier to decrease than to increase aid, *ceteris paribus*. With this three-dimensional schema in mind, I will consider the following seven kinds of decisions:

1   *Gatekeeping decision: potential recipients that have not received aid in the past and continue not to receive it*
    The general process of the aid decision for potential recipients is one that for most donors is primarily guided by institutional inertia. The default in most budgetary decisions is the decision that was made in the previous year. Therefore, it is a much greater challenge to move a potential recipient from the 'no aid' list to the 'aid' list than it is to keep a potential recipient on whichever list it was on the year before.

2   *Gatekeeping decision: potential recipients that have received aid in the past and continue to receive it*
    Again, the general process of the aid decision is one that for most donors is primarily guided by institutional inertia. It is much harder to move a potential recipient from the 'aid' list to the 'no aid' list than it is to keep a potential recipient on whichever list it was on the year before.

3 and 4 *Gatekeeping decision: deciding to terminate or initiate aid to a recipient*
    It is more difficult and requires more justification to change a state's aid status than to maintain the status quo. As a result, one might expect greater impact of many of the independent variables. Whether the 'drop' or 'add' decision faces more institutional hurdles is unclear. On the one hand, adding a recipient requires additional expenditure of resources for the donor. On the other hand, dropping a current recipient risks harming relations with the

recipient, as well as forfeiting the kind of 'negative benefits' discussed below.

5   *Allocation decision: when aid remains the same*

Again, in most cases, the default in most budgetary decisions is likely to be the decision that was made in the previous year. Therefore, setting aside any economic stake the donor might have in the recipient, it is much easier to leave aid amounts unchanged, in real terms, than to increase or decrease the amount of aid a recipient receives.

6 and 7   *Allocation decision: when aid is increased or decreased*

Again, the general process of the aid decision is, as at the gatekeeping stage, one that for most donors is likely guided by institutional inertia. The default in most budgetary decisions is to repeat the decision that was made in the previous year. Therefore, it is much harder to change the amount of aid a recipient receives than it is to leave it unchanged. In addition, it should be harder to increase the amount of aid a recipient receives than to decrease it, due to budgetary pressures.

Other institutional factors

While we can predict patterns of aid disbursement based on these major aims of aid, there are some other assumptions common to aid policy-making processes that need to be taken into account as well. For example, aid is seldom withdrawn altogether from recipients because policy-makers in donor countries see 'negative benefits' in granting aid to many developing countries (Spicer 1966: 50). Negative benefits refer to the fact that the situation for both donor and recipient is likely to be even worse if aid is withdrawn. As a result, policy-makers believe that even if aid does not succeed in bringing about ideal trade relations with a recipient or making major strides toward internal improvements, the situation for both donor and recipient is likely to be even worse if aid is withdrawn. (During the Cold War this meant, most importantly, the risk of losing another 'domino'. Since 1990, the emphasis has shifted toward considerations such as maintaining access to foreign markets, and since 2001, the US war on terrorism has been a key determinant as well.) Therefore, donors may sometimes grant aid to potential recipients with poor human rights records, not in response to current conditions, but in hopes of influencing *future* conditions in that recipient – a strategy suggested, for instance, by Breuning (2004) and Matthews and Pratt (1988). (For instance, we will see that British, Canadian and Australian aid at the allocation stage demonstrate patterns commensurate with this kind of strategy.)

Hypothesis derivation

It follows from the above discussion that there are seven possible decisions for any donor state in a given year (though these are logically limited by the potential recipient's prior aid status; i.e. a recipient can only have aid initiated if it did NOT receive aid in the previous year).

Note that there are, however, only five outcomes for a recipient state:

1   it gets aid for the first time;
2   the aid it already has goes up;
3   the aid it already has stays the same;
4   the aid it already has goes down; or
5   it does not receive aid.

However, the last of these outcomes could have been produced by either a decision to continue no aid or to drop aid, depending on the recipient's status in the previous year. These are of course two dramatically different decision processes signifying radically disparate things about the relationship between the donor and the recipient. (The same is true for the decision to continue aid versus initiate it). For example, it is much more significant for a recipient who has received aid in the past to suddenly be dropped from the aid list, as it means there has been a change either within the recipient itself or in the relationship between the recipient and the donor. In contrast, when a potential recipient has not received aid in the past and continues not to receive it, this is a continuation of the status quo and probably reflects a certain continuity either in the situation within the recipient state or in the relationship between the recipient and the donor. So, though the gatekeeping stage may appear to entail a simple 'yes' or 'no' by the donor, there are two different 'worlds' in which this decision is made and, thus, four very different outcomes for this decision: initiate aid (usually the result of a significant change either within the recipient or in the donor–recipient relationship), continue aid (continuation of status quo), continue lack of aid (continuation of status quo); or cease aid (usually the result of a significant change either within the recipient or in the donor–recipient relationship).

From the foregoing considerations, I derive the following hypotheses:

The gatekeeping decision

1   Potential recipients that are more economically valuable are more likely to receive aid.
2   Potential recipients that are more economically valuable are less likely to have human rights taken into account in decisions about their aid status.
3   Potential recipients that are more strategically valuable are more likely to receive aid.
4   Potential recipients that are more strategically valuable are less likely to have human rights taken into account in decisions about their aid status.

Changes in status for a given potential recipient:

•   The greater the potential economic value of a recipient to a donor state, the less likely it is that that potential recipient will be dropped from the aid list, and the more likely it is to be added to that list (for any reason).

The allocation decision

5   Recipients that are more economically valuable will receive higher levels of aid.

6   Recipients that are more economically valuable are less likely to have human rights taken into account in decisions about their aid amounts.

7   Recipients that are more strategically valuable will receive higher levels of aid.

8   Recipients that are more strategically valuable are less likely to have human rights taken into account in decisions about their aid amounts.

Changes in status for a given recipient:

•   The greater the potential economic value of a recipient state to a donor state, the more likely it is that that recipient's aid will be increased, and the less likely it is to be decreased.

4 Methodology

Means, not end

Hypothesis testing

How can we know what role rights really play in foreign aid policy? To answer this question requires a two-pronged approach. No methods at the disposal of social scientists are sufficient in and of themselves; because they are meant to demonstrate different types of things, we need to make use of as many as possible.

First, we need to examine what aid policy-makers are saying – not just to the public, but to each other, when they can be at their most candid about what decisions are being made and why. How often proportionally are rights considerations brought to the table as opposed to other foreign policy goals? And what factors influence how large the role of rights is? Does a valuable trading relationship between donor and recipient mean that the rights issue is considered less frequently, or that violating recipients are less likely to be punished? Do human rights fall by the wayside for strategically important recipients?

Next, we might want to see how these considerations play out in practice. What characteristics of recipients are most influential in determining whether they receive aid and how much they receive? Are trade and strategic concerns in fact more important than recipient rights? And do these affect the role that the rights issue plays in aid decisions?

The specifics of these two components of the research are covered in greater detail below. First, a few basic points about the purview of the research.

Time period covered

My analyses cover the years 1980–2004. This is a particularly illuminating time period for a number of reasons. It encompasses over 1000 cases in the decade before the Cold War ended, and over 700 in the decade after. One can compare treatment of recipients that were allied with the West during the Cold War with treatment of Commonwealth of Independent States (CIS) states. This period also features major changes in the institutionalization of aid in two of the donor cases. It also includes the beginning of the US-led 'war' on terror as well as Western responses to genocide in both Africa and Europe, places with which donor states have vastly different relationships.

Case selection

The key donor states I examine are the United Kingdom, Canada and Australia, chosen for five reasons. First, all are donor states who spend a significant proportion of their Gross Domestic Product (GDP) on foreign assistance, and therefore states for which foreign policy actions have a clear cost, as opposed to states whose policy preferences are expressed through generally less costly means such as diplomatic measures. Second, all can be broadly defined as democracies. All are Commonwealth countries, allowing me to control (somewhat) for cultural differences often posited to affect the 'moral commitments' of a state. All were allies of the US during the Cold War. Finally, I deliberately avoid inclusion of superpowers; many past studies have focused almost exclusively on the US to the exclusion of the majority of aid-granting states, which are middle-powers.

This sample gives us both a 'great power of the second order' as Britain has been called, and true middle-powers. These middle-powers have some interesting similarities as well as important differences. Canada's foreign policy is dominated by its relationship with 'the Elephant to the south', as an internal memo put it, while Australia's foreign policy reflects a national identity marked by a sense of geographic and cultural isolation. Both have shared unusually close relationships with the United States. Canada's has been largely an unsought one, result of geographical and historical destiny. Australia's is one that has been, at times, so much the nucleus of Australian foreign policy that it has been the most important factor in foreign policy-making.[1] Andrew Cooper, Richard Higgott and Kim Nossal, in their comparative study of Australian and Canadian foreign policy (1993), draw attention to additional commonalities that bear on the analyses in this book: the trade and more explicitly commodity dependence of Australia and Canada (something that has become more true for Britain as well) and an increase in this focus since the end of the Cold War, especially given their increasing vulnerability in a more intensively interdependent, but also more unpredictable, global economic environment. (Another valuable discussion of the similarities between middle-powers in aid policy specifically can be found in Stokke 1989).

Many other key attributes (size, location and wealth of country, colonial background, dependence on trade) are allowed to vary substantially.

An introduction to the three individual donors whose policies will be examined in subsequent chapters may help to illustrate why they represent a particularly telling sample.

United Kingdom

In 1989 Cunliffe asserted,

> analysis of the flow of economic aid from London to the less developed
> world over the past fifteen years does not reveal any enduring, concerted

attempts by successive British governments to utilize the flow of concessional finance for the promotion on international human rights.[2]

(Cunliffe 1989: 115)

If this is still the case, what attempts *have* been made and what has generally driven aid decisions instead? Writing in the late 1980s, he argued that 'such concerns are subservient to other political and economic ambitions' in British aid decisions. While I will argue that the rights issue has entered the dialogue in much more meaningful ways in recent years, there were examples of response to rights abuses *in extremis* even in the earlier years of the UK aid programme. In 1977, Britain suspended aid to Bolivia because of the poor working conditions in the mining industry there. Aid was suspended because it was perceived that it would serve to increase economic inequality within the country, rather than ease the plight of the miners. The suspension attracted international media attention to the status of human rights in the country.

Canada

Canada has an ostensible commitment to human rights concerns in the allocation of Official Development Assistance. This commitment has been expressed in at least three major policy documents. The first two of these (the 1986 Hockin–Simard Report and the 1988 Winegard Report, *For Whose Benefit?*, which explicitly charged that business and trade interests too often trumped human rights and development concerns in aid allocation decisions) were reports to special committees in Parliament; the last is a report by the Canadian International Development Agency (CIDA) (1987's *Sharing Our Future*) This last claimed that the framework presented therein would 'help make it more feasible to take human rights under serious consideration in the formulation of our aid policy' (CIDA 1987: 25).

However, Canada's actual approach has been far more pragmatic than these principles suggest. Even today, when there is significant potential for trade with a country (in general more quickly developing recipients or Newly Industrialized Countries (NICs)), human rights have been argued to matter little (Gillies and Brecher 1989). Gillies contends that this discriminatory treatment of countries is a result of the extent to which an incumbent government's quest for political survival is predicated on economic growth. 'This imperative is the foundation of the privileged position that business develops in the policy arena' (Gillies 1989: 455). As the examples throughout this study suggest, this is a pattern that has been borne out in Canada's bilateral relations with several of its aid recipients.

Australia

Australia's potential as a regional power for influencing human rights abuses appears to be great, especially given the regionalism in Australia's foreign policy. However, the Australian government has a record of subsuming human rights concerns to economic ones in aid and other foreign policy decisions. For instance, in response to the initial Indonesian invasion of East Timor in 1975, the Australian ambassador in Jakarta wrote to the Foreign Affairs Department:

> I would suggest that our policies should ... leave events to take their course, and if and when Indonesia does intervene, act in a way which would ... minimize the public impact in Australia and show privately understanding to Indonesia of their problems.
>
> (Scharfe 1996: 99)

Critics have argued that the sole goal behind this hands-off approach was ensuring access to the Timor Gap – the second most productive oilfield in the world, which lies between Australia and Indonesia.[3]

Though this strategy was purchased at a high price,[4] it appears to have been effective. The timeline is highly suggestive: When in 1978 the Australian government gave de facto recognition to the Indonesian occupation, it began to drill more extensively in an area of the Gap claimed by Indonesia. After *de jure* recognition was granted, discussions on the Gap area began almost immediately (Budiardjo and Soei Long 1984: 170, cited in Scharfe 1996: 101). Finally, when the Australian government recognized the integration as complete, discussions moved on to a new phase: joint development with the Indonesian military and finally, an official 'zone of cooperation' between the two governments (*Canberra Times* 18 April 1984, cited in Scharfe 1996: 171). Finally, on 11 December 1989, the Indonesian and Australian Foreign Ministers signed a treaty officially dividing the area into zones of exploration rights for each country. While this sequence of events could be mere coincidence, and while it is, of course, impossible to know what Australia's stance on East Timor would have been in the absence of this economic incentive, this is a striking case where potential rebuke was put on the back burner for fear of jeopardizing an economically important relationship. Australia in fact continued to challenge the autonomy of East Timor through the International Court of Justice.

Strategic concerns have consistently loomed less large in Australian foreign policy than have economic ones and, when they have mattered, they have mainly been driven by the import accorded them by the United States. For instance, a strategic reason Australia has been opposed to an independent East Timor is that East Timor's boundaries contain the Ombai–Wetar straits (Taylor 1991, cited in Scharfe 1996). These have been rated, with Gibraltar, as the most important deep-water straits in the world to US defense planning. After the 1974 left-wing coup in Portugal, Australian and US policy-makers refused to consider self-determination for East Timor under socialist Fretilin for fear of jeopardizing access to these straits.

Commonalities

These three donors have much in common. Among the most obvious is rhetorical commitment to human rights that has not always panned out in practice (or has only been implemented very inconsistently). Policy-makers in all three donors have acknowledged the tradeoffs I predict to drive aid patterns. This implies that all of these donors rank their foreign policy goals and only aim to meet those lower on the list (where human rights probably usually falls) when those higher have either already been met, or conversely, when there is no chance of attaining them.

On the other hand, the differential geopolitical and economic situations of these donors suggests important differences in their aid patterns, in their view of their own economic interests, and in the likelihood that human rights will play a role in their aid decisions.

In terms of geopolitical position, for instance, Australian foreign policy-makers traditionally see themselves as far more isolated and trade-dependent than do policy-makers in the other two nations, so Australian aid is more regionally focused. Scholars of Canadian foreign policy perceive it as highly affected by its relationship with, and perceived dependence on, the US. If they are right, we should see a greater proportion of Canadian foreign policy directly taking into account US interests than is the case with the other two donors (Barratt 2004).

Qualitative approach

Tomasevski suggested that

> in order to be able to incorporate human rights into development aid, one would need to adopt a different approach from that pursued today by donors. The starting point would be to focus on aid itself – at the policy as well as the project level – and assess it by human rights criteria.
>
> (Tomasevski 1993: 154–5)

She went on to lament the dearth of country-level evaluations by many donors, and the secrecy of surrounding ones that did exist. This is an area in which donors have actually made great strides; since the 1980s most donors have carried out regular country-level evaluations.

But by and large, as Tomasevski and indeed the DAC itself (in its annual reports) has lamented, these have been internal documents and in many cases not even shared with other government agencies or parliaments. While this situation has improved somewhat, it has made it very difficult to really assess what is being taken into account in decisions about specific recipients. No wonder that so little analysis of internal evaluations and decision-making correspondence has been conducted – it has been almost entirely off limits.

This research presents the first systematic analyses of country strategy reports from the three donor countries in question. While specific access issues and reports covered are discussed in the individual donor chapters, all documents were analyzed around the content of several basic themes reflecting the goals of aid discussed in the previous chapter. These included development and poverty reduction, good governance (including democratization, elections and corruption), fiscal reform and management, security (including communism, internal disturbances and terror), trade (including specific considerations regarding petroleum), Commonwealth or colonial history, aid effectiveness, humanitarian crises and rights.

Quantitative approach

The question of selection effects

Before getting into the specifics of my quantitative approach, it is important to address the issue of selection effects.[5] There are at least two points in such a research design at which selection effects could be introduced. First, countries that are currently or potentially valuable to the donor may also be those that are less likely to be candidates for aid. However, this is not always the case. Growing economies in fact frequently request aid for infrastructural or industrial construction. For instance, Indonesia has been one of the greatest recipients of aid from both Canada and Australia, and it has a rapidly expanding import market, which has been the focus of numerous Canadian export offensives (Scharfe 1996).[6]

In another instance of this reverse-need prioritization, until the release of *Sharing Our Future* in 1988, Canada's aid disbursement was based in part on a 'Categories of Eligibility' list. It ranked recipients according to the nature and intensity of Canada's interests in the country, as well as by the mechanism of aid disbursement, and so relegated 'some of the poorest LDCs to marginal status as Canadian aid recipients' (Gillies and Brecher 1989: x).[7]

Another set of selection effects might be operating if one were to look solely at states that receive aid, rather than at all potential recipients. The design of this research, however, overcomes this potential problem. It explores two aid decisions (the first of which includes *all* potential recipients, not just those that actually receive aid, as discussed in the previous chapter), and therefore it should be possible to determine when these selection effects are operating, and to mitigate any bias they might introduce.

These decisions are examined for each donor–recipient dyad year, through which I evaluate the relative role of humanitarian, economic, strategic and other criteria. The first is the donor's decision to give the recipient aid, and the second is its decision about the amount to allocate. While the answer to the second question is contingent on the first, there are solid theoretical and epistemological reasons for modeling disbursement in two stages, as discussed in Chapter 3.

Quantitative research design

Assessing the goodness of fit of these hypotheses ideally necessitates three different analyses for the gatekeeping decision.[8] The first assesses the determinants of whether in any given year the recipient state received aid (1 if yes, 0 otherwise) from the donor. The second and third analyses look at determinants of specific changes in the pool of recipients from year to year. The dependent variable in the second analysis is whether the donor initiated aid to the recipient in question when the recipient had not received it for the year immediately preceding (1 if yes, 0 otherwise). The third analysis examines factors associated with whether the donor denied aid to the recipient in question when the recipient had received aid for the year immediately preceding (again, a 1, 0 dummy variable).[9]

I also look at several different types of decisions at the allocation stage. The first of these concerns the raw amount of aid to be allocated to each recipient in a given year. The second and third examine the decision to increase or decrease aid to a given recipient.

Though as we will see, substantial differences can be observed between the gatekeeping and allocation stages, few differences were observed between the different sub-decisions at these stages and therefore, for the sake of parsimony, the results of analyses of the different sub-decisions are presented only in Appendix 2.

Finally, and most importantly, I divide recipient states into groups based on their potential economic and strategic importance to donors, and explore whether concern for human rights matters more for some groups than others, at both the gatekeeping and the allocation stages. In the previous chapter I described the way I expect importance to condition the effects of human rights.

Because I explore two stages in the aid-allocation process, I employ two models in the quantitative portion of this research. The unit of analysis is the dyad year.

For the gatekeeping decision, I estimate models using pooled, cross-sectional logit, a technique appropriate to dichotomous dependent variables whose probability distribution is more logistic than it is normal, over a universe of cases that includes a large group of observations, each of which is taken at several points in time. A control is included for aid at year t−1 to control for serial autocorrelation.

The reduced[10] form of the model to be estimated is the pooled, cross-sectional logit function:

Aid given (0 = no, 1 = yes) = b1 human rights record + b2 potential economic importance of recipient + b3 vulnerability of donor state ruling party + b4 potential economic importance * human rights record + b5 donor government vulnerability * human rights record + b6 strategic value of recipient + b7 strategic value * human rights record + b8 end of cold war + b9 recipient need.

For the allocation decisions involving continuous dependent variables (raw aid amounts), pooled cross-sectional time-series regression analysis is conducted of the factors influencing aid amount. This method is, again, appropriate for examining a large group of cases over the duration of several temporal points.

The reduced form[11] of the model to be estimated for each of the donors under consideration is the regression function:

*Aid amount = b1 human rights record + b2 potential economic importance of recipient + b3 vulnerability of donor state ruling party + b4 potential economic importance * human rights record + b5 donor government vulnerability * human rights record + b6 strategic value of recipient + b7 strategic value * human rights record + b8 end of cold war + b9 recipient need.*

Aid

The operational forms of the dependent variable for the gatekeeping decision are discussed above. Of course, this does not capture the value of the aid to the recipient country, which the donor may also anticipate and give only when it thinks aid will be especially valuable to the recipient (and therefore reap the donor reciprocal benefits). However, the value to the donor is assumed by this approach to figure more prominently in its calculations than does value to the recipient.

Annual data on bilateral aid to all recipients from Australia, Canada and the UK are available from the OECD's publication *Geographical Distribution of Financial Flows*.

In order to test the central hypotheses, I include the following independent variables, 11 of which measure main effects. The rest are interactive terms.

Human rights record of the recipient state

Human rights abuses in recipient countries are measured, for the years 1980–2004, using the Purdue Political Terror Scale,[12] originally compiled by Michael Stohl, now maintained by Mark Gibney at UNC-Asheville. It is a dual scale derived from two sources: the US Department of State's annual country reports and those of Amnesty International. This is a 5-point scale ranging from 1 ('Countries … under a secure rule of law, people are not imprisoned for their views, and torture is rare or exceptional…. Political murders are extraordinarily rare') to 5 ('The violence of Level four has been extended to the whole population…. The leaders of these societies place no limits on the means or thoroughness with which they pursue personal or ideological goals') (Stohl 1973).

Unfortunately, for some regions, little early data on the status of human rights is available at all. This is due to inconsistent record-keeping, to varying definitions of human rights, and to opposition to documentation in systematic violators (in fact, persecution of human rights observers is often a major form of human rights abuses in violator states). Second, many characteristics of recipients associated with high levels of human rights abuses (frequent changes of government, general governmental instability, authoritarian control, etc.) are also associated with inconsistent and inaccurate record-keeping.

Given that the scale provides one with two measures, which should be adopted? It would be possible to take an average of the two scores, but the Amnesty scores suffer many more cases of missing data for than the State Department scores, so that using the averages for cases where both scores were present, but just State Department scores when that was all that was available, would lead to estimations that were not comparable across recipients. State Department scores are employed because they exist for a greater number of the cases than do the Amnesty scores. However, there are non-trivial differences between them that serve as an important caveat to the use of the State Department figures, especially if one is trying to obtain a measure of human rights violations as they are perceived by donor states (for an excellent discussion of this see Carey and Poe 2004).

First of all, there are significant differences in the source data for the State and Amnesty scores. Amnesty's data-collection protocols reflect a deep skepticism towards succinct quantitative comparisons between different states, because of lack of comparability due to data-collection problems, lack of adequate record-keeping, and deliberate governmental obfuscation. (After all, the focus of the Political Terror Scale is *governmental* abuses of citizens, the very data governments are most likely to suppress.) Therefore, Amnesty's country reports are almost entirely in the form of narrative records, often focusing on individual cases rather than overall counts of various types of violations. State Department accounts, while still in narrative form, tend to include more statistics and counts of various types of incidents, making State Department reports for any one country are more standardized across years, and more directly comparable with those for other countries, than are the Amnesty reports. This was a first major reason that State measures were chosen over those for Amnesty.

Missing values were a second. There were many cases for which *both* measures were missing, but there were significantly fewer for the State (1422 out of 3491 cases) than there were for Amnesty (1615 out of 3491). The fact that values were missing matters for convenience and for having as large a sample as possible. It does not *necessarily* indicate anything fundamentally different about the way the two sources assess human rights violations.

But obviously it might influence the choice of indicator if one was systematically 'easier' or 'stricter' in evaluating violations. An easy way to assess this is to examine the average of each. For the State Department's measure, the average of all 2000+ scores between 1980 and 1997 was 2.7 – right about in the middle of a scale which assigns the most serious violators a score of 5 and the best protectors of human rights a score of 1. For Amnesty International's measure, the average of all 1800+ scores was 2.94. While this is not, by most standards, an egregious difference, it does indicate that Amnesty tends to assess governmental human rights violations a bit more strictly (about 7 percent more strictly) than does the State Department (or at least the Purdue compilers perceive that it does).

However, this apparently small difference in means obscures more substantial discrepancies in the data on the level of individual cases. When one looks at the 1854 observations where there are scores for both scales, the two measures only correlate at 0.75 – lower than would be expected given the closeness of the means. Therefore, there must be a substantial number of states on which the two scales disagree. Of those 1854 observations, the two scales rate the state differently in 823 of those cases – over 44 percent of the total sample. In 297 of those cases, the State Department evaluated the country more harshly than did Amnesty International. In 526 of them, Amnesty evaluated the country more harshly than did the US State Department. Therefore, in choosing State Department scores, I may be underestimating the true level of state violence within the evaluated countries – as well as introducing an explicitly American (and explicitly governmental) view of which potential recipients are guilty – and not guilty. Fortunately, discrepancies in the sets of scores have become smaller over time, so differences in the analyses based on measurement error become smaller as one moves forward in time.

To test whether this made any difference to the statistical analyses in my research, all analyses for the OECD were conducted using both the State and Amnesty measures. While violations that made it onto the State Department's radar screen DO appear to have an effect on OECD aid decisions under certain conditions, rights records of states as assessed by Amnesty almost never did. It is important to keep in mind that no matter which of these scales I adopt, it does not reveal the entire story, and that the story told by the other measure may be quite different. This is especially true because many of the cases where the discrepancy between scales is the greatest (two points or more) are cases of countries with close ties to the donors of interest in this study.

This is particularly significant given that some past studies have used Amnesty measures and substituted in State measures when no Amnesty data were available. Given that there are 215 cases (or about 11 percent) where no Amnesty data are available, a great many cases of human rights violations are being judged with measures that are not comparable to those utilized for the other cases for which Amnesty measures *are* available. Since many of these include gross violators ranking a score of 4 or even 5 in the State Department's estimation (such as, for instance, Nicaragua in 1980, Cambodia in 1987 or Serbia in 1992 and 1996), this may indeed give one pause.

Nonetheless, it is probably preferable to proceed with the data available than to refrain from investigating human rights/policy linkages. So to provide a better understanding of what the State scales look like in real-world terms, some examples of the countries who received the worst (5) human rights scores in the last year in the study (of all potential OECD aid recipients) include Afghanistan, Iraq, as well as a number of African states in the midst of armed conflict including Algeria, Angola, Burundi, Liberia, Rwanda and Sierra Leone.

This variable is lagged one year to allow for collection of data in the donor country, as well as for the budgeting process to take place. In addition, given concerns about the State scales, it seemed wise to run these analyses substituting in other proxies for the status of rights in the recipients, such as levels of demo-cracy and counts of internal disorder incidents (riots, demonstrations etc). Similar results were observed, lending validation to the analyses discussed below.

Potential economic value of the recipient state

I take into account not only the current, but also the potential economic value of the recipient, because donor state policy-makers do so.[13] Potential characteristics capturing the economic value of the recipient state to the donor include import/export ratios and volumes, and the size and growth rate of the recipient country's economy.[14]

Potential economic value of the recipient to the donor is measured in two ways. First, what is the size of the economy of the recipient state (GDP)? Second, how fast is the economy growing (annual growth rate of GDP)? Together, these two figures suggest how promising a trade partner the recipient state looks to be.

I also control for recipient state population (Central Intelligence Agency (CIA), various years). While population is included as a control for per-capita ratios, it may also serve as a valuable clue as to whether donors take into account how many people will potentially benefit from their aid contributions.

In addition, I construct measurements that more specifically tap the recipient country's trade potential, since trade is often the most important dimension of the economic relationship between the donor and recipient. For individual donor states, percentage and total volume of trade between donor and recipient are available from the International Monetary Fund's Direction of Trade Statistics. For the OECD, by multiplying the country's total volume of exports (and imports) for the year in question by the percentage of exports (and imports) to and from the OECD, it is possible to calculate the recipient country's total export and import volume with the OECD. The import/export ratio between recipient and donor is also included because it is a widely applied measure of a recipient's economic robustness and of the donor/recipient relationship, access-ible to donor policy-makers. Finally, in order to test whether, as postulated, the economic value of a recipient conditions whether its human rights record is likely to impact aid, an interactive term is included that consists of the recipient state's human rights record multiplied by its import/export ratio with the donor.[15]

Finally, volume of trade is not always synonymous with importance of trade. A total of $30 million in video games is unlikely to be viewed in the same way as is $30 million in petroleum. Therefore, in analyses of individual donor coun-tries I also include a measure of whether the aid recipient is a major exporter of oil or other natural resources.

Party in donor state

The vulnerability of the government in the donor state is best captured by the robustness of its control of Parliament. This can be operationalized categorically, by whether the government is strong majority, bare majority, minority or coalition. To be more precise, I include a measure of number of seats controlled by the ruling and opposition parties. I predicted in the last chapter that this vulnerability conditions the precedence that economic interests take over human rights on the foreign policy agenda.

Strategic value of the recipient state

A prevailing argument in much US-focused aid literature (for instance, Organski 1990) is that it is strategic interests that predominantly trump human rights – and economic – concerns. These arguments predict that a recipient with whom a donor has had recent conflict or anticipates future conflict should be less likely to receive aid, because such conflict would disrupt any benefit the donor would be deriving for its investment. (For instance, such relationships involving aid have been documented by Morrow *et al.* 1998). However, such conflicts, at least militarized ones, are relatively rare, due to the vast power and wealth asymmetries between most donor and recipient states.

Therefore, the strategic value of the recipient is measured in several other ways. These measures include the geographic location of the recipient (proximity to donor, to trade intersections, and to areas of instability); existing alliances between the two states;[16] recent tensions between the donor and recipient, and whether the recipient possesses nuclear capabilities.

Obviously many of these do not apply in any meaningful way to aggregate aid levels recipients attain, examined in the next chapter. However, two measures of potential strategic value that are not donor-specific *are* included in the OECD analysis. The first of these is the nuclear status of the recipient. Current lists of the members of the nuclear club were taken from the *Historical Statistics of the United States* (2005). The second is whether the recipient state is located in an area of current instability (whether internal or external). This admittedly broad measure is derived from disputes compiled for that year by the CIA in which the recipient state (or a state on which it borders) is a party of any kind (CIA, various years).

End of the Cold War

Donors might see themselves as being less constrained by strategic concerns and freer to allocate aid according to other considerations. Whether the Cold War is still being waged during any given year is measured dichotomously. This variable is likely to matter more for donors who are closer strategic allies of the US, such as Britain.

Five other variables are included in the functions to be estimated as control variables.

Recipient democracy

All donor states in this study have very high democracy scores (as measured in Marshall and Jaggers' most recent update of Polity IV (2005)). Much discourse around human rights, as we have seen, treats 'democracy' and 'respect for human rights' as essentially synonymous (e.g. Beitz 1979: 179; Franck 1992: 46–7). When two states mutually possess high democracy scores, it is also a powerful predictor of trade volumes (Morrow *et al.* 1998). This variable is included to test the extent to which democracy is indeed a proxy for respect for human rights, and to hold constant the added boost to trade volumes one might expect when two states share high levels of democracy. Similarity in democracy levels is measured as the distance between the donor and recipient's scores.

Immigrants from recipient state in donor state

A large, well-organized immigrant population can have a decisive effect on aid allocations to its country of origin. This argument has, for instance, been made consistently about US aid to Israel (Organski 1990). The presence of nationals of the recipient country in the donor country is measured in raw numbers and as a percentage of total donor country population. Sources for each donor country are described in subsequent chapters. Electoral and financial importance of that immigrant group, the extent of organization of that group, and media coverage of the source country would require assembling these data from archival research on each donor country individually, and are beyond the scope of the present project, though they would be important inclusions in future research.

Past aid

Past aid is a significant determinant of present aid, because appropriations are often left unchanged as a result of bureaucratic inability to agree on changes and due to institutional inertia described above. Aid may remain at similar levels, or at a similar status (in the gatekeeping model), as something of a default (Apodaca and Stohl 1999: 188). In the gatekeeping model, this variable is measured as a zero, one dichotomous variable. In the allocation model, this variable is measured in raw terms.

Activities of human rights interest groups in donor country

As discussed at the beginning of this chapter, there are limited avenues open to human rights interest groups as they compete against better-funded business interests for the ear of the public and policy-makers. One of the most important of these is public action, which can increase the salience of human rights as a policy issue. These attempts at agenda-setting by such groups as Amnesty International and Human Rights Watch (HRW) are currently measured by reports of demonstrations and protests in each of the donors (based on the PANDA subset of KEDS data, (Protocol for the Assessment of Nonviolent Direct Action, www.wcfia.harvard.edu/ponsacs/research/PANDA_IDEA.htm (last accessed 2 March 2006), regarding the relevant recipient, because neither Amnesty nor HRW in the donor countries have systematic data available on activities around specific campaigns, such as the number of public campaigns launched, number of demonstrations, and size of such demonstrations.

Mass-mediated humanitarian crises

This control is included both in the interest of replicability (it is standard in studies of US aid (Cingranelli and Pasquarello 1985; Poe 1990, 1991)) and because a measure of humanitarian crises serves as a gauge of altruism. Mass-mediated humanitarian crises refer to humanitarian crises in the recipient that are widely covered in news sources in the donor. They are also another measure of public awareness, and hence salience, in the donor country.[17] There may be some collinearity between this variable and a recipient's per capita GDP. While exogenous shocks which cause humanitarian crises (such as earthquakes, floods, droughts etc.) can occur anywhere, poorer recipients are likely to have the least infrastructural ability to respond to and recover from such shocks. Therefore, humanitarian crises which occur in the poorest countries are on the one hand likely to receive the most coverage, but are also occurring, at least according to a needs-based model, in places that are already getting high amounts of aid. Because they would be more likely to be receiving aid from the international community at large and from multilateral granting organizations, poor recipients with mass-mediated humanitarian crises may actually receive less from any one of the individual donors, because such donors might know the recipient is getting aid from other sources. This data is drawn from the UN's Humanitarian Affairs Relief Web database, online at www.reliefweb.int/rw/dbc.nsf/doc100? OpenForm (last accessed 7 May 2007).

5 The global context

Cross-national aid patterns 1980–2004

This chapter presents the results of quantitative tests of the general approach and specific hypotheses laid out in the previous chapters, in the context of the donor members of one international organization – the Organization for Economic Cooperation and Development, or OECD. These analyses are designed to provide evidence on the following broad questions. First, in both the gatekeeping and allocation decisions, what is the relative weight accorded the human rights records, economic importance and strategic importance of the recipient states? Second, are these factors weighted in a way which is symmetrical? That is, do the same factors have the same relative weight in the decision to initiate or increase aid as they do in the decision to terminate or decrease it? Finally, are different factors weighted differently for different kinds of recipients – that is, are all recipients or potential recipients judged by consistent criteria and processes when aid decisions are being made?

Why look at aid decisions by all members of the OECD when the approach and theory laid out in the previous chapters is built around the decision-making process in individual donors? Looking at the OECD overall furnishes a baseline context of aid determinants in a group comprised largely of the kind of wealthy Western democratic donors that are the subject of this study. This allows me to examine the determinants and processes of aid decisions in each of the donor countries of interest in the context of a more generalized donor community.

Of course, there are certain aspects of the model laid out in Chapters 1 and 2 that cannot be examined in the context of aid from all OECD members pooled together. Vulnerability of the donor government, for example, is not a factor that can be evaluated in any succinct and meaningful way in the context of aid from all OECD members pooled. For similar reasons, the analyses of individual donors will contain greater emphasis on the *processes* behind aid decisions, and thus will draw more heavily from comparative case-study methodology. Nonetheless, most of the other major relationships that are key to understanding why aid goes where it does (such as when human rights versus economic concerns are likely to matter, and whether these factors weigh differently for different kinds of aid and diverse categories of recipients) can be meaningfully tested in the OECD context.

For untied aid, the same hypotheses apply with stronger relationships posited between both moral and economic concerns and amount of aid. This possibility is discussed in Appendix 3.

As mentioned in the previous chapter, several permutations of the dependent variable will be examined. The first is simply whether in any given year the recipient received aid (1 if yes, 0 otherwise) from the donor. This will provide a straightforward overall look at the gatekeeping decision.

Next, I move on to the second stage of the decision process: the allocation of specific amounts of aid once a state has made it into the pool of recipients. Regression analyses are conducted of the raw *levels* of aid in order to determine the relative influence of human rights, economic characteristics of the recipient, and strategic factors.

There still remains one crucial question, however. *Do different kinds of recipients receive different treatment?* That is, are recipients (or potential recipients) which are economically valuable more likely to be rewarded for 'good' internal behavior, and less likely to be punished for 'bad' behavior? In order to determine whether all recipients are indeed treated as equals, the sample of aid recipients from 1980 to 1996 was divided up on the basis of how economically valuable they might appear to the donor, or, in this case, OECD members in general. (As it seemed unwise to make assumptions about which measure of economic value might be most important to donors, the sample is divided up according to different measures of economic value, as described in Appendix 2.) If indeed economically important recipients 'get away' with more than do economically unimportant ones, human rights variables should have more of an impact for less economically valuable recipients than they do for economically important ones. In turn, it is likely that donors' economic self-interest has an increased relative effect in aid decisions about economically important recipients than it does in aid to economically unimportant ones.

Data issues

Variable operationalization and data sources are described in detail in the previous chapter. All analyses address total aid; differences between tied and other kinds of aid are discussed at the end of the chapter. As noted, there are a number of characteristics of both donor and recipient states which simply cannot be measured in any meaningful way in the context of aid decisions of all OECD members pooled. Among these are donor government vulnerability and the strategic value of the recipient. In addition, many of the economic value and trade variables are not quite as easily interpretable for the overall OECD as is the case for individual donors, and they do not mean quite the same thing. For example, if 70 percent of France's trade were with a specific recipient country, one might expect that recipient's economic and trade value to have a significant impact on French aid allocation to that recipient. But such considerations may be dramatically diluted in a multilateral setting.

Pooled figures do not reveal whether many donors are each giving a small amount, or one state is giving a substantial amount, or something in between.

For instance, countries that receive large amounts of aid from the OECD and also engage in a large volume of trade with OECD countries could be receiving aid because nearly every member country has a small amount of trade with that recipient and hence *some* interest in it. But a large amount of aid would also be recorded in the OECD's pooled figures if just one donor was responsible for it because, for instance, it did a great deal of trade with it and therefore had an intense interest in it. In short, statistical analyses of OECD aid decisions can indicate something about broad funding trends, but it is harder to assess much about the intentionality or reasoning processes behind these decisions without disaggregating to the level of the individual donor, as I do in subsequent chapters.

There are further data availability and analysis issues particular to the case of the OECD that bear discussion since they are relevant to the validity and interpretability of the results presented below. Most importantly, the quality of data on percentage of exports and imports to and from OECD members varies greatly over time and across recipients. Especially in earlier editions of the CIA publication, trade partners are simply listed with no indication of how large a percentage of trade occurs with them. In most cases, it was possible to estimate from these lists the total amount of trade that occurred with the OECD, but some of these estimates are rough.[1] For the individual donors examined in subsequent chapters, these data will be drawn from the World Bank's Direction of Trade data set which lists very specific bilateral trade volumes, so these measures are much more exact in later chapters.

Whether the recipient was located at a key trade intersection and whether it was located in an area of instability are also by necessity measured rather broadly, since for overall OECD aid levels it is difficult to include in the analysis the perceptions and estimations of which intersections are 'key' or which areas of instability matter to individual donor governments. Yet both of these are defined very specifically by the OECD itself as being explicit considerations in the aid decision-making process.

For example, in 1997 the DAC issued a set of guidelines and a formal policy statement on 'Conflict, Peace, and Development Cooperation on the Threshold of the 21st Century'. This document makes a strong argument for the utility of development assistance in lessening the likelihood of armed conflict, as well as mitigating its destructive effects. Specifically, the document presents various forms of aid and the ways that they can be used at each of four stages in a conflict: in situations of potential conflict, during open hostilities; in the transitional period directly following armed conflict; and in reconstruction operations (OECD 1997). These guidelines would lead one to predict that potential recipients in conflict, ceteris paribus, are more likely to receive aid than other states, and to receive more aid. What my analyses actually demonstrate, as will be discussed below, is that these states are *less* likely in any given year to receive aid, but more likely than other states to be *added* to the aid list. To an extent, then, OECD members' actions follow policy guidelines.

Both the measures of conflict/instability and location at a trade intersection rely on CIA data (various years). If a recipient is listed as a participant in an interstate dispute or as a site of government-threatening civil unrest, or borders on such a state, it is coded as a site of instability. A potential recipient is coded as being located at a key trade intersection if it contains major pipelines, key ports or is on a major natural resource shipment route.

Finally, some of the key variables discussed in detail in Chapter 2 bear closer examination in the context of aid from all OECD members pooled together.

For the allocation decision, aid is operationalized as total aid from OECD countries to that recipient in a given year. Of course, this does not capture the value of the aid to the recipient country, which donors may also anticipate, giving only when they judge aid especially valuable to the recipient. Annual data on aid to all recipients from OECD donors are available from the OECD's Creditor Reporting System (online at www.oecd.org/crs/o).

Table 5.1 yields a sense of the universe of (189) potential aid recipients. Potential recipients are defined as all states who are *not* members of the OECD and are poorer than all OECD member countries.

The analyses demonstrate that it is much more unusual to *not* be granted aid than it is to receive it. In fact, Table 5.1 shows that 164 of the 189 potential recipients got aid. Therefore, a look at the potential recipients who were *not* granted aid is in some ways more revealing. Five of the 25 who did not receive aid (Brunei, Kuwait, Oman, Qatar and UAE) are oil exporters and relatively wealthy; while this does not explicitly exclude them from consideration for aid, it is not surprising that they would not be seen as priorities for disbursement of OECD member countries' resources. There are also few clear patterns evident in terms of the human rights records of the potential recipients who did not receive aid. The numbers in parentheses indicate the human rights scores of these states (higher numbers designate worse violation levels). Fifteen of them were not evaluated by the State Department in 1996. Five had the best possible human rights score at 1, and three had scores of 2. Only two had poor scores of 4. Clearly human rights concerns do not matter for every aid decision. The question is: *when do they?*

Results

Gatekeeping

When we examine which aid-eligible states receive aid from at least some member of the Development Assistance Committee (DAC), we see that only a few characteristics of recipients are regularly taken into account (Table 5.2). These include both economic and strategic aspects. For example, recipients with stagnating economies are likely to receive more aid, while nuclear states get less and those with internal crises get more (in line with OECD recommendations) a fact that could be read as indicating a certain amount of altruism. For states in conflict are likely to be less lucrative trading partners and are less attractive for donor-state investors – but they may still be places that can put aid to good

Table 5.1 Aid recipients and non-recipients, 2004

Recipients

Albania	Algeria	Angola	Anguilla	Argentina
Armenia	Azerbaijan	Bangladesh	Barbados	Belarus
Belize	Benin	Bhutan	Bolivia	Bosnia
Botswana	Brazil	Bulgaria	Burkina	Burundi
Cambodia	Cameroon	Cape Verde	Cent. Af. Rep.	Chad
Chile	China	Colombia	Comoros	Congo
Cook Is.	Costa Rica	Croatia	Cuba	Czech. Rep.
Djibouti	Dominica	Domin. Rep.	Ecuador	Egypt
El Salvador	Eq. Guinea	Eritrea	Estonia	Ethiopia
Fiji	French Pol.	Gabon	Gambia	Georgia
Ghana	Guatemala	Guinea	Guinea-Bis.	Guyana
Haiti	Honduras	Hong Kong	Hungary	INDI
Indonesia	Iran	Iraq	Israel	Ivory Coast
Jamaica	Jordan	Kazakhstan	Kenya	Kiribati
N, Korea	S. Korea	Kyrgyzstan	Laos	Latvia
Lebanon	Lesotho	Liberia	Libya	Lithuania
Macedonia	Madagascar	Malawi	Malaysia	Maldives
Mali	Malta	Marshall Is.	Mauritania	Mauritius
Micronesia	Moldova	Mongolia	Montserrat	Morocco
Mozambique	Namibia	Nepal	New Caled.	Nicaragua
Niger	Nigeria	Niue	N. Marianas	Pakistan
Palau	Panama	Papua N.G.	Paraguay	Peru
Philippines	Poland	Romania	Russia	Rwanda
South Africa	Sao Tome & P	Saudi Arabia	Senegal	Serbia
Seychelles	Sierra Leone	Singapore	Slovakia	Slovenia
Solomon Is.	Somalia	Sri Lanka	St. Exupery	St. Helena
St. Lucia	St. Vincent/G	Sudan	Suriname	Swaziland
Syria	Tajikistan	Tanzania	Thailand	Togo
Tonga	Trinidad	Tunisia	Turks/Caic.	Tuvalu
Uganda	Ukraine	Uruguay	Uzbekistan	Vanuatu
Venezuela	Vietnam	Virgin Is.	W. Samoa	N. Yemen
S. Yemen	Zaire	Zambia	Zimbabwe	

Non-recipients

Afghanistan (4)	Ant/Barbuda (na)	Aruba (na)	Bahamas (na)	Bahrain (2)
Bermuda (na)	Brunei (1)	Cyprus (1)	Falk. Is. (na)	Gibraltar (na)
Grenada (na)	Kuwait (2)	Macau (na)	Mayotte (na)	Myanmar (4)
Nauru (na)	Oman (1)	Qatar (na)	St. Kitts (na)	Taiwan (1)
Timor (na)	Tokelau (na)	Turkmenistan (2)	UAE (1)	Wallis/Fortuna (na)

Note
Numbers indicate Political Terror Scales coding for that recipient in 2004.

effect, as the OECD leadership has suggested. It should be noted, however, that there are very few states in any given year that get no aid at all. In fact, in the last year of this study, no country in the study that was eligible was absolutely bereft of aid. This leads to a very skewed distribution, an insignificant model, and low explanatory power for the model.

Table 5.2

Variable	Gatekeeping allocation coefficient	Allocation decision
Year	−0.04	6862.38**
General characteristics of recipient		
Recipient GDP	2.42^{-10}	-4.90^{-09}
Human rights measures		
Human rights violations	0.00	−3308.40
Recipient polity score	−0.00	−496.05
Economic value measures		
DAC exports to recipient	2.42^{-09}	-2.20^{-07}
DAC imports from recipient	8.44^{-09}	1.12^{-07}**
Recipient oil exports	0.00	116.29**
Recipient GDP growth	−0.03*	−1004.38
Recipient population	1.92^{-07}	8.00^{-06}
Strategic value measures		
Recipient nuclear capabilities	3.76***	335,751.90***
Internal dispute	1.29*	33,445.02
External dispute	−0.59	−22,710.78
Post-Cold War	0.71	−90,674.03**
Trade intersection	−0.99	66,072.97**
Need measures		
Humanitarian crisis	0.38	48,860.30**
Policy history		
Aid previous year?	7.56^{-06}	0.64***
Significance of model		0.00
N	2396	2444
R^2 within groups, between, overall		0.06, 0.92, 0.52

Notes
*** = significant at $p < 0.001$; ** = $p < 0.01$; * = $p < 0.05$; (marg) = $p < 0.075$ (one-tailed).

Allocation

When we move on to look at the overall levels of aid that recipients get, many more of the predicted variables have an impact. States with ongoing humanitarian crises receive more aid as do those that are strategically important in terms of their nuclear capabilities or being situated at a trade intersection. Each recipient gets a bit less after the Cold War, but analyses of aid patterns for the individual donors suggest this has to do with a wider disbursement of aid, especially to former Soviet and Soviet bloc states after the end of the Cold War. States with high levels of trade with DAC members get more, as do oil exporters. Improvements in rights do not appear to matter significantly.

The effect of a valuable trade relationship on the aid calculus

But economic and strategic value does not represent just an additional variable, but rather identifies fundamentally different processes of aid allocation. Those countries that have strong economic value are treated systematically differently than those that have comparatively less economic value. The process of aid allocation varies depending on the economic value of the recipient, so that variables such as *Human Rights* have different effects among high economic-value states than they do with low economic-value states. Two different processes require two different efforts to estimate variable effects and two error terms (Greene 2003; Hanushek and Jackson 1977; Studenmund 1992).

To capture these different processes of aid allocation, I use a method that I will here describe in some detail, because it is applied in the analyses of individual donor-aid programs in the chapters that follow.

I want to identify those observations (country years) that represent especially valuable OECD economic activity. Which criteria determine a recipient state's economic value to the OECD? I initially focus on a recipient's imports from OECD countries. I do this for a number of reasons. First, the notion of deploying aid to foster expanding markets for developing world exports has a long history in the justifications of aid allocation (dating right back to the Marshall Plan and expressed legally in, for instance, Britain's now abolished Aid and Trade Provision) and is a key part of other arguments about the interconnectedness of aid and development (Cardoso and Galetto 1979; Evans 1979), making imports both an obvious candidate and an important factor to examine. Second, exports to OECD countries are greatly influenced by oil (and to a lesser extent by other natural resources), making exports a more complex factor. Third, I want a value that OECD states can clearly identify and recognize as belonging to those states that are most economically important. Thus more subtle notions, such as levels of technological innovations (for instance, patents) or educational investment, might have important long-run economic value, but are unlikely to represent a visible criterion used to allocate aid annually. But critically, as I will show in the section on diagnostics, the choice over which factor, statistical method or operational procedure to use to split the sample into high economic-value states and other states has virtually no effect on the results (for example, exports work almost identically to imports). Therefore, given that imports are a little easier to interpret and represent a concept tightly connected to traditional arguments about the role of aid and trade, I employ recipient state's imports from all OECD members to split the sample.

The variable *High OECD Imports* is coded one (1) if it is in the top quartile (25 percent) of OECD importers. A one for *High OECD Imports* signifies that an observation is seen by the OECD states as among the economically most valuable nations. I code the observation a zero (0) for *High OECD Imports* if it is in the bottom 75 percent of all OECD imports. The *High OECD Import* group has 311 observations and the *Low OECD Import* group has 930 observations.[2] *High OECD Importers* received on average aid allocations of $369,850, ranging from (in millions of US dollars) $12.6 to $749,487, while *Low OECD Importers* averaged $109,594.9, ranging from $7.8 to $357,750. Thus, those who imported the most from OECD countries received on average over 300 percent more aid than those who imported less. Similarly, the minimum and maximum aid allocations are higher for the *High OECD Importers* than for *the Low OECD Importers*. A bivariate analysis of *High OECD Import* status on *Untied Aid* results in a positive strongly significant estimate, suggesting that recipient economic value is systematically correlated with aid levels.[3]

Thus, both descriptive and inferential statistics suggest that high economic value, as determined by import status, fundamentally leads to greater aid allocations.[4] Next, I want to identify both which factors influence aid allocation within each group and whether the allocation processes are similar between groups. In order to answer these questions, I conduct two new analyses also displayed in Table 5.3. The first, shown in the third column, represents the aid-allocation process for *Low OECD Importers* (those in the bottom 75 percent). The second, in the fourth column, examines aid allocation for *High OECD Importers* (those in the top 25 percent of importers).

The last analysis demonstrated that states with a high level of trade engagement received more aid. Does a state's level of trade engagement with donors affect not only the amount of aid it receives but the extent to which it can 'get away' with higher levels of human rights abuses? My analyses suggest that, at least in the aggregate, there are differences between what affects aid for high-importing and low-importing recipients, but that human rights improvements or failings matter for neither. This is only demonstrated for aid amounts, though – as noted above and demonstrated in Table 5.1, it is extremely rare for eligible states to receive no aid whatsoever and, when analyzing simply whether or not a state received aid, no variables achieved significance for either high- or low-importing recipients. The factors that matter to aid amounts, however, do differ somewhat for high and low importers. For low importers, poorer states and those with a high volume of exports to the DAC receive higher aid amounts. For high importers, we see more consistent aid as well as higher amounts. There is less volatility year by year, though we do actually see a more complex set of factors systematically mattering: the presence of a humanitarian crisis (states in crisis get more), the relative economic performance of the recipient (those performing worse get more), its level of democracy, and whether or not it is an oil-exporting state (they get more). Interestingly, rights actually matter for neither category.

Different calculi apply to states that are more economically engaged with DAC states and more strategically positioned because of their geopolitical circumstances as well as their apparent vulnerability. Interestingly enough, the high importers actually have a more complex set of factors connected with their aid amounts – something that would not have been predicted by a trade-trumps-all sort of model.

The effect of a valuable strategic relationship on the aid calculus

The results presented in this section should be treated with caution, as it is difficult to distinguish between objectively 'strategic' and 'nonstrategic' recipients. Such categories are always constituted by the bilateral relations between recipient and donor. In the donor chapters that follow, therefore, strategic

Table 5.3

Variable	Gatekeeping decision		Allocation decision	
	Coefficient (standard errors) low importers	Coefficient (standard errors) high importers	Coefficient (standard errors) low importers	Coefficient (standard errors) high importers
Year	-0.04	-30.81	3624.65**	14,862.22
General characteristics of recipient				
Recipient GDP	1.18^{-09}	1.29^{-07}	-3.72^{-06}**	-1.50^{-07}
Human rights measures				
Human rights change	-0.00	-190.00	-2697.74	-6521.35
Recipient polity score	-0.01	19.85	54.76	-4919.47**
Economic value measures				
DAC exports to recipient	-2.05^{-08}	2.02^{-06}	0.00	-1.69^{-07}
DAC imports from recipient	-2.86^{-08}	0.00	0.21**	9.73^{-08}
Recipient oil exports	-0.00	1.53	19.76	188.35*
Recipient GDP growth	-0.02	-20.56	720.56	-15,794.52**
Recipient population	-1.29^{-08}	0.00	0.30	0.00
Strategic value measures				
Recipient nuclear capabilities	-1.98	-1147.24	63,862.31	445,956.80
Internal dispute	1.12	753.65	2963.31	4454.16
External dispute	1.10	-557.96	-16,985.03	-86,918.70
Post-Cold War	0.07	297.30	-33,749.92**	-224,818.80*
Trade intersection	0.14	-550.94	5730.01	61,144.85
Need measures				
Humanitarian crisis	0.61	201.49	5839.50	68,045.66***
Policy history				
Aid previous year?	2.76^{-06}	0.01	0.65***	0.57***
Significance of model		1.00	0.00	0.00
N	1611	785	1510	734
R^2			0.32, 0.84, 0.67	0.04, 0.82, 0.48

Notes
*** = significant at $p < 0.001$; ** = $p < 0.01$; * = $p < 0.05$; (marg) = $p < 0.075$ (one-tailed).

relationships are defined by an index of a recipient's contiguity to and colonial history with a donor, as well as its nuclear status and presence at a trade intersection. The presence of any two of these characteristics demarcates a 'strategic' recipient in the donor case chapters. In the context of aggregate aid patterns, however, we are forced to rely on blunter, monadic measures of a state's potential strategic value. For the purpose of these analyses, I have chosen nuclear status, presence at a trade intersection and oil exporter status. The presence of any one of these recipient characteristics was treated as a signal of strategic significance to the donor community.

At the gatekeeping phase, we can have limited confidence in our model due to overall insignificance, caused by substantial skew in the data. However, at the allocation stage, we see evidence that there are differences in the sets of factors guiding aid decisions about the two groups. Yet the differences are not as dramatic as those we saw between high and low importers, suggesting that strategic value is less straightforward in its effects on the overall aid calculus. Even once the two groups have been divided, within-group strategic differences and exports continue to affect aid amounts. For the 'low-strategic' category, amount and nature of exports increase aid amounts, as do the recipient's nuclear capabilities and geostrategic location. For the 'high-strategic' category, recipient exports, GDP growth, war, geostrategic location, past aid and crises all influence aid amounts. Notably, there are many similarities between the two groups: export amounts, geostrategic location, past aid and humanitarian crises boost current aid amounts for all states. Therefore, it does not appear that the aid calculus is affected as much by recipients' (bluntly measured) strategic qualities, as it is by their trade with the donor community.

Conclusion

The results presented in this chapter offer mixed support for the four hypotheses at the heart of this research. I have examined a number of relationships and done so across various categories of recipients based on how economically valuable they are perceived to be by donors.

The bottom line is that economic and strategic value both play a crucial role in delineating two populations of states and that both the process generating aid and the amounts of aid vary between groups. These differing results are robust to variation in method and the employment of any combination of spatial and temporal fixed effects, variation in the economic quality used to split the sample, and the coding rules used to determine the sample split cutoff point.

Appendix 1: Diagnostics for pooled analyses

In a pooled cross-sectional time series, there is always the possibility of unspecified systematic temporal and spatial variation. These were addressed in a number of ways. First, checks were performed for serial auto-correlation; systematic variance across time in the error term. The Durbin–Watson into each analysis for each year, minus one is 2.04, 1.91, 1.98 and 190, respectively. Since proximity to 2.0 (on a 0–4 scale) is an indicator of no auto-correlation, these results strongly alleviate that concern. Second, I included temporal dummies into Models 1, 2 and 3 for each year, minus one, of the study. Results were largely the same – human rights matter for the low economic-value states, and not for high economic-value states or in the pooled sample (not shown). Third, group measures might apply differently to particular states. To check for this a Fixed-Effect Regression was conducted, controlling for the effect of each state. Again, results were the same (not shown). Fourth, I conducted a Fixed-Effect Regression controlling for state and included year dummies. Controlling for year and state in a pooled cross-sectional times series presents an especially demanding test. I have not reported here analogous diagnostics for the more straightforward strategic measures.

For *Low OECD Importers*, the variable *Human Rights* continues to have a strong and negative effect on aid allocation – even when year and state fixed effects are included. *Population*, *End of the Cold War*, and *GDP growth* are each positive and significant. For the *High OECD Importers*, state population is again the only significant factor. Explanatory power for the model of *Low OECD Importers is* high, with an overall R^2 is 0.41, while between group R^2 is 0.82. Explanatory power for the *High OECD Importers* is again quite small, with an overall R^2 of 0.11 and within group R^2 of 0.15.

I also employed economic indicators other than imports to bifurcate the sample. I analyzed all three models using *Exports to OECD* and *Log of GDP* to split the sample. That is, I determined high economic value as those in the top 25th percentile of either exports or GDP. I found that splitting the samples by those above or below the 75th percentile for either exports to the OECD or log of recipient GDP generated very similar results to those obtained and presented using imports (results not shown).

Finally, I examined the robustness of the coding of *High OECD Importer* in a number of ways. I first recoded the cutoff point two ways – splitting the sample of *High OECD Importers* as those that exceeded the 75th percentile or those that met or exceeded the 75th percentile – identical results (not shown). I next made a more dramatic effort to test the sensitivity of the coding criteria. I recoded the cutoff four times, alternatively employing the 60th, 65th, 70th and 80th percentiles of recipient-state imports from OECD countries (sample sizes get too small past the 80th percentile for the purposes). All eight models (those above and below each of the four new cutoffs) behaved very similarly to those shown. Human rights records were consistently significant and negative in the group that imported less and never a factor for the states that imported more (results not shown). Rarely, a control variable changed significance (i.e. *End of the Cold War* is significant in the above 80th percentile group), but both variable estimates and model effects are strikingly similar whether 60 percent, 65 percent, 70 percent, 75 percent or 80 percent sample cutoff points are used. The results are highly robust to a wide variety of ways to identify those states that have high economic importance.

Table 5.4

Variable	Gatekeeping decision		Allocation decision	
	Coefficient (standard errors) low strategic	Coefficient (standard errors) high strategic	Coefficient (standard errors) low strategic	Coefficient (standard errors) high strategic
Year	−0.04	−25.60	6448.45*	15,706.61
General characteristics of recipient				
Recipient GDP	2.42^{-10}	1.70^{-08}	8.08^{-08}	$−1.34^{-06}$
Human rights measures				
Human rights change	−0.07	21.71	−2529.35	−32,550.08
Recipient polity score	−0.00	−1.34	−201.14	−1712.43
Economic value measures				
DAC exports to recipient	2.43^{-09}	$−3.49^{-08}$	$−2.05^{-07}$	$−1.07^{-06}$
DAC imports from recipient	8.44^{-09}	4.91^{-08}	1.07^{-07}*	4.38^{-06}***
Recipient oil exports	0.00	2.01	114.93**	193.50
Recipient GDP growth	−0.31*	−0.33	2075.77	−16,663.27***
Recipient population	1.91^{-07}	0.00	−0.00	0.00
Strategic value measures				
Recipient nuclear capabilities	−3.76***	147.38	394,894.30***	197,907.30
Internal dispute	1.29*	−83.92	19,150.42	815,509.00***
External dispute	−0.59	−137.56	−33,620.87	617,705.00**
Post-Cold War	0.70*	9.16	−88,473.74**	−313,224.80
Trade intersection	−1.00	−337.09	42,809.35*	808,874.20***
Need measures				
Humanitarian crisis	0.38	48.06	48,421.04***	72,389.96*
Policy history				
Aid previous year?	7.56^{-06}***	−0.00	0.64***	0.51***
Significance of model	1.00	1.00	0.00	0.00
N	1375	1585	1107	1391
R^2			0.08, 0.92, 0.55	0.08, 0.80, 0.47

Notes

*** = significant at $p < 0.001$; ** = $p < 0.01$; * = $p < 0.05$; (marg) = $p < 0.075$ (one-tailed).

Appendix 2: Making changes at either stage of the aid decision process

As discussed in Chapter 3, there are good reasons to believe that there are real differences between the following decisions: to continue *not* to grant aid to a state that is not currently receiving it, to start giving aid to a state that has not been receiving it, to continue to grant aid to a state that is already receiving it, and to cease granting aid to a state that has received it in the past.

For instance, we know from organizational theory that the inertia of a foreign policy organization can have a significant impact on the policy outcomes that emanate from that organization. Inertia results in part from the fact that continuance of past policies allows for increased usage of standard operating procedures (and the savings in terms of time resources this is assumed to produce) and in part from the costliness of evaluation. Gartner cites Van Evera's observation that 'evaluation and organization, it turns out, are to some extent contradictory terms' and goes on to note that 'because organizational interests are generally assumed to change rarely or at most slowly, this also suggests that policy preferences change infrequently' and that organizations have little incentive to evaluate policy (Gartner 1997). Of course this may be less the case with development assistance agencies, which explicitly react to humanitarian crises, political changes in the recipients, and their own budgetary realities.

However, the decision to leave a state's status the same is likely to be less controversial and to require less justification than the decision to either initiate or terminate aid. Therefore, we should see that – because it takes relatively dramatic developments in the granting organization's evaluation of either the human rights, economic or strategic performance of the recipient to get it to change the recipient's aid status – all these variables should exhibit more variation in cases where there has been a *change* in whether a state is receiving aid.

There are also real differences in the decision to initiate or terminate aid. It may be more difficult to make decisions that will disappoint (i.e. denials or decreasing of aid). Another reason aid is so rarely withdrawn from recipients is that policymakers in donor countries see 'negative benefits' in granting aid to many developing countries (Spicer 1966: 50). That is, despite urges to focus aid more on places where it can presumably make a difference, policy-makers believe that, even if aid does not succeed in bringing about ideal trade relations with a state or represent major strides towards internal improvements in the recipient, the situation for both donor and recipient is likely to be even worse if aid is withdrawn.

Knowing the answers to these questions can help us determine how seriously to take decisions that appear to be 'rewarding' or 'punishing' states.

In order to determine the differences between the decisions to initiate and terminate aid, and between the decisions to increase and decrease aid, I developed dependent variables measuring changes in the pool of recipients from year to year. At the gatekeeping stage, I analyzed the determinants of when aid to a potential recipient is initiated, when it is terminated, and when a potential recipient is left at the same aid status as the year before. For the allocation stage, I analyzed the factors leading to each of three different kinds of decisions: to increase aid, to decrease aid, and to make no change in aid. If the decision calculi are symmetrical for each of these decisions, We should see similar factors having similar influences on the decision to *decrease* aid and on the decision to *increase* aid.

In order to examine the differences between the various decisions at the gate-keeping phase, the universe of cases was narrowed to those cases in which the recipient had *not received* aid in the year before. A variable was created that designated whether the state then began to receive aid in the present year. Pooled cross-sectional probit analysis was conducted to determine which factors were associated with the occurrence of this new variable. While space constraints do not allow full presentation of results, the most important conclusions follow.

Initiating aid

Some of my expectations were borne out for the initiation decision, while I fail to see evidence of others. Human rights and the size and expansion rate of a recipient's economy are all marginally significant in predicting when aid will be initiated to a state. But, as I would predict based on the assumption that trade concerns would prevail in most human rights decisions, a state's exports to the OECD are far more significant predictors of whether a recipient will be added to the aid list than either human rights concerns or general economic indicators. Finally, states with nuclear capabilities are more likely to have aid initiated to them – but this finding must be interpreted with care because the number of recipient states with nuclear capabilities is so small that this finding is not very robust. Past aid levels were dropped due to collinearity, and caution must be exercised in general about the interpretation of these results because the model was insignificant overall, owing in large part to the skew in this variable (as discussed below).

Terminating aid

Poor human rights records and low GDP both make it more likely that a state will be removed from the aid list. Surprisingly, a high volume of trade with OECD members also makes a state more likely to be removed from the aid list. Larger states are, on the other hand, less likely to be dropped, which could be due to donors' perception of either greater need or greater potential value of these states. The interactive term between trade and human rights (which tests whether one conditions the other) is also significant for the termination decision. States at a trade intersection are less likely to be dropped, but interestingly, ones in areas of instability are *more* likely to be – contrary, again, to the OECD's official directive. Aid is terminated less often after the Cold War than before, suggesting again that aid is a more widely used policy tool in the post-Cold War world. But states which have had mass-mediated humanitarian crises are, surprisingly, *more* likely to have aid terminated. It should be kept in mind, however, that this analysis only measures tied aid, which is not synonymous with humanitarian assistance, and such states generally receive large amounts of emergency assistance from alternative sources. Finally, states with high levels of aid in the previous year are, unsurprisingly, less likely to have aid terminated. In terms of the overall explanatory power of the model, the percentage of outcomes predicted correctly (PPC) is very high, though the highly skewed distribution[5] means there is little proportional reduction in error.

A more intuitive way to compare whether extremes are really required to move a state from one list to another is to examine the means of some of our key variables for different samples of states: states which stayed on the same list they were on in the previous year, states to whom aid was terminated, and states to whom aid was initiated. For most of the variables of interest, more extreme values are indeed associated with policy changes, as institutional inertia would suggest. But for a number of the most theoretically interesting, such as human rights and recipient GDP, this is not the case. Clearly, a closer examination is necessary. How do these relationships apply at the allocation phase?

Increasing aid

The results of these analyses indicate that the calculi for changes in aid are not symmetrical, because the same factors do not seem to be associated with a decrease in aid as with an increase. Interestingly, and contrary to the trade-driven model of aid disbursement, states with GDP growth are less likely to see aid increased. But as a trade-driven approach would predict, all indicators of trade volume are *positively* associated with aid increases. Since this same pattern persists across many of these models, it appears it is not necessarily states with the healthiest economies that are favored, but those that are most willing or able to open themselves to international trade. In addition, more states see their aid go up in any given year *after* the end of the Cold War than before it. States with more aid are, interestingly enough, less likely to see it increased, so there appears to be some equalizing process taking place. (As is the case above, the proportional reduction in error (PRE) is rather small, but this is due in part to the skewed nature of the data).

Decreasing aid

In a symmetrical manner, states with higher GDP growth rates are more likely to see their aid amounts decreased, but states with large trade volumes with the donor states are much less likely to have their aid reduced. Though more states receive less aid after the end of the Cold War (perhaps owing to a more globalized distribution of resources by donors), once they receive it, it is less likely to be reduced. States with less aid are, again, less likely to see it cut back.[6]

Differences between different categories of recipients

Gatekeeping – initiation

I also examined whether there were differences between low- and high-value recipients for the initiation and termination decisions, but the multiple division of the sample resulted in too few observations to produce meaningful results.

Allocation – increasing aid

These analyses offered some supporting evidence to the idea that less economic-ally viable states may be held more accountable for domestic human rights abuses. States engaged in less trade with donor nations are negatively affected in decisions to increase aid if they have poor human rights records. Those with more significant trade are not affected.

Allocation – maintaining or decreasing aid

When we look at differences in the decision to decrease aid across different cat-egories of recipients, my two main predictions are borne out. First, poor human rights records are indeed punished with a decrease in aid for states in the lower half of the sample. This effect disappears for the top half of the sample.

Next, I turned to determinants of aid staying the same. No clear pattern emerges that can be linked to a recipient's trade relations with OECD states. While states with more stagnant economies are more likely to be punished and less likely to be rewarded on the basis of their human rights records, there seems to be little difference between what keeps states with high trade volumes with the OECD at constant aid levels and what does the same for those that do not enjoy the same trade volumes.

To summarize, for cases where aid was decreased or remained the same, analyses revealed significant effect of both economic and human rights variables. While I would predict that more variables would be important in the 'increase' and 'decrease' decisions than in the cases where aid levels are left at the status quo, this only seems to be the case when I compare 'no change' cases with 'decrease' cases. This is to an extent surprising because conventional wisdom holds that it takes more policy rationalization to increase spending on something than to decrease it or keep it the same, due to competition over scarce resources.

Appendix 3: Tied aid versus untied aid

A significant portion of Chapter 3 was devoted to an examination of the differ-ences between the main types of aid distinguished by the OECD. It is pretty clear that different things are taken into account for different kinds of aid (for instance, a regime that is a human rights violator is in many cases denied budget support but not humanitarian assistance). Other ways we could disaggregate of course are by sector, by degree of control maintained by the donor, by grants vs loans, and by bilateral vs multilateral. It is beyond the scope of this book to dis-aggregate aid on every possible dimension, and its focus is whether different kinds of recipient states are held to different standards, not whether different kinds of aid are disbursed differently. However, I want to at least examine some suggestive differences between the major categories of tied and untied aid.

To review, tied aid is by definition aimed at benefiting both recipient and donor alike. Hence, one should see both economic and human rights concerns having less of an effect on tied aid than on untied aid, where states are likely to be much more selective. Therefore, one might predict that both donors' economic interests and moral priorities would be more clearly expressed in the disbursement of this kind of aid than of tied aid.

But although there are good reasons to predict that more independent variables have an impact on the untied aid decision, few real differences emerge between the two kinds of aid for most of these decisions. A few illustrative examples follow.

Gatekeeping and allocation decisions

I analyzed the determinants of the major gatekeeping decisions regarding untied aid. As predicted, measures of strategic, economic and humanitarian considerations are more highly significant for the gatekeeping decision about untied aid than for tied aid, demonstrating that states use untied aid as a way to pursue a range of policy interests, while tied aid serves in a more focused way to pursue donor economic benefit. This also means that taking tied aid as the base category in the analyses in this chapter presents the hardest task as far as the expression of human rights and strategic considerations are concerned.

Similar differences exist between tied and untied aid for the allocation phase. While four variables of interest, touching on economic, strategic and moral concerns, affect the decision to decrease all OECD aid, only two – human rights and instability – have an effect on the decision to decrease untied aid. One would predict most variables of interest to be less significant for tied aid than for all aid; states often choose to give generously of tied aid because it ends up benefiting the donor in the long-term analysis. In line with these expectations, while still significant, the model overall explains a smaller percentage of the variance than is the case for all DAC aid above. The State Department's measure of human rights continues to be significantly and positively associated with higher aid levels, as does recipient state population. Recipient GDP growth becomes insignificant, which makes sense due to the fact that tied aid theoretically benefits the donor no matter what, so there is less incentive to just give it to economically valuable states. However, clearly economic concerns still come into play as the volume of a recipient's imports from OECD countries continues to be significant. This finding is supported by the positive association of large aid amounts with the one interactive variable included here – the interaction of the recipient's import/export ratio with the OECD and its human rights record. This suggests that it is something about the combination of a recipient's economic value and domestic adherence to democratic principles that may be a guiding factor in aid decisions – a possibility explored above when the different relative effects of different determinants of aid on various categories of states (more economically valuable versus less so) are compared. Finally, as was the case for all aid above, a state's location at a key trade intersection is *positively* associated with higher aid levels, while instability in the region of a recipient state is associated with *lower* aid levels.

I predicted that untied aid would be most sensitive to concerns like human rights considerations. In fact, most of the variables measuring economic value of the recipient state appear to have little effect on untied aid either. The only coefficients which reach reasonable significance levels are those for population and whether the recipient is located at a trade intersection (both positively associated with higher aid levels) and the recipient's location in a region of instability (associated with lower aid levels). The overall model is significant and the R^2 is 0.13, down slightly from the last analysis in which it was 0.29. Why would one see so few variables achieve significance for untied aid, which the hypotheses above might predict would be most sensitive to the widest array of influences? It seems clear that something must be missing from the operationalization of the model for untied aid – perhaps the domestic politics variables that come into play for the individual country cases.

Allocation – increasing aid

Few differences exist between tied and untied aid for three possible decisions about recipients at the allocation phase. Here we see few major differences for any of these decisions in terms of one type of aid being systematically more affected by one kind of consideration than the other type. This approach predicts that untied aid may be where states display their true preferences, as they are not muted by the automatic economic benefits to the donor that are built into, for instance, tied aid. It is difficult, however, to really compare these two analyses as neither is significant overall and both explain very little of the overall variance in aid. Even once one turns to the coefficients and their significance, it is rather difficult to assess whether one is more affected by moral and economic concerns than the other, since moral concerns appear to come into play in the case of the untied aid decision while for aid overall, it is the interaction of moral and economic concerns that appears to make a difference. An interesting pattern emerges, however, when one looks at tied as well as untied aid. Moral concerns appear to play a role in untied aid, while economic ones appear to be associated with tied aid decisions (though in the opposite direction to that which one might expect). This is surprising because untied aid is generally seen by recipients as more valuable than tied aid, and so one might predict that tied aid would be used to woo potential trading partners rather than states with good human rights records. This does, however, suggest another possibility as well: that human rights records, especially as assessed by the State Department, sometimes function as a proxy for cooperation with Western goals and hence are more likely to be rewarded than they might be otherwise.

When one looks at aid continuity for untied aid, the model is highly significant at 0.0001, but the pseudo R^2 is still very small at 0.04. The human rights record of the recipient is negatively and significantly related to a lack of change in aid – that is, an improvement in human rights is associated with a change in aid. Location in an area of instability also makes it more likely that a recipient's aid levels will not change, perhaps indicating a 'wait and see' attitude on the part of donors. It is *not*, however, surprising that of the forms of aid I have so far examined, this one seems most sensitive to human rights and concerns about instability. Untied aid should be less constrained by economic considerations than other forms, and thus allow for the expression of ethical and other concerns. Once again, it is relatively difficult to compare these results to those for increases in untied aid because the overall model is insignificant and the pseudo-R^2, at 0.005, is miniscule. It might be predicted that untied aid would be the category most sensitive to concerns like human rights considerations, and, in fact, this variable achieves marginal significance, but no other independent variables achieve significance. Interestingly, there once again seem to be more factors having an impact on the decision *not* to increase aid than on the decision to increase it.

Allocation – decreasing aid

I then analyzed when aid was decreased for both tied and untied aid. How do these compare to the determinants of when aid went up? It is usually easier for a donor to cut aid budgets than to spend more, so increasing a state's aid should require stronger justification than decreasing it. For cases where untied aid was cut, the model is significant, at 0.0126. Interestingly, a high human rights score appears to be positively and significantly correlated with a decrease in untied aid, again perhaps reflecting that once a state has achieved a relatively high level of human rights, it is no longer seen as needing the economic persuasion that comes with aid. Instability is also negatively and significantly associated with a decrease in aid. Donor states and multilateral lending organizations may not want to pull money out of areas which are already unstable, as might be expected. How does this compare to the decision to *increase* untied aid? Again, fewer variables achieve significance in the model for increasing aid. While human rights concerns are of marginal significance, the overall model is insignificant and no other independent variables achieve significance.

Are decisions different for different kinds of recipients?

In most cases, the results for breaking down the sample based on GDP or GDP growth produced similar results for untied aid as for tied aid. Given the large number of tables included for this set of decisions for tied aid, only one is included here for untied aid, for illustrative purposes. I analyzed determinants of total aid amounts for untied aid, when recipients are categorized according to the growth rates of their economies. As was the case for untied aid, here human rights are only a factor in aid amounts for states with stagnant economies, while greater numbers of strategic and economic considerations come into play the stronger the economy of the recipient state.

6 Imperial pieces to global preeminence

British development assistance and human rights

British foreign policy has been, unsurprisingly, far more scrutinized than that of Canada or Australia. A substantial body of literature has been devoted to the history and purposes of British overseas development assistance. Rather than review that in its entirety I will here consider the ways that British foreign policy generally, and aid policy and practice more specifically, have reflected changing ideas of what the concept of human rights means and how it can and should be pursued. The first portion of this chapter reviews the role of human rights in British foreign policy rhetoric and practice more generally, with special attention to the last 25 years, before turning to the tool of development assistance specifically. I will also consider whether pursuing human rights is generally commensurate with or conflicting with other goals, for it is only in the latter cases that we will be able to see what choices are made when priorities must be set.

Certainly others have assumed a tension may exist, that, as Vincent puts it (1986: 1), 'the rights of states ... are likely to pull in a different direction from the rights of individuals'. Even those who argue that 'we [should not] accept the use of free trade as an argument for excluding human rights from interstate relationships' implicitly acknowledge that a tradeoff exists (Hill 1989: 10).

A caution applies here and in the following three chapters about the evolution of development policy. Development has become much more visible in international discourse over the time period considered in this study. Combined with macroeconomic and political changes in the world, this has resulted in radical changes in the discourse surrounding development assistance. For example, the very term 'foreign aid' is increasingly giving way to the more comprehensive and holistic notion of 'development assistance'. 'Anti-corruption' is referred to less than the more holistic but more fluid 'good governance'.

There is an unfortunate temptation, however, when agencies are increasingly evaluated, to base this evaluation on their adoption of rapidly evolving goals. Especially when any development project arguably fulfills more than one goal, the ways in which projects are reported may change without the projects themselves changing proportionately. Most aid programs now require individual bilateral programs to produce matrixes delineating which of their programs meet which goals, and this can lead to a temptation to think, essentially, about which boxes a project allows you to tick without necessarily changing the underlying motivations behind project choice or implementation.

Therefore the first half of the chapters will carefully consider major policy papers and statements, to determine what they indicate about the shifting priorities of aid. This discussion is followed in the last pages of each chapter by a quantitative description of the frequency with which particular terms are mentioned in individual bilateral strategies, to determine whether the priorities expressed in central policies are reflected in individual bilateral program policies (as well as consistencies and inconsistencies between those policies). Finally, I present statistical analyses that show which characteristics of recipients are actually associated with getting aid in the first place, and with higher aid amounts. This allows for a comparison of apparent emphases with the actual policy results. While reasons for discrepancies can only be speculated on here, any discrepancies observed suggest important avenues of future inquiry, as they indicate possible slippage between policy-making and policy implementation.

Human rights in British foreign policy thinking and practice

Human rights defined

Before identifying the most important moments of evolution in the status of 'human rights' as a goal of UK foreign policy, it is necessary to consider what the term 'human rights' has meant in British foreign policy dialogue. The fact that 'human rights' is one of the most culturally and contextually variable terms in international relations was discussed at some length in earlier chapters. The key conclusion: human rights means different things, both formally and informally, for each donor state, as well as across different governments and leaders and across time within the same donor state.

In earlier chapters I discuss the choice of a single definition of rights for the quantitative portions of this study. But if we are to determine the extent to which public and rhetorical commitments are carried out in internal decision-making and practice, we must also evaluate donor performance based on the conception of human rights that the donor government actually claims to be pursuing. This is a better guide to what to look for in policy outcomes.[1]

The evolution of the role of human rights in British foreign policy rhetoric and practice

Morality – in some form – has played at least a rhetorical role in British foreign policy for centuries. The rhetoric of morality is 'at least as old as party manifestos', if 'only at times as a matter of lip service to impress an audience whether at the hustings or at the UN General Assembly' (Dickie 2004: 117). But the role of morality generally, and human rights specifically, was rather difficult to pin down through much of the late twentieth century. Former Foreign Secretary John Coles remembers that 'my first job in the Foreign Office in 1964 was that of desk officer for human rights, together with a number of other issues which had limited prominence...' (Coles 2000: 98–9). It often disappeared in the shadow of more important aims.

The 1964 Plowden report, for instance, put commercial work at the top of the list of priorities to be pursued with Britain's foreign policy tools and a committee appointed in 1968 to reevaluate British foreign policy effectiveness was charged particularly with attending to trade and economic interests. In particular the committee concluded that Britain's evolving status as 'a major power of the second order' compelled it to focus on export promotion (Coles 2000: 71–3).[2]

This was not to say that the promotion of democracy overseas, or of development, was absent altogether. It had its roots in the obligations of Empire, though institutionalization and path dependency would give these obligations a life of their own. In the 1970s

> Britain's objectives overseas were clear: to safeguard the country's security, to promote its prosperity, to uphold democratic values, to honour commitments and obligations to work for a peaceful and just world, and to provide assistance to developing countries. Assessment of our interests could not be confined to economic or exporting considerations alone.
>
> (Coles 2000: 190)

A colloquium held in 1978 yields one snapshot of the current thinking about the role of human rights in foreign policy decisions. FCO staff claimed to take human rights into account in foreign policy decisions and listed the range of possible responses as follows: a

> statement of our concern in semiprivate form, such as letters to MPs or members of the public; confidential representation to the government, joint confidential representation with other governments, public statement of concern in Parliament or elsewhere, cancellation or postponement of ministerial visit, restraints on cultural and sporting contacts, embargoes on arms sales, *reduction in our aid program*, withdrawal of our Ambassador, *a cessation of all aid*, the breaking of diplomatic relations, trading sanctions.
>
> (*Human Rights in US and UK Foreign Policy:*
> *A Colloquium* 1979: 14, my emphasis)

Military force, so often put to use in the name of democracy today, is notably absent. This most costly step would not be advocated in the name of human rights.

FCO staff noted that human rights was always viewed as the concern of 'other countries'. What changed things, according to one report, was the ratification of the Optional Protocol to the European Convention on Human Rights (ECHR). Attitudes changed sufficiently for the UK to even begin to encourage other states to ratify (*Human Rights in US and UK Foreign Policy: A Colloquium* 1979: 36).

So what have formal foreign policy statements and practice defined as

a   human rights and
b   the appropriate way for the UK to pursue them and why and
c   the place of human rights in the hierarchy of other foreign policy goals and
    reasons for this?

One source of priorities is a nation's perception of its own role (Holsti 1970;
Breuning 1995). Thus postwar Britain saw itself torn between the new Cold-War
context of the old 'special relationship' on the one hand, and a perceived relative
decline among the states of Europe (necessitating a focus on commercial
competition) on the other. This tension is revealed in both the rhetoric and
reality of foreign policy developments during the first two decades after World
War II. Against these more traditional concerns the profile of human rights as a
foreign policy goal has grown dramatically from its inconsequential position at
the middle of the twentieth century, mirroring its rise in foreign policy rhetoric
the world over.

There are at least two key moments that can be identified in the evolution of
human rights from something seen by many policy-makers as the kind of thing
that got in the way of 'real' foreign policy-making to something widely perceived as a legitimate foreign policy goal.

The first of these was the added emphasis given to human rights by the Carter
administration in the US during the mid-1970s, including his establishing of the
Human Rights Bureau within the US State Department and his initiating of the
annual country-specific Human Rights Reports. But as of the late 1970s, the UK
had only cut off aid completely to two countries in response to human rights
abuses. When human rights had any effect at all, it was highly conditional. For
instance, in aid policy,

> London's relations with the Third World ... have been dominated by ...
> political, historical, and economic constraints which have drastically limited
> the extent to which ... concern for ... human rights has led to changes in ...
> aid relations ... [human rights] concerns are subservient to other political
> and economic ambitions in determining the quantity and direction of the aid
> programme.
>
> (Cunliffe 1985: 112, 116)

By the mid-1980s observers still concluded that 'calls for the protection of
others' rights have not led to serious commitments' (Brewin and Vincent 1986:
189), part of an overall realist turn that foreign policy took under Thatcher.
'Power politics was seen as the true nature of international relations...' (Larsen
1997: 93–4). In 1989

> analysis of the flow of economic aid from London to the less developed
> world over the past fifteen years does not reveal any enduring, concerted

effects by successive British Governments to utilize the flow of concessional finance for the promotion of international human rights.

(Cunliffe and Hill 1989: 115)

The second and arguably more important watershed moment in the emergence
of human rights as a more central priority was Blair's choice of Robin Cook as
Foreign Secretary upon Labour's victory in the 1997 election. Before the election human rights found a place in Labour's pre-election statement of foreign
policy aims, *Britain in the World*, which was produced in response to a set of
consultations conducted between 1994 and 1996. The most important points of
this were incorporated into the 1997 Labour Party manifesto.

1997 Labour Party manifesto

International relations functions mainly as a backdrop in the manifesto itself.
The document includes human rights as one among many international goals
addressed in the document, including global stability and free trade. The document refers to the importance of the ECHR and Britain's obligations under it, to
discrimination, to reform of the justice system and to the processing of asylum-
seekers. In the section on British leadership in Europe, the key initiative areas
include a referendum on a single currency, reform in the EU, defence cooperation, UN reform and, crucially, tackling global poverty. A sense of constraint,
however, pervades the document and suggests that priorities must be set.
Though Britain's heritage exacts important obligations to the rest of the world,
the manifesto is careful to note that Britain is an island nation with 'limited
natural resources'. Hence it must stay connected to the global economy and to
powerful allies. This leads the party to pledge that

> with a new Labour government, Britain will be strong in defence; resolute
> in standing up for its own interests; *an advocate of human rights and demo-
> cracy the world over*; a reliable and powerful ally in the international insti-
> tutions of which we are a member; and will be a leader in Europe.

(Labour Party 1997)

Perhaps not surprisingly, international issues constitute the last section of the
manifesto. The section on 'leadership in the international community' includes
the goals of UN reform 'and a more effective role in peacekeeping, conflict prevention, the protection of human rights and safeguarding the global environment'. The manifesto also emphasizes the importance of the Commonwealth, to
which Labour will accord 'renewed priority'. It pledges that Labour will 'seize
the opportunity to increase trade and economic co-operation'. A separate
section addresses 'promoting economic and social development', discussed
below.

Human rights is also accorded its own subsection – though the briefest in the
manifesto's discussion of international priorities. The manifesto asserts that

Labour wants Britain to be respected in the world for the integrity with which it conducts its foreign relations. We will make the protection and promotion of human rights a central part of our foreign policy. We will work for the creation of a permanent international criminal court to investigate genocide, war crimes and crimes against humanity.

(Labour Party 1997)

(That is, in fact, the entirety of the wording of the section.) Human rights are not defined and potential conflict between human rights and other foreign policy goals is not addressed.

The other two international sections address the environment and free trade. The latter of these, similarly brief, focuses on the dangers of isolationism and 'protectionist policies' (Labour Party 1997).

FCO Mission Statement of 12 May 1997

Immediately the general election of 1997 was concluded, major changes in policy orientation became evident. The FCO's new Mission Statement sets out several priorities, many of which speak to the promises of the Labour Party manifesto. Security and prosperity are the first goals addressed ('We shall make maximum use of our overseas posts to promote trade abroad and boost jobs at home'), followed by quality of life ('We shall work with others to protect the World's environment and to counter the menace of drugs, terrorism and crime') and finally mutual respect ('We shall work through our international forums and bilateral relationships to spread the values of human rights, civil liberties and democracy which we demand for ourselves') (FCO 1997). The question of human rights appears last. Again the rights are not defined, and potential conflicts between the goals are not acknowledged.

However, the new Foreign Secretary, Robin Cook, immediately foregrounded human rights in his foreign policy rhetoric, pledging to put 'human rights at the heart of our foreign policy' (Dickie 2004: 117).[3] This led many in the press to skeptically question the depth or consistency of his commitment to a goal that might make for hard tradeoffs with more directly measurable and self-interested aims,[4] but Cook's changes in the Foreign Office soon made it clear that there would be substance behind the rhetoric.

A new Human Rights Department was established with 20 staffers (to the two at the desk until the early 1990s – who were actually assigned to the UN office), and an 'innovative activist from Amnesty International', Harriet Ware-Austin, appointed as policy advisor (Dickie 2004: 117). This department has funded more than 500 projects in 90 countries since 1997, some of which – notably – have been quite unpopular with the host government, indicating that the British government is willing to act in ways that might have a detrimental effect on its relations with other governments in the name of human rights. In 2001 these included exhuming graves in Guatemala for legal investigation and helping set up the truth commission enquiring into the Fujimori regime in Peru.

The largest amount to any country went to China to fund work on women's rights, civil education and investigations of the judicial process and police procedures investigations. The funding also provided for the appointment of a human rights advisor (another former member of Amnesty International) to the British Embassy in Manila. Other advisors have been sent to Kiev and to Nepal. The five countries where over £100,000 have been allocated are inspected each year to ensure projects are being fully carried out (Dickie 2004: 117–18).

Perhaps the clearest way to identify an administration's priorities is to examine what it funds. One of Cook's key achievements was the creation in April 1998 of the Human Rights Projects Fund (HRPF), 'which enables diplomatic missions to secure funding to achieve their human rights objectives in the country in which they are stationed' (Dickie 2004: 48). This is a dramatic change from the traditional tendency to sideline human rights in favor of competing objectives when scarce resources caused diplomatic missions to choose geopolitical and economic goals over human rights. Funding designated to human rights funds mitigates the zero-sum nature of these calculations. In its first three years the HRPF dispensed over £15 million to fund a total of 400 projects across 90 countries (Dickie 2004: 48). Currently the HRPF has an annual budget of £5 million, and, according to FCO figures, had provided £15 million to 400 projects in 90 countries as of 2001. Funding decisions prioritized freedom of expression, religion, and assembly, the rule of law, group rights, and human rights education and institutions (Amnesty International 2001: 11).

For the first time an FCO Annual Report on Human Rights was instituted with the purpose of recording gains and suggesting avenues for future improvement. The annual human rights reports issued by the FCO differ from, for instance, the US State Department's human rights reports, in two major respects: only one report is issued for each year, rather than one for each country annually, and they focus as much on what the UK is doing to combat human rights abuses as on the abuses themselves. Therefore, human rights is explicitly acknowledged as a valid and desirable goal of foreign policy, and the full range of tools the UK has at its disposal to address such rights can potentially be discussed. Also, we find, at last, clear definitions of human rights, though to many advocates they will seem quite limiting. In addition, in the most recent of these reports, described below, the contrast between Cook's more assertive role in pursuit of human rights goals, and the Jack Straw's more conservative one, will be very obvious. The contents of the most recent report are discussed in some detail below.

In 1998, the FCO established the Global Citizenship Unit, which met with approval even from groups like Amnesty International which tend to be among the FCO's sharpest critics. The same year saw the reframing of its military assistance program with clear orientation toward security-sector reform. The program is now known as ASSIST – Assistance to Support Stability with In-Service Training. It is administered partly by the Foreign Office's geographical directorates and by the Security Policy Department. Its activities in 2001 included sending police to conduct human rights training in Brazil, promoting penal reform in Latvia, training officers in the United Arab Emirates (UAE) on the sensitive handling of rape cases, and sending staff to Indonesia to create a new code of ethics for the police. The fund also supplies resources for education, peacekeeping, and disaster management (Dickie 2004: 118).

These sorts of developments are all the more significant given Labour's determination to have a limited and focused set of priorities so as to increase the chance of them being achieved. This is a commitment clearly laid out in its 1997 manifesto.[5]

Since 1997, rights considerations have been instilled in diplomatic culture in less formal ways. For new members of the diplomatic corps 'the high profile given to human rights is underlined in a whole-day session conducted by an outsider, usually from the organization Justice or Amnesty International' (Dickie 2004: 48). Cook boasted after four years as Foreign Secretary that 'more than three hundred members of the Diplomatic service' had taken this course (Dickie 2004: 51).[6] However, this is among many training initiatives that new mandarins undergo, and it is possible that its leadership by an outsider negatively affects its perceived importance.

Amnesty International has noted that the increase in staffing and status has continued, with mainstreaming of human rights concerns into overall foreign policy through requests from the top that country desks and UK embassies and high commissions develop human rights strategies and increase monitoring (Amnesty International 2001: 11).

Yet it would be dangerous to characterize these changes as necessarily signaling the end of the primacy accorded political and economic considerations as priorities, as is clear from other key foreign policy strategy documents. For instance, in the socialization process of new Foreign Office staff, the primacy of economic and political concerns is also emphasized. 'The importance of trade promotion is instilled into the high-fliers during a day at British Trade International' (Dickie 2004: 48). Groups like Amnesty International are not likely to be easily convinced of the adequacy of the government's achievements in human rights when compared with political and economic imperatives. A Human Rights Audit on the Foreign Office by Amnesty International (AI) stated:

> [t]he key questions regarding the consistency with which foreign policy is applied – and whether it is driven by human rights concerns – rest in the relative importance given to trade or strategic interests as opposed to human rights, and whether the UK is prepared to criticize publicly its trade partners where they are responsible for human rights violations.

AI's conclusion was that there was 'a mixed record on this count'. In its 2001 audit there was praise for the 'significant positive contribution' by the FO in East Timor, Kosovo, and Sierra Leone, but the audit expressed concern about policies towards China and Saudi Arabia, with whom, it claimed, greater priority was given to 'business as usual' than to challenges over human rights failings

(Dickie 2004: 51). Even Cook aimed to find representatives from British industry to serve as ambassadors to countries with strategic markets (Dickie 2004:
155).

In fact, Dickie cites trade promotion as the only specific policy area with
which heads of mission are consistently concerned (Dickie 2004: 53). The new
joint board for 'joined-up decision-making' that was formed when the Board of
Management and the Policy Advisory Board were abolished includes the Group
Chief Executive of British Trade International (BTI) (Dickie 2004: 111). In
addition, the traditionally close relationship between the Department of Trade
and Industry (DTI) and the FCO means that a Foreign Secretary is never likely
to be allowed to forget about the economic aspects of a policy for long. For
instance, in the area of arms sales Cook was clearly torn between the rights
implications of arms sales and the fact that arms sales produce half a million
jobs (by some estimates) in the UK annually. This can lead to some rather dual-
istic messages from the highest levels of government.

> The chancellor ... while warning the HIPC [Heavily Indebted Poor Coun-
> tries] countries that their debt burdens would not be eased if they allow
> savings from debt servicing to be used to buy weapons, does not let the
> Foreign Secretary ignore the fact that arms sales account for vast export
> earnings – in 1997, in excess of four billion pounds. Most of the time the
> dilemma of steering a course between economic interest and principles is
> resolved in a process that rarely comes under the public spotlight.
>
> (Dickie 2004: 119)

These tensions are, and have been, plentifully evident. In 1993 the Conservative
government infamously linked aid for building the Pergau Dam to the sale of
British arms. In April 1996 a Saudi dissident was ordered to be expelled by
Howard on the grounds that his presence threatened arms contracts and jobs. And
of course many of these tensions are magnified many times over in relations with
China – a 'particularly difficult tightrope act for Britain's Foreign Secretaries'
(Dickie 2004: 120).[7] For instance, Cook incurred the condemnation of human
rights NGOs for failing to raise a single one of the individual human rights cases
on his list in high-level meetings in China in January 1998, declining to meet the
long-imprisoned human rights campaigner Weijing Sheng, who subsequently
denounced Cook for abandoning China's human rights victims.[8] Although human
rights abuses in Burma and Rwanda have been vigorously condemned,

> for a long time Foreign Office ministers confined themselves to platitudes
> over the violence against farmers in Zimbabwe when their land was invaded
> by President Mugabe's supporters. *It strengthened suspicions that the easy
> targets get the big stick* while the big powers and those that present a polit-
> ical problem are handled cautiously with a 'constructive dialogue' on
> human rights issues.
>
> (Dickie 2004: 139; emphasis mine)

Some of this inconsistency also indicates an incompleteness of institutionaliza-tion of human rights vis-à-vis other goals, resulting in a situation in which advo-cacy has depended on the personal attributes and inclinations of the Foreign Secretary (more will be said about this below relevant to the Minister of Inter-national Development).

In 2000, the main provisions of the European Human Rights Act came into effect in the UK, committing the UK to basic standards of human rights at home and abroad.

The 2001 General Election

The replacing of Cook with Jack Straw led not only to a less aggressive stance on human rights but to a less independent voice for the FCO all the way around. Straw did not hesitate to invoke morality and humanitarianism – for instance, he claimed that engaging in Afghanistan was a moral duty as well as a practical imperative. However, he refused to take a more robust approach to China, regard-less of the contents of the annual Human Rights Report. For instance, when Hu Jintao, China's Vice President, visited Britain in 2001 he was shielded from Free Tibet protesters by being brought in and out of Downing Street through a side entrance. Straw clearly defended human rights as coinciding with Britain's other interests, rather than acknowledging potential conflicts. For instance, in a March 2005 speech he defended interventions in Sierra Leone and Afghanistan 'because those situations both outraged our sense of morality and threatened Britain's interests' (FCO 2005: 244). While not going further in explaining how the goals were commensurate, he went on to assert that economic and altruistic goals were also mutually reinforcing: 'They coincide in our doubling of the UK's aid to the poorest nations, for poverty is both a scar on the world's conscience and a brake on its progress' (FCO 2005: 244). He linked economic progress and democracy again, more explicitly, in another speech in the same month: 'democracy and the open societies which support it foster dialogue, enquiry and innovation, essential ingredients for economic success. Greater freedom ... allows entrepreneurs to flourish; and creates dynamism and jobs' (FCO 2005: 245).

2003 FCO strategy paper

In December 2003 an FCO White Paper, its first ever strategy paper, was pub-lished. *UK International Priorities: A Strategy for the FCO* is meant to 'be the basis of our resource bid in the 2004 Government Spending Round, and of our new formal objectives and PSA targets in the next spending period' (FCO 2003: 62). It emphasizes security above all else, which comes as no surprise in the first command paper to be published after 9/11. It delineates four specific policy responsibilities. In order, these are

> promoting the security of the UK within a safer, more peaceful world;
> improving prosperity in the UK and worldwide through effective economic

and political governance globally; promoting a strong role for the UK in a strong Europe responsive to people's needs; and making sure that UK Overseas Territories are secure and well governed.

(FCO 2003: 9)

Note that the issue of human rights only enters this litany in the guise of good governance and there the UK's declared sphere of influence only extends to its overseas territories. (In fact, human rights concerns are only directly referenced nine times in the 66-page document, while security and economic concerns are referenced 58 and 57 times, respectively.) Prior to addressing the policy priorities that follow from the four overarching goals, the paper describes the changes expected to occur in the world over the next ten years. The first and longest of these sections deals with security, followed by ideology and religion, then economics (including, toward the end of the subsection, a discussion of global economic inequality and the Millennium Development Goals (MDGs)), population, environmental change, energy, technology, and 'wider participation'. While the FCO is careful to caution that the order in which the specific priorities are presented does not constitute a strict rank ordering, they are:

1   a world safer from global terrorism and weapons of mass destruction
2   protection of the UK from illegal immigration, drug trafficking and other international crime
3   an international system based on the rule of law, which is better able to resolve disputes and prevent conflicts
4   an effective EU in a secure neighbourhood
5   promotion of UK economic interests in an open and expanding global economy
6   sustainable development, underpinned by democracy, good governance and human rights
7   security of UK and global energy supplies
8   security and good governance of the UK's Overseas Territories.

(FCO 2003: 10)

Points 3, 6 and 8 quite clearly deal with some conception of basic human rights, at least in part. However, the concept of security appears in fully six of the eight priorities. Interestingly, economic concerns are explicitly addressed only in point 5, though they are also implied by 6 and, less directly, by 4 and 7.

One could argue that these priorities are sufficiently interconnected that progress on each suggests progress on the others. For instance, in the section on global terrorism, the means to achieve a safer world include 'lead[ing] a systematic strategy across government for engaging with the Islamic world and promoting peaceful political and social reform in Arab countries', clearly steps that have relevance for promoting the protection of basic human needs and at least bodily integrity rights. And promoting democracy in the graduating states, as well as asylum policy, are explicitly components of #4. Similarly, development is clearly addressed as part of #5, but so is winning contracts for UK industry in foreign markets.

Priority #6 echoes the clear connections between sustainable development, democracy, good governance and human rights that have become common in UK foreign policy parlance over the last nine years. Interestingly, though, priority 6 is immediately justified in self-interested terms:

> For our security and prosperity to be lasting, we shall need to support the equivalent aspirations of the peoples of the developing world, including the most vulnerable in Africa. That means promoting democratic values, human rights and good government, and working for progress towards poverty reduction and sustainable development in all parts of the world.
>
> (FCO 2003: 42)

Rights beyond basic human needs and humanitarian assistance are discussed little further, with emphasis on poverty reduction, debt relief and sustainable development. The one exception to this is support for the International Criminal Court (ICC), as well as a mention of gender equity in a box profiling the Department for International Development (DfID).

The other priority that might seem to represent incorporation of some idea of human rights is #8, though it only applies to the UK's overseas territories. But while democracy, good government and quality of life are mentioned in this brief section, rights *per se* are not, except in a passage that advocates 'a proper balance between rights and responsibilities in the constitutional relationships between the UK and the Overseas Territories' (FCO 2003: 42).

In a separate chapter on 'Delivering High Quality Public Service', the report also details the services it will supply to business, with the most specific trade targets being those related to export promotion.

In fact, the place where the human rights question makes its most dramatic appearance in the paper is in a boxed profile, 'Human Rights: Global Issues, Global Influence' that appears on p. 55 of the 66-page document. However, it only focuses on torture and the Convention Against Torture (CAT), and the NGO and academic partnerships that have helped improve regularization of reporting procedures around torture. This, while laudable, is a very minimal definition of human rights protection.

2005: Most recent FCO Annual Report on Human Rights

The FCO Annual Report on Human Rights both includes clearer definitions of human rights than any of the other policy statements and also demonstrates what is being done to address them. Thus, it provides valuable evidence regarding whether rights are pursued consistently, and which interests prevail when two or more goals conflict.

In the most recent report, Straw's opening preface makes it clear that simply listing the countries of concern is in and of itself supposed to be a useful form of punishment (FCO 2005: 3). But is it? If it were, would not the US Department of State's Human Rights Reports over all these years have had more effect? In addition, *vis-à-vis* Cook, Straw backtracks in the 2005 report to the position of justifying human rights as a means to more self-interested goals, such as their role in creating greater security and prosperity (FCO 2005: 3, 14, 15). He sounds a clear pragmatist note, cautioning that it is important to distinguish between what can be achieved and what cannot (FCO 2005: 14) – a much more conservative stance than the human rights community came to expect from Cook.

In addition, a large number of proposed tools for pursuing human rights are multilateral, such as the use of the EU and G8 presidencies as well as Britain's permanent seat on the UN Security Council (FCO 2005: 14). This unwillingness to take direct responsibility for stopping human rights abuses abroad is emblematized by the following passage:

> The events of the past year epitomize both what we can achieve when the international community acts robustly in support of the victims of human rights abuses and the limits of what we can achieve when a government is unable or unwilling to address human rights violations on its territory.
>
> (FCO 2005: 14)

There are many clues about the FCO's *definition of human rights* in the 2005 report.

First, democracy, good governance and human rights are portrayed as integrally related (FCO 2005: 15), though, as discussed in Chapter 2, the three need not go hand in hand. Yet according to the report

> Democracy is a precondition for a true human rights culture, since only governments appointed through regular, free and fair elections are truly accountable to their people. In addition, human rights, such as freedom of information, expression, association and assembly, respect for the rights of minorities, non-discrimination and respect for the rule of law, are also essential attributes of democracy. Without these additional elements, elections can create the outward appearance of democracy but simply consolidate the power of undemocratic regimes in practice, as witnessed in Zimbabwe earlier this year.
>
> (FCO 2005: 16)

Within democracy and good governance, the FCO intends, specifically, to focus on four key factors in democracy (fair electoral processes; development of pluralist political systems and effective parliamentary institutions; encouraging the development of the Community of Democracies, and freedom of expression) and three key elements of good governance (participation of civil society in decision-making; a common approach to good governance in international bodies and in development cooperation; and the rule of law) (FCO 2005: 16).

Second, in conjunction with priority 6 of the 2003 FCO White Paper, human rights work is focusing on three particular human rights themes – rights of the child, abolishing torture, and doing away with the death penalty – which would seem wholly inadequate to many human rights defenders, especially those who argue for indivisibility of rights. The report does not defend the limitation of goals to these three areas. While other rights, such as free expression, are discussed in the context of democracy (FCO 2005: 16), this seems a rather circumscribed set of foci.

Again, the potential tensions between rights and other foreign policy goals are disregarded altogether. Rather, in keeping with the aims of a more integrated approach to government that has been one of the hallmarks of Labour policy-making, UK and global security, prosperity and rights are depicted as goals that reinforce each other and can therefore be pursued simultaneously.

For instance, security is depicted as something that can be provided with no threats to rights. The FCO has provided resources supporting human rights training in counterterror courses (FCO 2005: 17). It explicitly justifies the links in the following way:

> There is a particularly strong relationship between security and human rights, since violations of human rights (for example, discrimination against minorities or denial of vital economic and social rights, such as the right to food, health or education) are often the precursor to armed conflict. Some of the worst human rights abuses against vulnerable groups, such as refugees, women and children, take place during the course of a conflict.... The UK is convinced that respect for human rights is an essential element of an effective counter-terrorism strategy. We maintain our total opposition to torture and actively combat it around the world.
>
> (FCO 2005: 14, 16)

And '[a]lthough the Counterterrorism programme does not have an explicit human rights objective, in practice some of its projects have also had a significant human rights dimension...' (FCO 2005: 18). Critics might argue that without a clear definition of what rights are, it becomes easy to point to 'human rights dimensions' in nearly any policy without actively pursuing human rights. The nexus between conflict and human rights abuses are addressed in a separate chapter, as well, which argues, not incorrectly, that more secure conditions create the spaces for basic needs to be addressed effectively.

In an even more complex nexus, the FCO's Global Opportunities Fund (GOF) supports projects that simultaneously promote development, the environment, resource preservation, security and rights, because it argues that sustainable development is impossible in a context where the government does not have sufficient accountability to its citizens (FCO 2005: 16). The report also includes a separate chapter on human rights and development, which draws some familiar and important causal connections between the two. First, that focusing on development means privileging a certain set of human rights:

fulfillment of basic needs – economic or more specifically subsistence rights. Second, that the increasing emphasis *within* development on poverty reduction means that some of the more obvious tensions between development and security, or development and rights, are set aside. Development as poverty reduction implies but does not necessitate more or less statism, for instance, or more or less political democracy. It does, however, underline some of the most dangerous externalities of amoral globalization. Much more will be said about the relationship between human rights and development later in this chapter.

The Global Opportunities Fund was previously the Human Rights, Democracy and Good Governance (HRDGG) Fund. The rationale for its redesign and retitling is that this will reorient it more directly toward the aims of Priority 6. And as the GOF represents a combination of the HRDGG fund with the former Strengthening Relations with Emerging Markets Fund (FCO 2005: 18), there is an apparent dilution of HRDGG goals with commercial ones. That the commensurability between these goals is seen as being greater than the tension is reflected in the very wording of Priority 6, discussed above. Other structural changes are supporting these presumed links.

> On 14 March 2005 ... with the launch of the new FCO Sustainable Development Strategy ... the FCO finalized a three-year work programme on human rights, democracy and good governance. The two strategies are designed to take forward work on Strategic Priority Six...
>
> (FCO 2005: 16)

The problem, of course, comes when aspects of development conflict with HRDGG goals. Trade openness can lead to downward wage competition and overreliance on exports. SAPs can result in reduction in social-sector spending that helps the very poorest or the most affected by reorientation of developing economies.

Countries to be supported through GOF's Sustainable Development Program are selected based on 1) the country's strategic importance, 2) getting the greatest effectiveness for expenditure, 3) the importance of the issue in the recipient country. These issues are supposed to be commensurate with three broad themes: 1) transparency, information, participation and access to justice (including freedom of expression, rule of law and environmental governance); 2) core human rights priorities (including combating torture, child rights, and death penalty abolition); and 3) natural resource management (including sustainable forest management and reduction of illegal logging, biodiversity, and sustainable tourism) (FCO 2005: 19).

There are optimistic and pessimistic reads of this integrated approach. It may reflect a mainstreaming of human rights values into all other areas of foreign policy-making. On the other hand, critics wonder whether human rights a) is being interpreted so narrowly that the only rights being pursued are those not conflicting with other goals, or b) is an attractive label being applied to any policy that even incidentally improves the lives of poor people (e.g. Amnesty International 2001).

So a detailed read of the report still leaves us with ambiguity about the role of human right, because, if rights can be pursued simultaneously to other goals, there is no need to set priorities.

Therefore it is important to look at which kinds of sanctions have been applied to which kind of states in response to which kinds of violations – especially in cases where there are compelling reasons to maintain good relations with the government. For instance, the huge amount of coverage of Sudan and Burma in the 2005 Human Rights Report is made relatively costlessly, because the UK has few identifiable strategic or economic benefits to be derived from its relationship with these states. The longest component of the report goes into some detail on abuses in major countries of concern, in each case describing key concerns, *what the UK is doing to work on them*, and what the prospects are for the future. An examination of this section allows us to determine the actions the UK has taken vis-à-vis each country and whether the UK seems to engage countries with similar human rights problems in similar ways – questions that are systematically addressed later in the chapter. In general, most of these actions include relatively low-level activities such as funding human rights projects, health education, and calling on regimes to release prisoners. There are no examples of military intervention or economic sanctioning. The fact that a large number of positive tools is being implemented reveals a prudent mixture of carrots and sticks, but also raises moral hazard concerns.

A random sample of country programs revealed the following patterns: of 22 countries of concern, the most frequently taken actions, in order, were:

- criticism in high level talks: 8
- funding human rights projects: 7
- UN resolution: 6
- arms embargo: 3
- general sanctions: 3
- aid cessation of some types: 3
- calls for release of specific political prisoners: 2
- calls for investigations: 1
- support for peaceful opposition: 1
- visa ban: 1
- election monitoring: 1
- explicitly discouraging trade and investment: 1
- intervening for prisoner's rights: 1
- recall ambassador: 1
- EU resolution: 1.

Notable here are not only the high ratio of carrots to sticks, but to whom each is applied. For instance, the report covers very similar types of abuse in Burma and China (including torture, disappearance, denial of access to prisoners, denial of cultural rights). Yet the responses have been dramatically different. In the case of Burma, actions taken (through the EU) include:

an arms embargo; bans on defence links, highlevel bilateral government visits, non-humanitarian aid (with certain exceptions), the supply of equipment that might be used for internal repression or terrorism; and an asset freeze and visa ban on regime members, their families, the military and security forces and others who actively frustrate the process of national reconciliation. To put pressure on the regime to work towards democratic change and respect for human rights, unilaterally, the UK does not encourage trade, investment or tourism with Burma and offers no assistance to any British companies wishing to trade with, or invest in, Burma.

(FCO 2005: 39)

Burma has as many negative tools applied to it as any rights-violator in the report. When it comes to China, though, the bulk of the work is being done through the UK–China Human Rights Dialogue, even though the report notes no progress since the last round of the dialogue. The more aggressive measures applied to Burma are notably absent (FCO 2005: 41–5), and even the language of 'dialogue' expresses nowhere near the same level of condemnation directed at Burma. North Korea offers another interesting case, as the description includes a great deal of conciliatory language not evident in other cases. 'We recognize that human rights is a complex issue' but 'unless the DPRK [Democratic People's Republic of Korea] government is willing to engage with us we are unlikely to make any significant progress.' The report goes on to commend the DPRK's 'engagement' (FCO 2005: 54–6).

2006 FCO White Paper: active diplomacy for a changing world: the UK's international priorities

Immediately prior to the completion of this book a new White Paper was issued, updating the 2003 White Paper. Some of the key changes include an integration of economic and energy issues, greater focus on issues related to migration, with a continued emphasis on trade liberalization.

In order, the priorities addressed in the White paper include

1 making the world safer from global terrorism and weapons of mass destruction
2 reducing the harm to the UK from international crime, including drug trafficking, people smuggling and money laundering
3 preventing and resolving conflict through a strong international system
4 building an effective and globally competitive EU in a secure neighbourhood
5 supporting the UK economy and business through an open and expanding global economy, science and innovation and secure energy supplies
6 promoting sustainable development and poverty reduction underpinned by human rights, democracy, good governance and protection of the environment

7   managing migration and combating illegal immigration
8   delivering high-quality support for British nationals abroad, in normal
     times and in crises
9   ensuring the security and good governance of the UK's Overseas
     Territories.

(FCO 2006: 3)

It will be noted that the first four of these deal primarily with security interests, and points 4 and 5 with economic ones. Poverty reduction and environmental and social justice enter the equation at #6, in the second half of the priorities. If one counts priorities 7 and 9, one could argue that fully a third of the priorities in some way deal with rights. But they are clearly behind security and prosperity. A later section describing the best means to these ends suggests this is indeed the FCO's rank ordering of priorities. There the FCO reflects that 'our role is not to report on events or pursue good relations for their own sake. It is to exercise judgment and influence in order to shape the future for the benefit of our citizens and others' (FCO 2006: 4).

Still the language of rights suffuses the paper. In Jack Straw's preface the very first substantive policy mentioned is 'a world in which freedom, justice and opportunity thrive, in which governments are accountable to the people, protect their rights and guarantee their security and basic needs' (FCO 2006: 4). This is done not because they are a means to an end of stability or prosperity, but 'because these are the values we believe to be right '(FCO 2006: 4). The need to remain engaged in an increasingly globalized world (including for purposes of poverty alleviation) follows quickly on in Straw's preface. Security is next. Terrorism and organized crime are discussed along with disease and climate change as threats that can only be addressed by 'the global community as a whole' (FCO 2006: 4).

The first section of the paper describes the changing global context, citing specifically the post-Cold War increase in global trade and movements for national self-determination. The 'darker side' of some of these changes was evidenced by the events of September 11, claims the paper (FCO 2006: 6). But 'the emergence of fragile democracies in Iraq and Afghanistan is giving people the prospect of building a better future than they could have hoped for under tyranny' (FCO 2006: 7). It also warns, significantly, about the dangers of economic without political openness (FCO 2006: 16). Other key areas of crucial future change discussed are poverty and governance including progress toward the MDGs (or lack thereof) and accountable and just governments, security and conflict (surprisingly late in the chapter), and science and innovation.

The second chapter of the White Paper discusses the UK's key multilateral and bilateral relationships. Here we see human rights make a more explicit appearance (for instance in the discussion of China). Since they are raised only in certain contexts they have a rather *ad hoc* and less systematic presence in the paper than in some of the policy documents heretofore discussed. For instance, a profile on Turkey's EU accession later in the paper does not mention human rights.

The nine priorities laid out in the 2006 White Paper, listed above, are very similar to those laid out in the 2003 White Paper. Still, some shifts are evident.

Priority 6, comparable to priority 6 in the 2003 paper, again presents these most apparently altruistic of goals in light of the UK's interests. 'We need to support the aspirations of people around the world,' it says, 'including the most vulnerable, if our security and prosperity are to be lasting' (FCO 2006: 35). It should be noted, however, that rights abuses by governments are not the sole or even central thrust of this section, but rather are mentioned as one of several problems after systemic concerns such as environmental degradation and threats to global health. When 'democratic values, good government, and respect for human rights' are mentioned, they are defended not on their own merits but implicitly because 'these make conflict less likely, reduce poverty and support sustainable development across the world' (FCO 2006: 35).

Since, human rights, democracy and good governance are increasingly being referred to in a single breath, what are the differences between the terms? The FCO's official statement about priority 6 (FCO 2003: 2–3) reads as follows:

Human rights represent universal standards that transcend cultural and national boundaries, and that reflect principles and teachings in all the major faiths. They are encapsulated in the ... UDHR [Universal Declaration of Human Rights].... They are developed and codified in international law by individual UN treaties, of which six treaties are considered to provide the core of international human rights law. Human rights are indivisible, with civil, cultural, economic, political and social rights being mutually dependent and reinforcing.

Adherence to these core international human rights standards is increasingly seen as the benchmark by which to judge governments' legitimacy. Some elements, including the prohibition of genocide, slavery and torture, are now generally considered to be *jus covens*, or peremptory norms, that are binding on states and individuals, whether or not states have ratified the treaties which forbid them....

Good Governance concerns the State's ability to serve its citizens. It involves the rules, institutions, processes and behaviour by which human, natural and economic resources are managed, and powers are exercised, so that development is equitable and sustainable. Where there is good governance, even scarce resources are more likely to be well managed to ensure that maximum sustainable benefit is obtained from them, and equitably enjoyed.... Key characteristics of good governance are accountability, transparency, equity, participation and subsidiarity.... Another critical element of good governance, which also concerns human rights, is respect for the rule of law....

Democracy is the only system of government in which individuals have the opportunity fully to realize their human rights. It also provides the best foundation for good governance and the rule of law to flourish. It involves a process of decision making that respects a plurality of opinion, provides a framework for non-violent change, and manages conflict peacefully, based on equal opportunity to participate in the political process. It requires that government be representative of the people and accountable to them for the use of power and public resources. Civil society has a dynamic role in helping to shape policies and to monitor their implementation. Democracy provides the opportunity for competing interests in the management of resources, including natural ones, to be fully considered before decisions are taken that affect everyone. In democracies, the rights of persons belonging to minorities are much more likely to be respected. Freedoms of expression and of association are essential components of democracy, as are the principles of equality and diversity, and non-discrimination.

(FCO 2006: 2–3)

Most in the rights community would caution against uncritically combining HRDGG, as democracy and good governance are necessary but usually insufficient conditions for protection of human rights.

Priorities 7 and 9 need to be mentioned in passing because they too shed light on the UK's definitions of rights. Priority 7 deals with migration and asylum policies, while employing rather strict language regarding illegal immigration. Priority 9 concerns security and good governance of the UK's Overseas Territories. In terms of rights, it mentions the aims of improving quality of life and ensuring sustainable development. The issue of rights is explicitly addressed in this section through a profile of the joint Forced Marriage Unit (joint between the FCO and Home Office) that attempts to protect British nationals from this abuse.

An annex to the White Paper lays out 'specific aims of the FCO' (FCO 2006: 52) within the larger priority areas. In these guidelines for implementation, the interrelationship, and apparent consonance, between these goals, is more readily evident. Scant acknowledgement is given to the fact that these goals may in many cases be at odds with each other.

So for instance, the means to achieving security-oriented priority 3 include strengthening the rule of international law in order to protect ordinary people from crimes against humanity and genocide (FCO 2006: 54). And the economically oriented priority 4 includes more inclusive fair-trade practices (FCO 2006: 55). The means to achieving priority 6 give us still further insights into the types of human rights that are included in the FCO's strategic vision and their commensurability with other goals. The first 'specific goal' is to 'encourage the spread of democracy and good political governance, in particular through fair electoral processes, effective parliamentary institutions, public participation in decision-making, independent judiciaries and freedom of expression'. Democracy is defined in specific ways, even if these would hardly constitute a complete definition of democracy. In addition, these are individually based and clearly civil/political rights. Other kinds of rights are not specifically enumerated. Similarly, priority 7's interim goals include work on refugee issues and human trafficking – however, here the FCO will be working within multilateral settings, rather than bilateral ones.

Critical assessments

Despite the clear growth in the institutionalization of human rights in the last ten years, the extent to which it ever takes priority over other goals is still in question.

Amnesty International (AI), for example, has questioned the extent to which things that appear to be interventions on behalf of human rights really are, claiming that often what appears to be an intervention for human rights is actually an intervention for UK interests. AI's 2001 UK Human Rights Audit noted that the UK often expresses concern about rights violations and conflict not out of real care for the victims but concern over potential immigrant flows into the UK (Amnesty International 2001: 1). And as we have seen, Cook himself defended pursuing human rights based on UK interests, because countries that respect the rights of their own citizens are more likely to be good trading partners and less likely to threaten international stability and UK security (Amnesty International 2001: 10).

While certainly in some cases the pursuit of human rights and other goals is commensurate, it is those where it is not that allow us to truly test our hypotheses. NGOs such as Amnesty have regularly claimed that when the two conflict, the goal of human rights almost always loses out to state interests. Members of government admit this as well.

> [T]rade minister Richard Caborn told a parliamentary committee in February 2000 that the DTI is not responsible for human rights. The minister was giving evidence to an inquiry into UK support for a project to construct a dam in Turkey, with potentially very damaging effects on people … and the environment. Nobody expects the DTI to be the lead department on human rights issues, but it must accept responsibility for the impact of its actions.
>
> (Amnesty International 2001: 11)

In fact, according to Amnesty, many officials consider human rights (HR) 'an obstacle to 'friendly relations' (Amnesty International 2001: 11). The country cases of China, Burma and North Korea described above suggest that at the very least a state's military or economic power mitigates the aggressiveness with which the UK will pursue HR goals in that country. We return to this question presently, but first turn from foreign policy generally to the specific area of foreign assistance.

British aid

In 2005 Britain gave a little less than US$10.8 billion in ODA, 48 percent of its Gross National Income (GNI). Some 76 percent of this was bilateral. The largest proportion, over US$3 billion, went to Sub-Saharan Africa.

The play of priorities in British aid

Brief institutional history

While the British aid program has been accused of reaching beyond its grasp, and failing to set clear enough priorities (OECD 1994b: 9),[9] the Department for International Development is a leader among bilateral donor aid programs.

Priorities within development have varied dramatically depending on the institutional status of development vis-à-vis the Foreign Office. Traditionally, development administration has gained more formal and practical independence under Labour governments, and been able to prioritize developmental over political or commercial goals as a result. Under Conservative governments it has been reabsorbed back into the FCO and developmental concerns have often lost ground in aid decisions to other kinds of goals. The most recent institutional change, and one of the most important in the history of British aid policy, was the creation of the DfID as a separate department with its own cabinet-level minister upon the Labour victory in 1997. The 1997 Labour manifesto referenced above devoted a separate section to international development based on 'a clear moral responsibility to help combat global poverty'. It maps a route to reestablishing poverty reduction as a priority through 'strengthen[ing] and restructure[ing] the British aid programme and bringing development issues back into the mainstream of government decision-making'. This was a promise upon which it was quick to deliver after its victory, as will be discussed below. The manifesto also pledges to shift aid resources to the poorest and to reach the 7 percent GDP (now GNI) commitment level advocated by the UN. At the same time, it pledges to pursue the potentially contradictory goal of aligning 'the aid, trade, agriculture and economic reform policies of the EU'. Debt reduction is also advocated as is 'a fair deal' for developing countries in global trade – all while keeping overall budgetary levels from growing at a rate commensurate with past Labour governments.

DfID White Papers in 1997, 2000, and 2006 have laid out the new approaches to development that would be taken by the department. One of the most important of these was a focus on development policy understood more broadly than just aid provision, in part in response to international initiatives such as the MDGs.

The 2000 White Paper also foreshadowed the institutionalization of a major, and related priority shift in the International Development Act 2002 – the first new Act since the 1980 Development and Cooperation Act. The Act crystallized poverty reduction as the purpose of aid and required that only aims that ultimately furthered that goal were justifiably part of the mission of the development program.[10] This definition has been read expansively and creatively, however, to include rights, democracy and good governance, financial restructuring, infrastructural projects, and environmental reform, among other things – and DfID, especially under strong ministers, has been able to claim the right to have input on a wide range of policy initiatives across government. The Act also got rid of aid-tying once and for all. Together the focus on poverty reduction and the ending of aid-tying (following the abolition of ATP in 1997) meant that more assistance would be going to poorer countries – those with the most progress to make toward the MDGs – rather than the richer countries who were more likely to be able to absorb the capital-intensive projects that tended to be generated under ATP and to a lesser extent under tying.

DfID has been quite explicit that a) it will deal with root causes rather than symptoms of poverty where at all possible and that b) aid effectiveness would be given increased emphasis, commensurate with new Labour's results-based focus. (This has led, in part, to the development of an increasingly thorough assessment process of country and regional progams).

Importantly, the 2006 DfID White Paper, *Making Governance Work for the Poor*, reflects both the continued importance of the MDGs and the promises made to civil society at the 2005 Gleneagles G8 meeting. More on the role of civil society follows below. The title of the White Paper reflects a clear shift to the governance component of the HRDGG triad, with an emphasis on increased transparency and anticorruption initiatives. However, the paper repeatedly casts this as a means to the end of faster growth through both distributing resources more equitably and attracting foreign trade and investment. This is the latest emphasis among several considerations that have driven development decisions.

Colonies   The original rationale for instituting a formal aid program, embodied in the Colonial Development Act of 1929, was the obligation of Empire. The perceived need to help provide for the colonies and, crucially, to encourage trade with them was the crucial factor in establishing the aid program in its first incarnation (Barder 2005: 3).

Commercial interests

Trade has continued to be a consistent theme in British aid policy. Even during the Cold War, 'the balance of trade was just as important as the balance of terror and counting jobs was as critical as counting Moscow's warheads ... the promotion of overseas trade became for a time practically synonymous with foreign policy' (Coles 2000: 112). And, of course, after 1991, 'no longer was reference to the Soviet threat available to defeat special issue groups from pressing their aims' (Coles 2000: 112). This goal was embodied in the 1980s and 1990s with the Aid and Trade Provision, which allowed businesses to propose projects for development. Policy-makers claimed that this was a defensive tactic meant to counter the use of strategies such as *credits mixtes* by the French. But it was roundly criticized by academics, the DAC and NGOs as distorting the aims and thus results of aid by allowing business rather than government (in consultation with the recipient country) to propose projects, likely sacrificing development criteria to commercial ones. In addition the program encouraged a shorter timeline for evaluation of projects due to the annual fiscal cycle of companies. This is problematic given the amount of time development projects generally take to plan, implement and evaluate, which is what drives the three-to-five year cycle on which DfID and its predecessor organizations have generally operated. In addition, ATP (and tied aid more generally) has generally been found to help the least competitive and future-trade-generating firms (see Morrissey *et al.* 1992) and therefore to be a suboptimal way of achieving either development or trade aims. Importantly, the DAC noted criticisms such as 1) a *'conflict of objectives between the commercial need for quick decisions and the need for full appraisals of the social, environmental and economic aspects of the proposal'* (emphasis mine), benefiting affluent rather than poorest recipients (in clear opposition to the 'more help for the poorest' approach or the 90–10 aim), and 2) the danger that concentration in a few sectors tends to creates vested interests and lobbies inclined to value criteria other than development (OECD 1994b: 25).

Geopolitics

If trade has been one of the most consistent goals of British aid policy, some of the most dramatic shifts therein have been in response to geopolitical changes. It was fear of instability in the colonies in the earliest years of the aid program that led to an increase in aid amounts as well as in length of commitment to individual projects (Barder 2005: 4). The successes of the Marshall Plan, clearly a political program, demonstrated the potential success of aid in a setting where there was a receptive cultural and infrastructural context, thus normalizing the attachment of political rationales to aid. In many cases commercial and political goals have of course gone hand in hand. As noted earlier in the chapter, commercial goals underlie much diplomatic work.

Given that aid has always had at least ostensible developmental content, the justification for development has varied dramatically over time. Development – as it has come to be understood in practice and defined officially in the 1997, 2000 and 2006 White Papers and 2002 IDA – subsumes several components.

Poverty reduction

As mentioned above, this is now the sole official *raison d'être* of the British development assistance program. But already by 1994 the DAC review was reporting that 'the stated purpose of British aid is to promote sustainable economic and social development in order to improve the quality of life and reduce poverty, suffering and deprivation in developing countries' (OECD 1994b: 34).

Good governance

As early as 1990, then-Foreign Secretary Douglas Hurd claimed that promotion of good government and political pluralism was Britain's official development assistance goal (Stokke 1995: 22). By 1994 the DAC noted that 'the objectives of the aid programme are to promote economic reform, enhance productive capacity, and to promote good government...' (OECD 1994b: 34), noting that Britain had been one of the leaders in elevating this last goal to the top of the development agenda. The integration of good governance under priority 6 (above) has been intended to mainstream good governance goals into broader foreign policy.

General social goals

The DAC report cited above goes on to note that these goals also include 'to help developing countries to define and carry out poverty-reduction strategies, to promote human development including better education and health ... and ... the social, economic, legal and political status of women...' (OECD 1994b: 19).

Environment

As early as the early 1990s, the same DAC report mentions environmental goals in its initial statement of the British aid program's aims. And the discussion of priority 6 above makes it clear that environmental protection is clearly one of the aims of good government,[11] as well as being a determinant of whether development can truly be considered sustainable. The 2006 White Paper dramatically shifts emphasis to environmental protection, devoting a chapter to climate change and incorporating the context of environmental challenges in every other section of the document.

Rights

As has been discussed, implicit and explicit definitions of rights, and their relationship to concepts like development, good governance and democracy, have varied over time, but in some form have been addressed by both Conservative and Labour governments alike. In 1990, John Major, then Chancellor of the Exchequer, advocated making aid conditional on democratic reforms in recipients. Now rights have been made, as we have seen, a much more explicit priority of foreign policy. But if we take priority 6 at face value, we have a potential conflict between the inclusive definition of rights found here and the narrower focus defined in the FCO's most recent human rights reports. Depending on which we assume is being pursued, there is likely to be a lower or higher level of potential conflict with other goals, especially as pursued through development policy.

If we assume the more inclusive definition, there are several kinds of situations where conflict could arise with strategic/geopolitical and commercial goals. For instance, this would be the case when governments of politically or economically important states domestically repress, which many lower-income states do, in order to extract more from their populations. Promoting human rights could also come into conflict with other developmental goals. For instance, when emergency and subsistence aid goes to regimes with poor human rights records it not only alleviates citizens' suffering but may mute discontent and allow those governments to stay in power longer – or the benefits may actually be captured by those governments.

If we assume the more restrictive working definition: foci on good governance and democracy, as well as the torture, death penalty and rights-of-the-child initiatives, then it is more likely that there will be commensurability between human rights and other goals, examples of many of which were mentioned above. And yet even here we know there are potential conflicts. For example, what if democracy produces a regime that is anathema to British ideological, strategic or trade interests? What if governance reforms are seen as imposed from above and therefore illegitimate?

The DfID itself issued a policy statement on human rights in 2000, rationalized on the basis that its main goal of poverty reduction could only be achieved through the full involvement of poor people in development processes. This led the DfID to suggest a 'rights perspective' on poverty, incorporating the idea that poverty is about lack of power in ways that go beyond the economic, and that it is the duty of governments to address disempowerment in all its forms, especially when it is unequally distributed (DfID 2000: 7). The report goes on to identify three 'operational principles' to help integrate a rights perspective into development: ensuring participation in decision-making processes, the building of socially inclusive values and societies, and strengthening of institutions to make sure that states provide these things to their citizens (DfID 2000: 7).

While the DfID's foci on democratic participation and social/economic empowerment go far beyond the three focus areas of the FCO, they do match up quite closely with the emphases of priority 6, discussed in depth above.

How British aid policy is made today

Parliament

Parliament's role falls short of what might be expected. Many have documented the difficulties of ensuring a legislative monitoring role without separation of powers (something true of all three case studies). Tony Wright (himself an MP) notes that 'this close connection between government and Parliament means conflict between them is by definition almost impossible' (Wright 2000: 197). While Parliament may debate key issues of the day, 'it is rare ... for a debate in Parliament to have a very significant impact on policy. It is the government that makes policy, not Parliament, and most of the ... policy-making process take[s] place outside Parliament...' (Wright 2000: 212). From the Whitehall side of the process, former Permanent Secretary John Coles writes that 'Parliament's influence on foreign policy is limited...' (Coles 2000: 94).[12]

The organ of Parliament that has the most potential to oversee Whitehall is the committee. The two main committees that have purview over development policy, the Foreign Affairs Committee (FAC) and International Development Select

Committee, have regularly complained that the FCO withholds information (Wright 2000: 220), part of a tradition of secrecy that prevailed through much of the twentieth century and to which I will return below.

In addition, while Parliament is responsible for raising revenue, it 'barely considers how it should be *spent*, even though the question of how money should be allocated across Whitehall departments is bitterly fought between government departments and the Treasury' (Wright 2000: 231). Theoretically Commons must approve final budgetary figures, on the basis of departmental reports from the previous year, overall macroeconomic constraints and overarching goals of government, but in practice it has 'all but abandoned detailed consideration of these figures ... the task is delegated to the departmental select committees ... but more particularly to the Public Accounts Committee and to the National Audit Office' (Wright 2000: 231).

Prime Minister (PM)

While the Prime Minister's power is often questioned, his power of appointment, especially in the areas of economic and foreign affairs, may be particularly powerful (Wright 2000: 263), as illustrated by the differences in goals and approach between Cook and Straw.

Whitehall

Nearly all the important action in aid policy-making happens in Whitehall. While the overall three-year DfID budget is agreed in Parliament through the Spending Review with the Treasury, DfID itself conducts the resource allocation process that results in specific amounts for geographic, sectoral and other programs. This process involves assessments of the efficacy of past aid, the needs and challenges within specific countries (see Content Analysis, below) and other high-level analysis and discussion, including with DfID's management board. Final amounts are approved by the minister.

The focus of power over aid policy within Whitehall has shifted over time, with changes in the status of the development unit – from dependence on the FCO, to independence, and back and forth again, as discussed earlier. This is additionally important because of regular conflicts between the FCO, DTI and DfID or ODA – an institutional reflection of tensions between development and other foreign policy goals.

Even when aid policy-making has enjoyed separate institutional status, the Minister for International Development's and Foreign Secretary's personalities and relationships with the PM and the Chancellor have affected the content of development policy and the status of development vis-à-vis other goals. This suggests that development has yet to enjoy consolidation in the pantheon of foreign policy aims, particularly since it is the minister who formally makes final decisions on budgetary priorities.

Overseas posts are important sources of input. Many countries have independent DfID offices, which have a set of interests and opinions that are often quite distinct from those of the embassies or diplomatic missions in country.

'Outside' interests

General public It will come as no surprise that the general public rarely bases many of its voting decisions on development policy. However, 'the potential for a strong domestic reaction to an overseas development is always there and policymakers must factor that potential into their thinking' (Coles 2000: 111). Immigrant populations may pose an important exception to this rule, especially in particular country-specific aid cases. While such populations generally comprise a very small percentage of the total population, they can have a real impact if they are well organized and concentrated, as around the urban centers of, most notably, London and Birmingham, the largest current countries of origin being Pakistan, India and Nigeria, in descending order. Two more 'attentive publics' certainly exist, though.

Business lobby Coles writes that 'a common theme of the formal reviews of overseas reevaluation ... was that more emphasis should be placed by government on support for British business in its overseas activities.' The business community has had a major impact on not only Whitehall but also overseas diplomatic posts over the last 10–15 years (Coles 2000: 97) and 'the Foreign Office itself, which conducts export and investment promotion activities jointly with the DTI, has a closer relationship with British business than at any time in its history'. Where business interests do not prevail, he asserts, '*it is because the target country is seen as not being valuable to British trade*' (Coles 2000: 96–7; emphasis mine). However, with the post-1997 changes in the professionalization and institutionalization of aid under the DfID the status of the business community has changed rather dramatically. The changes in 1997 made it clear that aid would unambiguously take development as its first priority, and the business community has learned since 1997 that its priorities are not generally able to compete with developmental ones.

Development lobby Traditionally the poor man out among outside players (see for instance Morrissey *et al.* 1992), the influence of the development lobby, dominated by NGOs, has increased in recent years (Coles 2000: 98–9). In fact, he says,

> during the period of my own career the role and stature of NGOs were transformed.... NGOs were [at the start of my career] seen ... largely as campaign organizations whose main function was to criticize government and who were therefore to be kept at a certain distance. Some thirty years later, as PUS [Permanent Under Secretary], I invited the heads of seventeen NGOs to a morning of discussion at the Foreign Office which concentrated

on the objectives of our foreign policy. This is but one illustration of the much closer links which the department now has with organizations.

(Coles 2000: 98–9)

It should be noted that this is part of a much more general effort on expanding the range of parties consulted in the policy-making process since the accession of the Blair government in a range of policy areas from health care to defence. The 2005 Make Poverty History movement which sparked historic commitments from the UK and the rest of the world at the Gleneagles summit, was driven by civil society and has been successful in shifting the emphasis of the aid program as reflected in the 2006 White Paper.

Media   Sometimes policy is adjusted to avoid a critical media response but the adjustment is usually more at the margins (Coles 2000: 101). Where there is concern, it is generally more that the media will impact public opinion, but even this is a serious factor in decision-making only in very high-profile and controversial cases, such as Burma or Russia (over Chechnya).

Europe   While European laws subsume UK ones in the areas where the two coincide, most observers believe that a European foreign policy is unlikely to replace a national one in any meaningful way.

Other contextual factors   The government of the recipient is also increasingly consulted in aid strategy formulation, to enhance aid effectiveness, appropriateness and coordination, and to create buy-in in the recipient country.

Implications for hypothesis testing

First, to assume that government acts as a unitary policy-making entity would be overly simplistic and there are a wide range of actors within and without government, as well as in the recipient country, whose opinion is at least officially sought. And yet rarely are variables capturing the width of this network, which is steadily increasing, included in quantitative analyses of the aid process. Additionally, past analyses have tended to emphasize the role of Parliament, looking, for instance, at the content of Parliamentary debate to determine the extent to which different policy goals are favored (e.g. Breuning 1995). And yet there appears to be little reason to expect Parliament to have much influence on the content of aid policy, certainly regarding something as specific as how it pertains to particular recipients.

Second, we should also not expect aid decisions to be symmetrical, as suggested in earlier chapters. For instance, as suggested at the 1978 colloquium, once begun, complete cessation of aid is a rarity. Even suspension, as in the case of military assistance to Nepal in 2005, is seen as an extremely strong statement. But aid is also sometimes halted due to budgetary shortfalls, or increasingly when former recipients graduate to donor status, as has occurred with some former Soviet bloc states. So, as we saw in the aggregate analysis in the previous chapter, the decision to drop states does not necessarily respond to the same kinds of considerations as the decision to add states.

Archival research

Given the supremacy of Whitehall in the policy process, remarkably little academic work has examined the content of correspondence within the DfID or its predecessor institutions, though this is something that has been suggested by former senior civil servants.[13]

> A critical assessment would no doubt consider whether any important objectives have been omitted, and seek to analyze the quality of the objectives in terms of their relevance to British interests and their internal consistency and examine the proclaimed achievements in some detail. It would also consider whether there have been significant cases of failure to achieve these objectives since these are unlikely to be highlighted in official reports. It would be right, too, to distinguish between aims which are purely declaratory in nature and those which are seriously pursued by sustained diplomacy.
>
> (Coles 2000: 121)

While not embarking on a comprehensive evaluation of all the important aims of each kind of foreign policy tool, I have attempted above to very briefly assess some of the most important recent foreign policy statements along the most important of these dimensions, particularly proclaimed objectives, which can be compared with the actual content of policy decisions regarding aid to particular states below. Of course one of the key problems with disentangling candid statements of policy from concerns about public response or scrutiny, is that often the material that would be most valuable is confidential and therefore not publicly available (Coles 2000: 122).

FOI and open government legislation in Britain

Following through on the promises of Labour's 1997 manifesto, the Blair government has initiated a number of changes meant to promote greater openness in government. One of the most important of these has been the passage of Britain's first comprehensive FOI legislation, which went into effect in January 2005.

The policy process has not been particularly open for much of British foreign policy history. This is due in part to the doctrine of collective cabinet responsibility, which necessitates that much policy debate remain closed so that unanimity can credibly be claimed later.

> [Foreign p]olicymaking used to be a highly confidential operation carried out with a level of secrecy rarely seen outside a Trappist monastery.

> Submissions on action … were the product of in-house analysis based on top-secret telegrams from embassies. No outside expertise or opinions were sought.
>
> (Dickie 2004: 6)

This level of secrecy has not gone unnoticed by international organizations such as the DAC and even Parliament itself, which has been further limited in its ability to monitor foreign policy-making by the FCO's and ODA's traditional refusal to provide the FAC with even the amounts allocated to various recipient countries, let alone the country assessments on which it bases these allocations.

Coles among others has justified this secrecy in strong but characteristically vague terms. 'To state the precise aims of Britain in each individual country would cause embarrassment and go a long way to defeat their purpose' (Coles 2000: 105).

Documents examined

Over the last 25 years, regardless of its incarnation, the development arm of British foreign policy-making has developed policy review papers for its major bilateral programmes, and often for its smaller ones. Today these are called Country Strategy Papers (CSPs) and Country Assistance Plans (CAPs), but they have also been called Country Review and Country Objectives Papers, and other bilateral assessments are produced under different names on an occasional basis. In addition, ODA/DfID produce more general (i.e. regional) or specific (a sector within a specific recipient country) strategies, reviews and assessments. These review bilateral relationships in particular and lay out the general aims and specific goals for a recipient in the coming three-to-five-year period. These play a large role in the allocation of the next round of funding as well, and the department has the potential to move funds around on a more short-term basis as circumstances dictate.

But as the OECD lamented in 1994,

> Country documents are prepared for internal programming purposes, which makes it difficult to assess their full influence. They are not made public, which some NGOs find incongruous since they must propose projects in line with British strategy for a given country. Availability of the country strategy document would take some of the guesswork out of fitting proposals to country strategies.
>
> (OECD 1994b: 34)

As noted above, even the budgetary figures for particular recipients have traditionally been kept internal to the department (OECD 1994b: 35).[14] Though this practice has changed since the DfID was established, there are still internal drafts, consultations and other documentation, which go into making the public documents, that are unsurprisingly kept internal.

Internal documents can tell us very different things than public documents.[15] They can represent a more accurate view of what policy-makers take into account, and how. Public documents are not only the sum of innumerable drafts and redrafts but are prepared with an eye to pleasing as many and offending as few as possible. One is left to read between the lines and hope not to mistranslate.

In undertaking the following content analyses, I examined all available current and past bilateral Country Strategy Papers (CSPs) and Country Assistance Plans (CAPs) [see Table 6.1]. Any of these before 1998 are entirely internal documents. Because I am interested in how priorities are weighed relevant to each other in particular bilateral instances, I have not included regional documents. And because I want to look at the overall weighing of all possible priorities *vis-à-vis* each other, I have not included specific sectoral strategies which will by definition focus on some priorities over others. I listed the key policy priorities discussed above (strategic aims, trade, human rights and so on) and then counted the relative frequency with which each appeared. The percentages refer to the proportion of all key concepts represented by that term.

I then used the key factors I have posited that donors employ to 'sort' recipients, and divided the recipient sample based on each of those factors, so that we could see if the donor at least rhetorically weighed factors differently in decisions about some recipients versus others. Besides comparing 'strategic' to 'nonstrategic' states, and 'major importers' to 'minor' ones (both splits opera tionalized as in the OECD analyses in the preceding chapter) I also looked for differences in factors considered between decisions:

- reflected in documents prepared for internal versus external circulation
- regarding recipients in different regions
- made under Labour versus Conservative administrations (with a three-month lag built in)
- made during a key minister's tenure versus other (with a three-month lag built in)
- in cases that have received substantial (operationalization: three stories or more) media attention in the international press versus those that have not
- regarding cases about which there has been substantial activism by human rights groups in the donor country (operationalization: at least one documented campaign or event) as opposed to cases that have not been the targets of such campaigns
- for recipients with large immigrant populations in the donor (operationalization: immigrant group is one of top ten immigrant groups by size in donor) versus those without
- regarding the very poorest countries versus other developing countries (operationalization: UN LLDC status, or $1/day average GNI per capita)
- regarding oil-exporting recipients versus those that are not oil exporters
- regarding recipients who have had a humanitarian crisis in the last year versus those that have not (operationalization: crisis listed with UN Office for Coordination of Humanitarian Affairs)

- regarding nuclear versus nonnuclear states
- regarding large (top 25 percent by population; arbitrary cutoff) versus small states.

These different distinctions capture a variety of other qualities that we have discussed which might be expected to delineate different classes of recipients that would have different calculi applied to them by donors. While difficult to include in the multivariate statistical analyses below (without a host of interaction terms or more tables than is possible here), at this stage we can rather clearly determine whether there are statistically significant differences in the ostensible rationale applied to different classes of recipients, as well as observe which sorting criteria change the ostensible aid calculus the most.

I also took into account differences in terminology that might apply in different donor cases, fortunately this effect was minimized by the fact that the vast majority of documents in these three donor cases was in English (in the case of the French documents encountered in Canada, I searched for the English term that was closest possible in meaning to the French term). In the case of Britain I performed these analyses on 250 total documents. I have not provided counts for specific documents in part due to considerations of space, and in part because of the internal nature of the documents.

Content analysis

Table 6.1 shows the relative concentration of what concepts figured most prominently in the papers. True to the ODA's/DfID's stated aims, references to poverty alleviation and development constituted a majority or at the very least a plurality of the core concepts considered. Trade generally follows, followed by good governance and rights. This largely parallels the set of considerations that successive White Papers lay out, and in fact in the drafting of the strategy papers, especially since 1997, there has been explicit effort to ensure that individual country strategies conform to overarching policy directives.

First, I compared internal documents to those prepared with an eye to public dissemination. There are a few significant differences between the internal and external documents. First, good governance and democracy appear in higher proportion in public documents than in internal ones, as do references to economic management and reform in the recipient. One interpretation of this could be that, as has been cautioned, when new concepts come into vogue they often lead to a 'repackaging' of aid strategies rather than a real change in the ends or the means thereof. Trade features much more frequently in internal than in external documents, and emergency assistance appears less frequently in internal documents. Interestingly the concepts that most reflect self-interested goals occur far more often in the internal than the external documents, suggesting that aid is packaged in an attractive and altruistic wrapper for public consumption, that might sometimes not be entirely matched by the more candid rationale discussed within.

I compared regional differences as well. Though t-tests are impossible given the multiple regions considered, some interesting differences between regions can be observed. Good governance appears most frequently in country strategies for states in Africa and Europe, where there are a high proportion of failing states and transitional states, proportionally. The concept of rights crops up in highest proportion in states of Asia and the Pacific, and trade references occur in highest proportion in the areas where, unsurprisingly, Britain enjoys the most trade. References to the other concepts are relatively consistent across region.

Next we see the effects of the donor's decision-making context on which sorts of concepts are considered in the strategy papers. The Blair government has been far more ready to cite economic restructuring and reform than were its predecessors, and less likely to emphasize both trade and the 'obligations' of former colonial ties. This is rather unsurprising given that the last 18 years of policy-making had been made under Conservative governments and even the change from Thatcher to Major resulted in few major changes of direction in the UK's foreign policy identity or orientation. Emergency assistance is less emphasized as well, perhaps reflecting the DfID's explicit attention to long-term poverty reduction over short-term poverty alleviation.

Strategies have significantly different emphases during Clare Short's tenure. Emphases on development and economic management are substantially higher. This reflects Short's own strong advocacy for development within the administration, the changing conceptualization of ODA from one of 'aid' to one of development assistance, and the new emphasis on transparency and the creation of recipient environments that would engender the most efficient possible absorption of aid. Emphasis on security is less pronounced, but this may be accounted for in part by the fact that a large number of the (post-Short) documents date from the post-9/11 era, and some from post-7/7, both of which spurred increases in attention to security issues. References to trade and colonial legacy are fewer as well, in line with the overall change under New Labour.

The human rights activist community can be very effective in focusing public attention on particular cases of abuse. Interestingly enough, documents concerning states that have been the focus of Amnesty campaigns in the UK are actually less likely to emphasize rights and security than other documents, and more likely to emphasize trade. This may reflect attempts to justify aid to poor human rights performers. Strategy papers regarding aid recipients that have a large expatriate community in Britain do not differ substantially from others. Perhaps it is assumed that few immigrants will pay attention to such documents? Interviews with DfID staff would be necessary to determine whether that is the case.

What of factors pertaining to the recipient itself? The strategy papers regarding LLDCs place less emphasis on good governance and security than do those of other states. Perhaps analysts believe that leadership in these countries has quite enough on its hands just getting its economic house in order. This possibility is supported by the fact that LLDC strategy papers are also more likely to cite economic reform.

Table 6.1

Proportion of references	Development %	Good governance and democracy %	Rights %	Economic management %	Security %	Trade %	Colonialism %	Emergency assistance %	Aid effectiveness %
External documents	67	9	5	1	1	19	0	2	1
Internal documents	62	6	5	0	2	25	0	1	0
P(T<=t)	0.08	0.00	0.36	0.00	0.11	0.04	0.49	0.07	0.22
Factors pertaining to geopolitical forces									
Africa	66	10	4	0	2	17	1	1	0
Americas	79	3	3	0	0	14	0	1	0
Asia/Pacific	63	5	7	0	1	27	0	2	0
Europe	58	12	4	1	0	24	1	2	1
Middle East	64	6	4	0	1	24	0	2	1
Factors pertaining to donor's decision-making context									
Conservative	62	6	4	0	0	26	0	2	0
Labour	66	8	5	0	1	21	0	2	1
P(T<=t)	0.15	0.04	0.30	0.00	0.13	0.04	0.00	0.00	0.13
Not short	63	8	4	0	1	23	1	1	1
Short	69	8	5	0	0	19	0	2	1
P(T<=t)	0.03	0.33	0.17	0.01	0.03	0.09	0.01	0.26	0.41
High activism	70	8	3	1	0	15	0	2	3
Low activism	65	8	5	0	1	22	0	2	0
P(T<=t)	0.17	0.47	0.04	0.18	0.00	0.03	0.43	0.39	0.17
Low imm. pop	67	8	5	0	0	20	0	2	0
High imm. pop	62	7	5	0	2	23	0	1	1
P(T<=t)	0.15	0.23	0.40	0.33	0.14	0.24	0.29	0.32	0.28
Factors pertaining to recipient									
Not LLDC	63	10	6	0	1	22	1	2	0
LLDC	67	7	4	0	0	21	0	1	0

P(T<=t)	0.14	0.02	0.13	0.07	0.06	0.44	0.25	0.29	0.31
Major importer	63	7	4	0	0	24	0	2	1
Minor importer	67	8	5	0	1	19	0	2	0
P(T<=t)	0.16	0.23	0.27	0.40	0.02	0.09	0.49	0.38	0.33
Not oil	66	8	6	0	0	19	0	2	0
Oil exporter	64	8	4	0	1	23	0	2	1
P(T<=t)	0.27	0.27	0.07	0.41	0.10	0.16	0.48	0.21	0.32
Strategic	58	9	7	0	3	24	1	3	0
Non-strategic	67	8	4	0	0	21	0	1	1
P(T<=t)	0.05	0.07	0.09	0.03	0.04	0.30	0.04	0.05	0.31
Human crisis	66	3	5	0	1	21	0	2	1
No crisis	63	9	4	1	2	22	0	1	1
P(T<=t)	0.15	0.17	0.39	0.10	0.11	0.45	0.18	0.30	0.38
Nuclear	67	4	4	1	0	24	0	2	0
Nonnuclear	65	8	4	0	1	21	0	1	1
P(T<=t)	0.44	0.00	0.28	0.28	0.01	0.42	0.45	0.29	0.05
Large state	71	3	3	4	0	23	0	2	0
Small state	65	8	5	0	1	21	0	1	1
P(T<=t)	0.33	0.00	0.06	0.42	0.01	0.44	0.31	0.21	0.05

The key hypotheses developed in Chapter 3 suggest that donor–recipient trade and strategic relationships should be the most important factors in aid decisions and in delineating different categories of recipients. Interestingly, whether a recipient is a major importer of British goods has relatively little effect on the concepts cited in the strategy papers. Importers are less likely to have security considerations cited, but that is about it. We do, however, see an inconsistency in the application of rights issues in the fact that oil exporters are marginally less likely to be cited for good governance issues – especially important since so many oil exporters also suffer from severe maldistribution of resources.

There are many differences, however, in the coverage of concepts for non-strategic states and strategic ones. Development is mentioned more often for nonstrategic states, but good governance is mentioned less (which is surprising if we expect states that are 'important' in other ways to 'get away with' poor governance and human rights infringements). This result bears further investigation. Economic management, colonialism and emergency assistance are mentioned more often in coverage of nonstrategic states (though we had no prior expectations about why that would be the case), and security is mentioned less (which makes sense; strategically important states are in part defined by their importance for local, regional or global security).

The presence of a humanitarian crisis essentially has no effect on what is covered in a country's strategy paper. This is in a sense not surprising. States with humanitarian crises tend to receive aid regardless and since, so many crises involve natural disasters, there is no reason to think that there would be political factors systematically making 'crisis' states receive different treatment from 'non-crisis' states. Nonnuclear states are more likely to have good governance cited, while nuclear states are more likely to have security cited.

Finally, nonnuclear states are far more likely to have aid effectiveness security, and good goverance cited. Small states are more likely to be cited for good governance, security and aid effectiveness and marginally more so for right, an observation that supports the hypothesis that rights often come to the fore when other issues drop out.

Aggregate statistical analyses

So much for the rhetoric. How does this all play out in the actual aid disbursement figures?

Variable operationalization

The operational forms of the dependent variable for the gatekeeping decision were discussed in Chapter 4. For the allocation decision, aid is operationalized as total aid from Britain to that state in the given year. Annual aid data was obtained from the OECD's Creditor Reporting System (various years).

If a state was a noncreditor country in a given year, it was included as a potential aid recipient. It is more unusual *not* to be granted aid than to be granted it. In a sample year, 2004, 85 of the 180 potential recipients received aid. Ninety-five states that did *not* get aid (Table 6.2), eight were oil exporters and relatively wealthy; it is not surprising that they would not be aid priorities. Many others were island nations who benefit from substantial amounts of aid from geographically proximate states. There are also few clear patterns evident in terms of the human rights records of the states that are left off the list. Only five have relatively poor human rights scores of 4 or 5.

Variable operationalization and data sources for most of the independent variables are described in some detail in Chapter 4. All analyses address total aid. Many of the economic value and trade variables are more easily interpretable in the context of the aid decisions in individual donor states than was the case for pooled OECD aid, which represented the results of the decisions in over 20 donor states. In addition, a great deal of data is available for individual donors that either could not be assembled for all OECD aid pooled together or would have not been meaningful if it had been assembled.

Economic value of the recipient   For instance, the quality of data on trade volumes to and from members of the OECD varies greatly over time and across recipients. Especially in earlier editions of the CIA publication, trade partners are simply listed with no notation of how large a percentage of trade occurs with them. However, for Britain and the other individual donors, these data are be drawn from the International Monetary Fund's Direction of Trade data set, which lists specific bilateral trade volumes. Therefore, these measures are much more exact in the analyses of aid decisions in specific donors.

Strategic value   Strategic value, including whether the recipient is located at a key trade intersection and whether it is located in an area of instability, are also measured more specifically in the context of individual donors. For instance, for analyses of overall OECD aid levels, it was prohibitively difficult to include the perceptions and estimations of which intersections were 'key' or which areas of instability mattered to every member government. Conversely, for individual donors, strategic interests are much more well defined, and I can examine the effect of measures that make a recipient strategically important to a specific donor. A potential recipient that is important in geopolitical terms to Britain, because of shared alliance membership or geographical proximity, for instance, may not be so crucial to the UK's overall strategic vision. Therefore, I take into account military commitments (measured as shared alliance membership taken from the alliance subset of the Militarized Interstate Disputes data set). In addition, donors that are geographically proximate to a recipient have a greater stake in that recipient's fate, because of spillover effects of phenomena such as political instability or economic softening. For instance, Australia (as we will see) provides, through aid, a significant proportion of the GNPs of several island nations in the South Pacific. Geographical proximity is measured as distance in kilometers between national capitals.

Table 6.2

Recipients, 2004	Nonrecipients, 2004
Afghanistan	Algeria
Albania	Antigua and Barbuda
Angola	Argentina
Anguilla	Aruba
Armenia	Bahamas
Azerbaijan	Bahrain
Bangladesh	Barbados
Belarus	Benin
Belize	Bermuda
Bolivia	Bhutan
Bosnia	British Virgin Islands
Botswana	Brunei
Brazil	Burkina Faso
Bulgaria	Cape Verde
Burma	Cayman Islands
Burundi	Central African Republic
Cambodia	Chile
Cameroon	Comoros
Chad	Cook Islands
China	Costa Rica
Colombia	Cuba
Congo (Republic of Congo)	Cyprus
Croatia	Czechoslovakia
Democratic Republic of Congo (1998)	Djibouti
Dominica	Ecuador
Dominican Republic	Egypt
Eritrea	El Salvador
Ethiopia	Equatorial Guinea
Gambia	Estonia
Georgia	Falkland Islands
Ghana	Federated States of Micronesia
Grenada	Fiji
Guinea	French Polynesia
Guyana	Gabon
Haiti	Gibraltar
Honduras	Greece
India	Guatemala
Indonesia	Guinea-Bissau
Iran	Hong Kong
Iraq	Hungary
Ivory Coast/Côte D'Ivoire	Israel
Jamaica	Kiribati
Jordan	Kuwait
Kazakhstan	Latvia
Kenya	Libya
Kyrgyzstan	Lithuania
Laos	Macau
Lebanon	Malaysia
Lesotho	Maldives
Liberia	Malta

Table 6.2 continued

Recipients, 2004	Nonrecipients, 2004
Macedonia (Former Yugoslav Republic of Macedonia)	Marshall Islands
Madagascar	Mauritania
Malawi	Mayotte
Mali	Mexico
Mauritius	Mongolia
Moldova	Nauru
Montserrat	New Caledonia
Morocco	Niue
Mozambique	Northern Marianas
Namibia	Oman
Nepal	Palau
Nicaragua	Panama
Niger	Papua New Guinea
Nigeria	Poland
North Korea (Democratic Republic of Korea)	Qatar
Pakistan	Samoa (1997)
Palestinian Territories	Sao Tome and Principe
Paraguay	Saudi Arabia
Peru	Seychelles
Philippines	Singapore
Romania	Slovakia
Russia	Slovenia
Rwanda	Solomon Islands
Senegal	South Korea (Republic of Korea)
Serbia and Montenegro	St Kitts and Nevis
Sierra Leone	St Lucia
Somalia	St Vincent and Grenadines
South Africa	Suriname
Sri Lanka	Swaziland
St Helena	Syria
Sudan	Taiwan
Tajikistan	Timor (East Timor)
Tanzania	Tokelau
Thailand	Tonga
Togo	Trinidad and Tobago
Uganda	Tunisia
Ukraine	Turkey
Uzbekistan	Turkmenistan
Viet Nam	Turks and Caicos
Yemen	Tuvalu
Zambia	United Arab Emirates
Zimbabwe	Uruguay
	US Virgin Islands
	Vanuatu
	Venezuela
	Wallis and Futuna

Colonial history   I control for whether a recipient is a former British colony (*Flags of the World*, 2003 www.crwflags.com/fotw); colonial ties promote a tradition of financial support and account for a good deal of variation in aid amounts between recipients (e.g. Lumsdaine 1993; Maizels and Nissanke 1984).

Domestic politics   While the human rights score of the recipient country is clearly static in a given year, the donor's perception of its importance may be conditional. That is, there may be ways that a donor can be convinced that human rights is the most important lens through which to examine a particular potential aid decision. This, as suggested above, is often the goal of human rights interest/activist groups. Ideally, I would have obtained measures of the amount and intensity of campaigning done on behalf of particular human rights crises from the major human rights interest groups themselves. These would include paid lobbyist/consultant hours spent on a particular project, amount of money spent on a particular project, number of publications circulated focusing on a particular problem, etc. However, both Amnesty and Human Rights Watch report that they do not keep records of this kind or any other that would lend itself to systematic analysis – not even a financial audit that would contain country-specific line items. I therefore turned to the Integrated Data for Events Analysis (IDEA) protocol:

> IDEA provides a comprehensive events framework for the analysis of international interactions by supplementing the event forms from all earlier projects with new event forms needed to monitor contemporary trends in civil and interstate politics. It uses a more flexible multi-leveled event and actor/target hierarchy that can be expanded to incorporate new event forms and actors/targets, and adds dimensions that can be employed to construct indicators for early warning and assessing conflict escalation. IDEA is currently being used in the automated coding of news reports (Reuters Business Briefs) and, in collaboration with other projects, in the analysis of field reports.
>
> (Bond *et al.* 2003: 733)

I also measure political congruence between the donor and the recipient, as expressed (rather bluntly) by similar degrees of democracy (distance in scores as reported in the Polity III data set).

Results

Table 6.3 presents one form of the dependent variable – whether or not a state received aid – for all potential recipients. Unlike the last chapter, here we do get some degree of variation. While there is a good deal of variability over time, several characteristics of both the recipient itself and of the domestic and international context have an effect on whether a state receives aid. States with internal conflict receive more aid, in keeping with OECD recommendations. I read this as an example of selflessness in aid patterns. Areas in conflict are not

Table 6.3

Variable	Gatekeeping decision	Allocation decision
	Coefficient (standard errors)	Coefficient (standard errors)
Year	-0.19**	1031.47
General characteristics of recipient		
Recipient GDP	5.05^{-12}	-2.52^{-08}
Human rights measures		
Human rights violations	-0.03	-26.44
Recipient polity score	0.00	6.81
Economic value measures		
UK exports to recipient	$-1.97^{\ 06}$ **	0.00
UK imports from recipient	-1.21^{-07}	0.01*
Recipient oil exports	0.00*	0.89
Recipient GDP growth	0.00	163.42
Recipient population	4.89^{-09}	0.00***
Strategic value measures		
Recipient nuclear capabilities	-0.68	$-18,281.33$
Internal dispute	1.47*	-2570.83
External dispute	0.21	2197.50
Distance from UK	-0.00	0.03
Post-Cold War	3.35***	957.73
Trade intersection	0.26	-6574.26
Need measures		
Humanitarian crisis	0.20	1489.12
Domestic politics measures		
Human rights activism	-1.65	$-49,160.50$*
Immigrants from recipient	0.00	0.19***
Britain GDP	-9.86^{-13}*	$-1.00^{\ 08}$
Britain GDP growth rate	0.23 **	745.71
Labour/Blair	2.40***	-4591.14
Colonial history measure	-0.24	-184.00
Former colony	Dropped	-183.77
Policy history	0.00	6.81
Aid previous year?	5.91^{-06}	0.49***
Significance of model		0.00
N	1044	619
R^2		0.01, 0.87, 0.64

Notes
*** = significant at $p < 0.001$; ** $= p < 0.01$; * $= p < 0.05$; (marg) $= p < 0.075$ (one-tailed).

likely to be good trading partners or good investments for the donor. Instead, this represents an attempt to help rebuild a country that needs it, rather than a country that can pay one back in any real respect. British decisions in specific recipient cases support this as well. For instance, a 1998 Rwanda country strategy paper explicitly justifies increasing aid to respond to not just past but ongoing violence in the country.

What about the importance of economic relationships? Contrary to the trade-as-driver thesis, expressed in hypothesis 1, in fact the level a state imports from the UK is negatively associated with its likelihood of being granted aid. This could very well be that the neediest countries are not likely to be large importers since the end of ATP and that the DfID more help for the poorest approach is affecting the results we see here for the entire time period. However, a recipient's oil exports are positively related to the likelihood of receiving aid, suggesting that one kind of trade at least still matters. As gas prices continue to skyrocket, this is only likely to become more the case. Contrary to hypothesis 3, strategically 'important' states are no more likely to be granted aid than are any others, a surprising finding that begs further investigation.

States were more likely to benefit from after the Cold War as aid became more widespread and dispersed following the softening of Cold War spheres of influence.

And what of the UK's own domestic context? Often domestic conditions are cited for aid reductions generally, and in fact we do see that in years where the UK's GDP is growing, more states get aid. And far more states get aid under New Labour than they did under the Tories. However, much of this may be being driven by the fact that New Labour's tenure takes place entirely in the post-Cold War era.

At the next stage – the allocation stage (in the second column) – we see that larger recipients get more aid, as is only fair, and so do states that import *less* (again) to the UK. Again, this flies in the face of hypothesis 5, reflecting support for a needs-based rather than interest-based interpretation of aid, quite in keeping with the rhetorical flourishes of both recent White Papers and the specific country strategies.

In terms of the domestic context, recipients with larger numbers of immigrants also get more aid, suggesting that they are seen as an important constituency, and also that those states have higher visibility in Britain. Of course, those states are nearly always former colonies as well. Though personal integrity rights themselves have no effect, human rights activism is effective in suppressing aid amounts. This suggests, interestingly, that it is not the violations that matter so much as an interaction between violations and visibility.

So, trade makes a difference in the two above analyses, but in the opposite direction of that predicted by the aid-for-trade thesis. But what of the impact of trade on other considerations?

Table 6.4 presents the differences between low UK importers and high UK importers at the gatekeeping stages. The first thing to observe is that there is far more inconsistency year to year in aid for low exporters than there is for high. This suggests that the high importers are less likely to be granted aid (and they are, just half as likely) in large part simply because of their important trade status. In terms of recipient characteristics, personal integrity rights violations again matter for neither group. So consideration of human rights violations, in practice, is not conditioned on trade relations – it simply does not figure. Trade (in either direction) with the UK actually has a small but significant negative effect for the low group, but no effect for the high group. Then again, given that the high group is the top quarter of importers, there is relatively little variation on that variable for that group. UK GDP growth rate affects the probability of receiving aid for low importers but not for high importers. Overall, the decision is more complex, and the receipts more variable, for the low importers than the high. Another example of this is that in terms of domestic context, the presence of a Labour government and a large immigrant community positively affect aid for the low importers but not the high importers. Only two substantive considerations come into play for the high importers that do not for the low importers – whether there has been a humanitarian crisis and whether the recipient has nuclear capabilities. The nuclear result makes sense as none of the low importers are nuclear states, but it is unclear why high importers would be more likely to be granted aid in response to a humanitarian crisis than the low importers. The only plausible explanation is that the high importers are less likely to be receiving aid already and therefore there are more of them to whom aid can be initiated following a humanitarian crisis than is the case for low importers.

At the allocation stage, we again see greater year-to-year volatility for the low importers than the high importers. Aid amounts to them seem less fixed – perhaps because they have a weaker relationship with the UK? For both high and low importers, larger states unsurprisingly get more. For both groups, states with higher numbers of immigrants not only are more likely to get aid, but also receive greater amounts. Human rights activism depresses aid more among the group of high importers than low importers – again the opposite of what we would expect to see if hypotheses 2 and 6 were to be supported, but very good news for the focus of assistance on the states that need it most.

So the trade relationship of a state with the UK delineates some key differences in what is taken into account in aid decisions – but not in terms of the role of human rights. What of the political situation and geographic 'strategicness' of a recipient? Table 6.5 indicates that those states of little strategic import are mainly judged on their stability and, to a lesser extent, on the content of their exports. Both conflict and being an oil exporter make nonstrategic states more likely to get aid. The first piece of evidence suggests altruistic motives, while the second suggests self-interest. These states are also more likely to get aid under Labour than Conservative governments (in other words, both parties give to strategic states, while Labour being in power significantly helps the chances of less strategic states, which is not surprising, given the strong orientation of the Thatcher government toward strategic concerns). For the states that are strategically located and have greater instability, we see a different set of factors being taken into account – recipients whose economies are doing better are less likely to get aid, in keeping with the 'more aid for the poorest' goal, and those with high imports from the UK are once again *less* likely to get aid, which does indicate altruism.

At the allocation stage, there are many similarities between the strategic and nonstrategic group. States with larger populations get more, regardless of the

Table 6.4

Variable	Gatekeeping decision		Allocation decision	
	Coefficient (standard errors) low importers	*Coefficient (standard errors) high importers*	*Coefficient (standard errors) low importers*	*Coefficient (standard errors) high importers*
Year	-0.23***	-0.15	304.04	5533.25
General characteristics of recipient				
Recipient GDP	3.25^{-11}	2.66^{-12}	-2.90^{-07}	-2.44^{-08}
Human rights measures				
Human rights violations	0.04	-0.26	1334.68	-6475.69
Recipient polity score	-0.00	0.00	2.28	-36.72
Economic value measures				
UK exports to recipient	-0.00*	-1.15^{-06}	0.09	0.01
UK imports from recipient	-2.24^{-06}*	6.02^{-07}	-0.01	-0.01
Recipient oil exports	0.00	0.00	-15.86	13.11
Recipient GDP growth	0.01	-0.04	149.13	-58.45
Recipient population	-6.38^{-09}	2.65^{-09}	0.00***	0.00***
Strategic value measures				
Recipient nuclear capabilities	1.42	-5.24*	-3980.26	-10,937.68
Internal dispute	0.52	1.96	-1840.29	6934.99
External dispute	0.01	0.69	-62.33	-2214.87
Distance from UK	0.00	0.00*	-0.77	2.46
Post-Cold War	3.30***	2.84	3238.61	-27,034.52
Trade intersection	1.33	-0.27	-214.24	-108.65
Need measures				
Humanitarian crisis	0.13	0.56*	2051.85	-223.00
Domestic politics measures				
Human rights activism	-2.74	-1.08	-7865.55	-88,005.61
Immigrants from recipient	0.00	0.00	0.15*	0.19*
Britain GDP	-4.76^{-13}	-1.64^{-12}*	-7.44^{-10}	-4.30^{-08}

Britain GDP growth rate	0.24*	-0.17	1002.43	1473.32
Labour/Blair	2.63***	1.68	-3781.41	-13,977.57
Colonial history measure				
Former colony	-0.01	676.00	-6258.92	-36.80
Policy history	-0.003		2.28	
Aid previous year?	-7.99^{-07}	0.00**	0.50***	0.38***
Significance of model			0.0000	0.0000
N	732	162	462	157
R^2			0.09, 0.88, 0.49	0.00, 0.92, 0.73

Notes

*** = significant at $p < 0.001$; ** = $p < 0.01$; * = $p < 0.05$; (marg) = $p < 0.075$ (one-tailed).

Table 6.5

Variable	Gatekeeping decision		Allocation decision	
	Coefficient (standard errors) low strategic	Coefficient (standard errors) high strategic	Coefficient (standard errors) low strategic	Coefficient (standard errors) high strategic
Year	−0.17**	−0.89**	1358.947	4523.88
General characteristics of recipient				
Recipient GDP	3.75^{-12}	$−5.77^{-12}$	$−4.31^{-08}$	$−4.34^{-08}$
Human rights measures				
Human rights violations	−0.04	−0.17	−182.98	−340.71
Recipient polity score	0.00	−0.02	−39.38	−56.08
Economic value measures				
UK exports to recipient	$−8.96^{-07}$	−0.00***	−0.00	−0.01
UK imports from recipient	$−2.92^{-07}$	3.11^{-06}	−0.00	−0.00
Recipient oil exports	0.00*	0.00	−5.49	−9.78
Recipient GDP growth	−0.01	−0.29*	167.12	321.79
Recipient population	5.85^{-09}	1.39^{-08}	0.00**	0.00*
Strategic value measures				
Recipient nuclear capabilities	−0.50	6.36	−41,368.60	−109,405.60
Internal dispute	2.00*	6.33	−8504.30	
External dispute	0.09	0.14	−0.07	8540.26
Distance from UK	−0.00	8.43^{-06}	−0.07	−0.11
Post-Cold War	3.10***	Dropped	1209.70	Dropped
Trade intersection	−0.72	8.05	−15,318.98	1581.80
Need measures				
Humanitarian crisis	0.21	Dropped	2445.02	−287.57
Domestic politics measures				
Human rights activism	−1.83	42.10	−63,713.45	−12,5821.60**
Immigrants from recipient	5.74^{-06}	0.00	0.24***	0.37***

Britain GDP	-1.00^{-12}	4.06^{-13}	-1.38^{-08} *	-1.62^{-08}
Britain GDP growth rate	0.25	-1.29	1081.52	9534.76 *
Labour/Blair	2.45***	Dropped	-3082.29	-9,049,561.00*
Colonial history measure	-0.37	Dropped	-128.00	-128.00
Former colony	-3.71	Dropped	-1278.89	16,860.21
Policy history	0.00	0.00	-39.40	56.10
Aid previous year?	0.00	-0.00	0.44***	0.35***
Significance of model			0.00	0.00
N	908	136	528	
R^2			0.01, 0.81, 0.43	0.02, 0.62, 0.50

Notes

*** = significant at $p < 0.001$; ** = $p < 0.01$; * = $p < 0.05$; (marg) = $p < 0.075$ (one-tailed).

strategic situation of a state, as do recipients with more immigrants in the UK. However, party comes into play for high strategic-value recipients when it does not for low strategic-value recipients. High strategic-value recipients get less under Labour than they did under the Conservatives, while low strategic-value recipients are unaffected. This is consistent with the observation at the gatekeeping stage about the greater emphasis placed on geostrategic motives by Conservative administrations. Human rights activism again depresses the receipts for strategic states in a way it does not for nonstrategic states, perhaps because the latter are more in the limelight.

Though not all results could be reported here, these analyses were also rerun with the key measure of human rights in the recipient being change in human rights over the past year rather than overall human rights conditions. The results were similar with minor, nonsubstantive exceptions. The same was true when the 'add' and 'drop' decisions at the gatekeeping stage were analyzed.

So if the impact of rights is not mitigated by trade or security considerations, are there other key variables that condition the effect of rights?

So when do rights matter?

So far, while we clearly see that different categories of recipients are treated differently, we have seen little impact of rights. But rather than assuming that the issue of rights does not matter at all and, given the changes that have taken place in the administration of British aid in recent years, it seems wise to more comprehensively test the extent to which the various other likely factors in the aid process might affect the role of rights, including whether this has changed since New Labour came into power and ODA became the DfID. I therefore ran one final analysis, presented in Table 6.6, testing for interactive effects of human rights with each of the other key variables.

The results of this analysis were very interesting. First, we see that rights concerns are more likely to be taken into account, at both stages, and in the

Table 6.6

Variable	Gatekeeping	Allocation
Year	−0.19**	1031.47
Year*HR	−0.18**	2353.34
General characteristics of recipient		
Recipient GDP	5.05^{-12}	-2.52^{-08}
Recipient GDP*HR	6.24^{-12}	-1.90^{-08}
Human rights measures		
Human rights violations	−0.03	−26.44
Recipient polity score	0.00	6.81
Recipient polity score*HR	0.00	4.94
Economic value measures		
Britain exports to recipient	-1.97^{-06} **	0.00
Britain exports*HR	-2.02^{-06}	0.00

Table 6.6 continued

Variable	Gatekeeping	Allocation
Britain imports from recipient	-1.21^{-07}	$-0.01*$
Britain imports*HR	-1.02^{-07}	-0.00
Recipient oil exports	$0.00*$	-0.89
Oil exports*HR	0.00	-1.04
Recipient GDP growth	0.00	163.42
Recipient GDP growth*HR	0.00	234.02
Recipient population	4.89^{-09}	$0.00***$
Recipient population*HR	5.33^{-09}	0.00
Strategic value measures		
Recipient nuclear capabilities	-0.68	$-18,281.33$
Recipient nuclear capabilities*HR	-0.32	$-43,034.00$
Internal dispute	$1.47*$	-2570.83
Internal dispute*HR	1.43	-3220.03
External dispute	0.21	2197.50
External dispute*HR	0.10	1209.52
Distance from Britain	-0.00	0.03
Distance from Britain*HR	-0.00	0.00
Post-Cold War	$3.35***$	957.73
Post-Cold War*HR	5.09	1003.20
Trade intersection	0.26	-6574.26
Trade intersection*HR	0.02	-7023.09
Need measures		
Humanitarian crisis	0.20	1489.12
Humanitarian crisis*HR	0.32	1502.84
Domestic politics measures		
Human rights activism	-1.65	$-49,160.50*$
Human rights activism*HR	$-2.22*$	$75,323.65*$
Immigrants from recipient	0.00	$0.19***$
Immigrants from recipient*HR	0.00	0.05
Britain GDP	$-9.86^{-13}*$	-1.00^{-08}
Britain GDP*HR	-10.98^{-13}	-0.39^{-08}
Britain GDP growth rate	$0.23**$	745.71
Britain GDP growth rate*HR	0.84	503.06
Labour/Blair	$2.40***$	-4591.14
Labour*HR	$-3.23***$	$3204.09*$
Colonial history measure		
Colony	$2.40***$	-4591.14
Colony*HR	5.29	-2203.30
Policy history		
Aid previous year?	$0.00***$	0.00
(marg)		
Significance of model	0.0000	0.0000
N	1044	619
R^2		$0.01, 0.87, 0.64$

Notes
*** = significant at $p < 0.001$; ** = $p < 0.01$; * = $p < 0.05$; (marg) = $p < 0.075$ (one-tailed).

expected direction, since the change of government and reorganization of the aid administration in 1997. In addition, while we saw that rights were less emphasized in the public rhetoric about violator states, it IS the case that recipients about which there has been significant HR activism are more likely to see their aid go up with improvements in human rights. This seems to confirm the increased role of NGOs in agenda-setting in recent years.

This final quantitative analysis, then, provides a glimmer of hope for a role for human rights in aid considerations, particularly in the last decade. Whether this will continue under the new administration of course remains to be seen.

More evidence from the documentary record

Just as importantly, in an area as complex as aid, it is very possible that considerations can have important effects that are not easily captured in aggregate analyses, as most analyses of aid tend to be. It would certainly be worthwhile to conduct further analyses that examined individual aid sectors separately, as well as distinguishing direct budget support from program aid and from project aid. However, perhaps the most direct way of looking at the nuanced ways that a consideration such as human rights can have an effect is by looking at individual decisions themselves.

In the thousands of pages of documentary evidence I examined, I found no instances in which a bilateral aid program was terminated solely on the basis of human rights violations. But I did find that human rights entered into strategies about recipient or 'partner' countries in four types of ways.

First, human rights come into play as background context. Most CSPs produced by the DfID today include a section called 'The Challenge' that is positioned at the start of the paper after the opening summary. In cases where substantial rights violations exist, they have been in every case I have seen included in this section. In earlier versions of CSPs produced under the ODA, there were sections similarly positioned on 'Programme Context' including (usually in this order) subheadings on Social, Political, UK Interest, Economic, Human Development Status, Security and Recipient Policies. Human rights references often appear in the Social and Recipient Policies portions of the 'Programme Context' section. While this does not mean that aid *per se* is cut or raised in a way that would be picked up by the aggregate analyses, it does mean that rights issues are acknowledged and that implicitly this may lead to more closely monitored programs, aid being given for specific projects rather than as direct budget support, or similar.

Second, human rights can be directly and explicitly incorporated as a goal of aid through the Policy Information Marker System (PIMS). The 1997 DfID White Paper established PIMS as a way of measuring how well DfID projects and programs were targeting key UK development priorities. Since 1997, most CSPs have included an annexe that delineates what proportion of commitments target each priority. Since human rights is one of these priorities, each CSP shows what proportion of assistance to that country was targeted to programs or projects that support human rights. In the majority of cases examined, this proportion (including good governance, see below) was between 4 and 10 percent. However, in some (e.g. in Indonesia's 2000 CSP) 17.9 percent of development assistance commitments targeted human rights, while another 7.1 targeted the rights of children. This is significant since Indonesia's rights problems have been so acute. Additionally, there are cases of even current CSPs that do *not* include human rights among PIMS markers (e.g. Yemen in 2000).

Third, human rights can enter the dialogue as 'context' or through the PIMS subsumed under the heading of good governance (sometimes called 'good government' in CSPs). On the one hand, it is of course important to distinguish between the two, and in fact individual country discussions often do this to an extent that White Papers or other overarching policy statements do not make clear. For instance, in a background paper for a visit to China to discuss 'cross cutting issues' such as human rights, DfID staff devoted substantial attention to the fact that Chinese officials needed to focus less on transparency in business and development of China, and more on transparency in *society* and development of the Chinese people. On the other hand, some CSPs explicitly discuss human rights under the heading of good governance (in both 'context' and 'goal' sections). For instance in a 1994–5 CSP,[16] human rights only came up once, in the last of four subsections under good governance. (And in that case all good governance goals in total only commanded 4 percent of commitments.)

Fourth, human rights concerns can more directly limit the willingness to commit to recipient countries. This tends to happen only in more extreme circumstances, however. For instance, in interdonor discussions in 2000 about further aid to Rwanda, both the Canadian and UK governments expressed caution about the level and manner of aid provision based on a skepticism about the Rwandan government's commitment to reform as well as concerns about Rwanda's ongoing role in regional destabilization (correspondence from Maria Minna, Canadian MP to Clare Short, received 17 January 2000, and from Joseph Diess, Swiss Federal Councillor to Clare Short, dated 23 January 2000). The most common response is to disburse aid in ways that allows it to be more closely monitored. For instance, this is explicitly the response that the 1996 CSP for Afghanistan says it will take, even though 'the goal of ODA forward policy is to create an enabling environment for all Afghans – men and women – to realize and promote basic human rights' (summary page, undated ODA draft 1996/7 CSP for Afghanistan).

It is also important to note that internal policy dialogue reflects the general tendency of donors to increasingly be constrained by what works – policy will rarely be employed to send signals unless they are seen as being effective So for instance, in discussions around preparation of the 2000 CSP for Indonesia, while concern was expressed about human rights and more particularly the corruption aspects of good governance in the country, bilateral action was explicitly dismissed twice as unlikely to be very effective.

Finally, there were several cases in which clear consideration had been given to the foregrounding of human rights concerns, and efforts had been made to not let human rights be a 'priming' factor for the rest of the report. (I borrow this term from media studies where it refers to the fact that readers tend to be disproportionately affected by the first concepts they encounter when reading a document, which then affects the lens through which they view the rest of the document.) There were several cases such as that of a 1995 CSP[17] where the target of human rights was the only key one taken out of the introductory paragraphs of a CSP, though it was left in unaltered form in the 'context' section later.

Conclusion

Despite, or perhaps because of, the increasing professionalization of aid policy in the UK, not all recipients are created equal. While there has been an across-the-board elevation of certain goals – aid for the poorest, good governance and democracy, for instance – these are applied differentially across different kinds of recipients. Strategically and economically important beneficiaries are still likely to get aid regardless of other kinds of considerations, suggesting that development policy still serves the broader interests of British foreign policy rather than a detached set of development goals. And perhaps this is only right. Despite the new attention being given to parts of the HRDGG triad, recipients' respect for basic personal integrity rights still does not have a systematic effect on aid receipts, rather coming into play in emblematic and highly publicized cases (this is not tested in the aggregate statistical analyses but is suggested by the examination of recent cases of response to rights violations). This suggests that, while the incentives to respect human rights, and to be *seen* as promoting them abroad exist and may be becoming stronger, a traditional mix of political and economic imperatives still pervades the new focus on development for its own sake.

7 Neither here nor there?

Canadian development assistance and human rights

Canada's foreign policy history has been both indelibly shaped by her relationship with the UK and yet steered in very different directions by the influence of, among other things, Quebec within and the US without. It has also attempted to navigate between two competing impulses. The first is idealism[1] and the public's tendency to be, as Rhoda Howard-Hassmann has called them, 'compassionate Canadians' (Howard-Hassmann 2003), and to want to be seen that way abroad. The second is the deep pragmatism that comes with being a middle-power. So for instance, Pratt has observed that 'If Canada is unlikely to be able to exert much leverage on the domestic policies of aid recipients ... then [it has not] sought significant policy leverage through its development assistance' (Pratt 1996a: 7). In addition, the Canadian International Development Agency (CIDA) occupies a place in the foreign policy-making hierarchy that is much weaker than that of the DfID in the UK (though stronger than that of AusAID in Australia, covered in the following chapter). This has constrained its ability to act as an independent advocate for development without being colonized by the priorities of other actors in the foreign policy-making apparatus.

Human rights in Canadian foreign policy thinking and practice

Human rights defined

Naturally the definition (or the definition that can be inferred) of human rights in Canadian foreign policy has varied dramatically over time. While Canada's Charter of Rights and Freedoms already goes far beyond the protections found in many constitutions (such as that of the US), the current official definition of human rights in foreign policy (rhetoric anyway) appears to be even more expansive. The official definition of human rights that Department of Foreign Affairs and International Trade (DFAIT)'s Human Rights, Humanitarian Affairs and International Women's Equality Division has posted on its website refers to all rights in the UDHR as not only universal but indivisible. But clearly through most of Canada's history the rights that have been seen as appropriate for focus have shifted – both in terms of what has been the focus and in terms of how that focus has translated into actual foreign policy practice – especially when weighed against more traditional foreign policy concerns with more immediate benefit – or cost – to Canada itself. From the 'human security' focus under Foreign Secretary Lloyd Axworthy to the unique role that Women in Development has played in decisions regarding the range of foreign policy tools, what is seen as potential and legitimate terrain for Canadian intervention has shifted dramatically.

The evolution of the role of human rights in Canadian foreign policy rhetoric and practice

While Morrison could conclude in 1998 that 'ethical values have been stronger at other times in Ottawa than now' (Morrison 1998: 438), perhaps this is only to be expected when everything from classical realism, a sense that most sanctions do not work, and respect for sovereignty (as Kim Nossal (Nossal 1988) has observed) make officials chary to risk other aspects of foreign policy in an attempt to influence human rights elsewhere.

The question of human rights was on the international agenda, of course, from the late 1940s on, and the issue became more and more politically fraught as the Cold War led the US to expect increased cooperation on geopolitical matters from its Northern neighbor.[2] But the explicit consideration in Canadian foreign policy discussions, and, to a lesser extent, in practice, dates to the 1970s and the increased global attention to the issue. (As will be discussed, it has been suggested that this 'moving with the crowd' is far more the norm than the exception in Canadian foreign policy generally (Black *et al.* 1996).) In a 1970 White Paper, the Liberal administration of Prime Minister Pierre Trudeau committed to a 'positive and vigorous' approach to human rights (Government of Canada 1970). And this interest did occur earlier and take on a more concrete form than was the case with most donors. In fact, Canada was the first donor to require recipients to adhere to international human rights legislation, and one of the first to offer its foreign service officers formal human rights training (Black *et al.* 1996: 279).

Several aspects of the national and international context combined in the 1970s to raise the profile of human rights discussions on policy agendas. Nationally, every Canadian province passed local anti-discrimination laws. Several members of Parliament sought to make overseas development assistance dependent on improvement in human rights conditions for those guilty of the worst violations. During this decade, Canada signed on to the UN Convention on Racial Discrimination and Covenants on Economic and Social Rights and Civil and Political Rights, and the discussion before and after these raised the public profile of rights as an issue. The passage of the Helsinki Final Act by the Commission for Security and Cooperation in Europe (CSCE) enhanced the new status of human rights in the public eye. In addition, during debates over the UN Conventions and Covenants, the government established federal-provincial committees to identify and capitalize on links between domestic and international human rights issues. And throughout the 1970s and 1980s there was increasing verbal support for human rights among high-ranking cabinet officials.

In 1982, under the Liberal Pierre Trudeau administration, the Canadian Charter of Rights was adopted and this process made the media, the public and policy-makers more prone to view foreign affairs through the lens of human rights. Trudeau's successor as PM, Conservative Brian Mulroney, frequently invoked rights as a prime motivator for foreign policy. While not always backing this up, Mulroney did in several cases take stands that revealed a genuine if pragmatic commitment to rights issues in extreme or well-publicized cases (e.g. his opposition to apartheid and frequent disagreements with Thatcherite realism in the UK).

By 1988, Victoria Berry and Allan McChesney could note with optimism that 'for over two decades the Canadian public has expressed rising interest in the place of human rights in foreign policy' (Berry and McChesney 1988: 60). And Matthews and Pratt (1988) noted the extent to which this was being put into practice:

> Canadian foreign policy, as it surely should, stresses strengthening of these institutions, using these arenas to mobilize international opinion against states that severely violate human rights ... we therefore conclude that Canada has legitimate foreign policy concerns with regard to a wide range of human rights.
> (Matthews and Pratt 1988: 9–10)

However, as human rights rose higher on the international agenda, activists began to cite what they saw as the gap between Canada's ethical foreign policy rhetoric and its lukewarm commitment to human rights in practice. This was particularly pronounced in aid policy (Nossal 1988: 47).[3] Gilles and Brecher (1989) charged that states that promised to be good trade partners did not face criticism for internal problems that drew condemnation in other cases.

Successive Canadian governments have deemed it rational to relegate human rights abroad to a secondary place among policy priorities. For one thing, many officials are pessimistic about what can be accomplished by such actions in defense of human rights or that such actions 'conflict with other, more important goals...' (Matthews and Pratt 1988: 15).

The victory of the Liberals in the fall of 1993 prompted a comprehensive foreign policy review in 1994–5. However, though Jean Chretien was a converted proponent of free trade, the review ultimately injected little new focus into the foreign policy agenda, favoring instead a reiteration of existing initiatives that kept a broad set of goals on the table (Hampson *et al.* 2001: 2).

The central public document that emerged from the review was called *Canada in the World*. Like the discussions before it, it

> shied away from declaring the primacy of development, projected less clarity about the priority assigned to poverty alleviation and the human side of development, advanced a weaker position on human rights, offered no further concessions on untying [of aid], and downplayed public outreach.
> (Morrison 1998: 399)

This was defended by some as, in part a reaction to the somewhat idealistic rhetoric of the 1988 aid strategy paper, S*haring Our Future*, which was seen by some as arrogant for the role it gave to 'Canadian values' and 'character' (*Sharing Our Future*, Introduction) in shaping aid policy abroad. For these critics, *Canada in the World* was a more candid statement about not only the potential of, but also the constraints on, Canadian foreign policy. In fact, in Morrison's assessment, 'for those held accountable, the policies in *Canada in the World* were a much safer and more honest statement of the reality, however lamentable, of multiple and often conflicting objectives' (Morrison 1998: 387).

The appointment of Lloyd Axworthy as Foreign Minister after the Liberal victory in 1996 gave an added boost to the status of human rights, a status which had been improving on the heels of the developments of the 1970s and the general policy orientation of the outgoing Progressive Conservative government. Human rights, especially those that could be classified as some of the most basic needs, were once again near the top of the foreign policy agenda.

Axworthy was the product of a history of progressive activism and was determined to make a difference, according both to his own memoirs (Axworthy 2004) and most assessments (see for instance Hampson *et al.* 2001: xiii), prompting comparisons to Gladstone and Woodrow Wilson, among others (Hampson *et al.* 2001: 2). He himself summarized his global vision at one point by citing Trudeau's imperative that

> the role of leadership is to encourage the embrace of a global ethic that abhors the present imbalance in the basic human condition and in access to health care, to a nutritious diet, to shelter, to education, one that extends to all space and through all time.
>
> (English 2001: 97)

Axworthy put this ethos into practice by spearheading a number of initiatives that ranged from progress on an international landmines convention to efforts to codify children's rights further in international law (including an international conference in Winnipeg in the fall of 2000, and drafting and promotion of an optional protocol to the International Covenant on the Rights of the Child). Other key initiatives included work in international law to protect human rights workers and to promote ratification of the Rome Treaty establishing the ICC. These raised Canada's profile internationally as well, as Axworthy made many televised appearances all over the world on behalf of these initiatives, something that reflected his belief that being a middle-power in no way precluded Canada from being a global leader on key issues.

Axworthy was quite successful in many of his efforts due, in part, to his ability to work across large parts of the national community to create a buy-in for his policies. He worked especially closely with NGOs (he himself had come out of the United Church, which had a strong social activist tradition) and was more open than most of his predecessors to members of the academic community (though he continued to come under substantial criticism from more realist members thereof). More on the role of NGOs follows.

In terms of balancing this concern for human needs with other Canadian foreign policy priorities, Axworthy was highly suspicious both of globalization, seeing it as 'a code word for a right wing agenda' (English 2001: 97), and of an uncritical cooperation with the US. Many criticized him for his lack of 'continentalism' or attention to the Southern relationship.

The reception of the Axworthy agenda within the foreign policy bureaucracy was mixed. The Defence Department

> actually did much better than Foreign Affairs in the Cabinet budget discussions where, despite the acclaim for Axworthy's work, the human security agenda failed to gain much support. Axworthy, moreover, responded to the critics by sharpening his definition of human security (to include prioritizing threats from military conflict) and abandoning soft power, the term that so irritated his realist critics.
>
> (English 2001: 103)

However there were two key institutional victories in the creation of both the Human Rights, Gender Equality, Health and Population Division within DFAIT, and the Human Security and Human Rights Bureau under the Assistant Deputy Minister for Global Issues.

Axworthy's two most immediate successors as Foreign Minister, John Manley and Bill Graham, paid little more than lip service to Axworthy's notion of 'human security', focusing instead on repairing strained relations with the United States (Hampson *et al.* 2001: 15).[4] Manley, for instance, had previously been head of Industry Canada and was particularly responsive to Canadian business (Hampson *et al.* 2001: 17).

Despite the return to focusing on defense and trade, some observers have rightly noted that if human rights and democracy are truly mainstreamed into the foreign policy culture and process, they can be promoted via defense and trade policy as well as through other avenues. For instance the 'FTAA [Free Trade Area of the Americas] process has been useful in terms of encouraging governments' commitment to democracy' as well as trade liberalization (Hampson *et al.* 2001: 15). And, as Hampson *et al.* have noted, many of Axworthy's initiatives will continue because they were not his alone but rather part of a larger national and global agenda. For instance, within DFAIT the new Bureau for Global Issues and Human Security is carrying on many Axworthy initiatives.

While progress on human rights has been an area in which successive Canadian foreign policy leaders have seen the potential to distinguish themselves from the US, clearly the tensions that exist between pursuing rights and pursuing other policy goals have been felt as strongly in Canada as anywhere. More to the point, perhaps because of the smaller size of Canada's economy and its different situation in the world, there has not been the same need to rhetorically assume the commensurability between human rights and other interests that has been insisted upon in much official rhetoric in, say, the UK.

So, for instance, after the 1994–5 policy review, a report of Special Joint Committee Reviewing Canadian Foreign Policy (SJCRCFF) noted that there were 'two alternative visions' of Canadian foreign policy:

> the bottom line is that there are major differences between the two agendas – one is focused on international trade and Canada's economic competitiveness, the other on global security and the problem of world poverty. The tensions between the two become apparent when it comes to policies regarding trade and international assistance. The question arises, is it possible to make a convincing merger of he two agendas?
>
> (Morrison 1998: 387, quoting minutes of proceedings and evidence 31 May 1994 Session 16)

Similarly, 'Axworthy's four and a half years as foreign minister have sparked widely conflicting assessments of his achievements and of where Canada's real foreign policy interests lie' (Hampson *et al.* 2001: 2). For instance, while some praised him for the high priority he put on human development, others 'charge that Axworthy's global crusades were an unwelcome distraction from more pressing national interests [and that] Canada had spent too much time worrying about winning Nobel prizes instead of tending to its vital trade relationships with the United States' (Hampson *et al.* 2001: 2).

Critics also saw contradictions in Axworthy's very focus on human security, and were disappointed when inevitably exceptions to this prioritization had to be made. (One is reminded here of some of the criticisms that Robin Cook sparked from both sides of the ideological spectrum after his declaration that human rights would become a new priority in British foreign policy.) For instance, those who saw him as above all a 'man of peace' were disappointed that he supported Canada's involvement with the NATO bombing of Kosovo, though its purpose was most immediately humanitarian. On the commercial front, he was seen as not adequately constraining firms that wanted to invest in governments that were clearly abusing human rights.[5]

Then again, there are those who would argue that this is only right. Stairs, (2005) argues that at heart the guiding force in Canadian foreign policy is trade, something many middle-power leaders assume. Canada's willingness to engage in diplomatic and trade relations with China on a level that it never has with, say, Burma is only one of the more obvious examples of the differential treatment a state might receive if it has great potential as a trading partner. It is important to remember, though, that the vast majority of Canada's trade takes place with its two neighbors to the immediate South, and therefore there are many developing countries with which Canada's existing trade is nearly negligible. For the purposes of hypothesis-testing, then, it will be important to pay particular attention to *potential* trade.

Canadian aid

In 2005 Canada gave US$3.76 billion in ODA, 0.34 percent of its GNI. Some 76 percent of this was bilateral. Canadian aid is much more geographically dispersed than that of the UK or Australia, but the region receiving the most (about a quarter of all ODA) is Sub-Saharan Africa.

The play of priorities in Canadian aid

While Pratt has observed that Canadian aid has seemed not to have been 'influenced significantly by either the relative poverty of the [recipient] country nor by the extent of Canadian exports to it – two factors that might have been expected to be influential' (Pratt 1996a/b/c: 8), it might be argued that this has been because the aid program has through most of its history attempted to pursue widely ranging and often conflicting goals that are therefore not necessarily reflected in aggregated aid patterns. While having its origins in the Colombo Plan and the Commonwealth (and therefore in British colonialism, thus sharing some similar historical patterns with British aid), trade promotion has been in many ways a more forthright and less contested goal of Canadian ODA than has been the case for Britain. Though this will be discussed in greater detail below, it is also reflected in the traditional terms of Canadian aid – generous in its concessionality level but closely tied to Canadian goods and services (OECD 1994a, 1998). How the relative primacy of goals and their expression has shifted over time bears a closer look. But we must also be careful to distinguish changes in rhetoric from changes in actual policy outcomes. As is the case in the donor community more generally, since most development projects often achieve multiple aims, they are prone to 'relabeling' as new development priorities come into vogue (Black and Thiessen 2007; Stairs 2005). Hence, the last part of this chapter compares the stated emphases of the development program with the statistical record on Canadian aid determinants.

Brief institutional history

The Canadian ODA programme dates to its membership in the Colombo Plan which began in 1950. The imprint of this beginning can be seen in, among other things, the early focus on the Commonwealth in aid disbursements, with an emphasis on Asia and the Pacific, disbursed through a variety of transitory arrangements and eventually solidified in the External Aid Office (EAO) under the Secretary of State for External Affairs (SSEA). The EAO was upgraded to more or less its present form, the Canadian International Development Agency (CIDA) in 1968, with a president who reported directly to the SSEA. As such it is a quasi-autonomous agency from the Department of Foreign Affairs and International Trade (the successor department to the Department of External Affairs). This puts it somewhere between the legislatively mandated, total formal autonomy of the DfID from the FCO on the one end of the spectrum, and the dependence of AusAID on Department of Foreign Affairs and Trade (DFAT), as will be seen in the following chapter. While it has seen fewer dramatic changes in its institutional structure in terms of its independence than has the British aid institutional structure, its relative power and direction has still ebbed and flowed, in part with the predilections of particular prime ministers, secretaries of state and ministers of external/foreign affairs, junior ministers with specific responsibilities for Canadian aid, and the men and women chosen to lead the EAO and later CIDA itself.

For instance, during the administration of Liberal Prime Minister Lester Pearson, development rose among foreign affairs priorities, reflecting the Prime Minister's sense of the most pressing demands in global affairs as well as the general turn of attention in the West to issues of social justice. (After he left office Pearson was to go on to chair a key commission on international development and to be a key author of its report, *Partners in Development: Report of the Commission on International Development*, which recommended in strong terms a more progressive assistance strategy not just for Canada but for the entire Economically Developed Country (EDC) community.

Unfortunately, the pursuit of all the goals of aid discussed below has been severely constrained since 'at least 1986' (Gillies 1989: 204). From that point on 'the principal determinant of Canada's aid budget had been control of government spending and deficit reduction. All other considerations have become subordinate...' (Gillies 1989: 204).

Nonetheless, *Sharing Our Future*, the report issued following the review of 1988, focused on far-reaching moral and practical commitments to assisting developing nations. But the end of the Cold War, far from leading to a renewed idealism, brought with it an intense resurgence of pragmatism upon the victory of the Liberals in fall 1993, discussed above. Morrison (1998: 369) notes that this year was a 'particularly anxious one' for CIDA, between the pending policy review and the nearly simultaneous departures of Monique Landry as Minister of External Relations and Marcel Masse as President of CIDA. Moreover, CIDA officials knew that the organization's performance was a major concern of the new administration.

1995's *Canada in the World* (Department of Foreign Affairs and Trade 1995) represented a retreat from the proactive pursuit of development goals with regards to nearly every foreign policy tool. In fact, it did not even promise to sustain the existing volume or geographic scope of aid.

The aim of recent changes at CIDA have been to incorporate this retrenchment in a positive-sounding form, based on effects rather than input, to create what Morrison has called 'less aid, but better aid?' – note the question mark (Morrison 1998: 422). And in fact this reduction of aid has been, in Morrison's estimation, the dominant reality of foreign aid-giving between 1993 and 1998. CIDA presidents Jocelyne Bourgogne and Huguette LaBelle had to address this dramatic effect on their resources before making any major policy choices, and this greatly decreased their freedom of action (Morrison 1998: 369).

Commonwealth/Francophonie

While the emphasis on the Commonwealth that started under the Colombo Plan certainly marked the first several years of Canadian aid policy, internal political pressures led to an expansion to the Francophonie during the 1950s and 1960s. Foreign policy and the aid program in particular have at times reflected the more basic competition for primacy of the two in Canadian political life. Morrison notes that PM John Diefenbaker's enthusiasm for the Commonwealth in fact catalyzed French Canadian support for Francophone developing countries (Morrison 1998: 49). In late 1960, the Canadian Ambassador to France, Pierre Dupuy, embarked on a fact-finding mission to Africa and came back recommending a distinct aid program for French-speaking Africa. While the initial commitment of C$300,000 in educational assistance was hardly overwhelming, it did mark the beginning of a combined development/diplomatic/trade policy that was specifically oriented to Francophone Africa. Notably, the site selected by the Secretary of State for External Affairs, Howard Green, for a new multiply accredited Canadian Embassy was Yaounde, Cameroon, because Cameroon was also a bilingual country (Morrison 1998: 49).

Though response in most of Africa to Canadian aid was at first underwhelming (though commensurate with the amount of aid allocated and the speed with which operations on the continent were set up), things developed substantially to the point that Morrison could in 1998 call Canadian aid to Francophone Africa 'an exceptional use of development assistance for specific international leverage' (Morrison 1998: 14).

Canada has had a harder time than many donors imposing a geographic focus on its choice of aid recipients due to its membership in two communities of cultural commonality across the globe. Morrison juxtaposes the ideological and geographical focus of other middle-power donors like Japan and Australia with that of Canada whose geographical reach is more along the lines of a superpower – without a superpower budget (Morrison 1998: 17). Still, this dispersion has been done in a deliberate way, with an attempt to apply specific rules for meeting obligations to both communities while recognizing practical limitations. For instance, in Africa, Canadian ODA has reflected an attempt to distribute equitably between the Francophonie and the Commonwealth, while in other parts of the world (e.g. Asia and the Americas) there has been a much clearer focus on the Commonwealth (Morrison 1998: 17).

Development assistance policy has increasingly tried to project an equitable approach to the two. For instance, when debt forgiveness for Africa was instituted in 1987, it was done nearly simultaneously at Commonwealth and Francophonie heads of government conferences held in Canada that year.

Commercial interests

Gillies has concluded that up through the early 1990s 'the case for deliberate commercialization of aid is not fully proven ... export promotion remains a powerful, but not an overriding, determinant of policy' (Gillies 1996: 204). However, as mentioned, many other commentators have claimed that trade promotion is the core *raison d'être* of Canadian foreign policy. In fact the very structure of Canadian aid, with its traditionally high tying ratio, has contributed to this. 'Because aid was tied significantly to Canadian goods and services, what CIDA chose to do was influenced heavily by what could actually be done with those goods and services, as well as which sectors of the Canadian economy CIDA and Ottawa wished to favor' (Pratt 1996a/b/c: 9).

Perhaps this focus has been clearest when budgetary cuts forced difficult choices to be made in the Canadian aid program, such as was the case during the 1993 round of cuts, when Axworthy claimed that changes were 'diverting assistance from 'those in need to the support of the private sector and developing market opportunities. You're turning CIDA into a business-finance-trade agency' (quoted in Morrison 1998: 374). And in fact the guidance paper for that very policy review 'asked departments to keep in mind the government has an overall commitment to job-creating economic growth' (Morrison 1998: 384). And Pratt (1996b) has actually gone further to contend that *Canada in the World* actually entailed the government *requiring* CIDA to pursue commercial objectives.

While this led some, including Axworthy, to suggest shifting the Industrial Cooperation Program (CIDA-INC) out of CIDA altogether and back into DFAIT, both Andre Ouellet, the new Minister of Foreign Affairs, and Roy McLaren, the Minister of Trade, opposed this, wanting instead to retain INC in the development portfolio as 'a convenient source of patronage for international business ventures' (Morrison 1998: 384).

In addition, the tools used within CIDA to pursue export promotion have varied over time – and perhaps been less blunt than they might have been. For instance, Black *et al.* (1996) found that CIDA did not initially favor Structural Adjustment Programs (SAPs), though it has more recently come to accept SAP-like requirements, particularly under the rubric of good governance. Private-sector support in LDCs was one of six key ODA priorities listed in *Canada and the World* and has been borne out in evaluation of particular country programs in Africa. Black *et al.* note that the move toward SAP-like conditionalities has roots in the trends of the donor community as well as domestic pressures. 'After all,' they write,

> commercial opportunities for Canadian companies in Africa are limited at best. Over time, then, Canada's aid policy towards Africa has increasingly conformed to the premises and priorities of structural adjustment, even as these regime based priorities have themselves evolved. The same process can be traced in relation to other key dimensions of international aid doctrine.
>
> (Black *et al.* 1996: 272)

Geopolitics

For some more realist observers of Canadian foreign policy, this is of course the proper guiding light of not just aid policy, but all foreign policy. As Nossal puts it, there is a 'mandated limit to altruism' (Nossal 1988: 37–8).

Spicer, in his groundbreaking *A Samaritan State*, dismissed aid as a

> confused policy stimulant, derived exclusively from personal conscience. It is not an objective of government. Love for mankind ... can stir only individuals – never bureaucracies or institutions. Governments exist only to promote the public good; and as a result they must act purely in the selfish interest of the state they serve.
>
> (Spicer 1966: 11)

However, the effect of geopolitical concerns has waxed and waned over time. Freeman, for instance, suggested that geopolitical concerns held sway in aid policy until the middle of the 1970s as a response to the combined imperatives of the Cold War and the pursuit of international influence more generally (Freeman 1985: 109, cited in Morrison 1998: 430).

And a more inclusive definition of security, presaging the Axworthy vision, was evident in the guidance paper for the 1994–5 policy review, which 'suggested a revised conception of security reflecting sustainable development, and support for democracy and human rights' (Morrison 1998: 391). And yet some of the most conflict-torn countries, such as Sri Lanka, with the clearest threats to human security, had been hit hardest in the 1993 cuts. And when struggling Tanzania, which enjoyed one of CIDA's largest African aid programs, was cut, it was done so when other country assistance programs were retained due to 'foreign or domestic policy reasons: Egypt, an External Affairs favorite because of the Middle East conflict and commercial potential, the Southern African Development Community, because of the South African situation, [and] SADC's potential for regional cooperation' (Morrison 1998: 372).

Development

To what extent was development, the presumptive central goal of ODA, actually prioritized? And to the extent that it was pursued, what facets of it gained most prominence: poverty reduction, sustainable development, democracy, good governance, rights?

The Axworthy 'revolution' as it has been called, affected development policy dramatically as well. It called for a development assistance policy that 'emphasized human needs and environmental sustainability', and criticized the extent to which trade was currently foregrounded in regional priorities for Latin America and the Asia-Pacific region. However, the dramatic budgetary cuts that CIDA was suffering during the Axworthy era mitigated the impact of even the most sincere reprioritization within the agency's goal structure.

Pratt, who laments the failure of ODA to respond in a more regular way to ethical concerns, says humanitarian ones should be the 'main rationale for international development efforts' (quoted in Morrison 1998: 428). Morrison quotes him speaking at a 1970 conference: 'Inefficiencies, corruption, authoritarian regimes, these and similar factors in parts of the developing areas would lead to a diminishing Canadian international development effort unless underlying that effort there is a constantly renewed sense of moral obligation' (quoted in Morrison 1998: 428). In short, the existence of a bad government should not lead to a punishment of its people through development assistance policies.

The most recent policy review did lead to some policy initiatives that were positive from a pro-development perspective, such as a commitment that 25 percent of ODA should go to meeting basic human needs, and a promise to account to Parliament and the public in a more open and honest manner (Morrison 1998: 381). More on this openness later.

Poverty reduction

The idea of poverty reduction as a central component of development assistance goes back at least as far as the mid-1970s (Morrison 1998: 439). It was a central thrust, as well, of *Sharing Our Future*, and was reportedly taken very seriously by CIDA's policy branch (Morrison 1998: 405). Six years later, when a draft discussion paper on poverty reduction was circulated in August 1994, in anticipation of the 1994–5 foreign policy review, there seemed reason to hope poverty reduction would retain its pride of place. The paper made recommendations for a comprehensive approach, and was seconded by the fact that the SCJRCFP report in 1994 'declared that the central purpose of Canadian development assistance is to reduce poverty by providing effective assistance to the poorest people in those countries that most need and can use help' (Morrison 1998: 388). It goes on to say that self-interested justifications for aid (e.g. trade) have never done well with public opinion and that many polls have shown this, but that help for those in need expresses the basic moral vision of aid and corresponds most closely to what the vast majority of Canadians believe development assistance to be about (Morrison 1998: 388). The final version of *Canada in the World* rejected a focus on poverty alleviation or relief in favor of poverty reduction and attention to underlying causes rather than symptoms. It also included a renewed focus on basic human needs. Morrison notes that this in part reflected the international donor-community agenda and the beginning of discussions about the MDGs in the UN (Morrison 1998: 405–6).

As might be expected, the Axworthy revolution led to a further elevation of poverty reduction among developmental and human security goals, and this meant elevating Africa in the list of geographic concerns.

Inconsistencies in the rhetorical commitment to poverty reduction have been magnified in practice, as Morrison documents. For instance, Bangladesh, the poorest state in Asia, was hit particularly hard in the 1993 cuts, and programming was either dropped or dramatically cut in six other minor low-income recipients. Meanwhile, 'no middle-income or high growth country was appreciably affected'. Sub-Saharan Africa suffered severest repercussions.

> Of five countries in the downgraded region – Cameroon, Kenya, Rwanda, Tanzania, and Zaire – three had already experienced a suspension (Zaire) or curtailment (Kenya and Rwanda) of Canadian aid *in response to human rights abuses* and political unrest. However, the decision to withdraw from Tanzania, CIDA's largest country program in Africa since the mid-1970s, was shocking. By terminating conventional bilateral aid in Ethiopia as well, the Agency pulled back from the world's second and third poorest countries.
>
> (Morrison 1998: 372; emphasis mine)

Good governance

However, two new thematic funds were announced among the budgetary bloodshed of 1993: one for Human Rights, Democracy, and Good Governance (HRDGG), and one for private-sector development.

This was in part a response to the international environment. The 1993 UN conference on human rights

> underscored heightened international interest in questions of human rights and democracy, especially since the end of the Cold War. Although the aid regime has only a limited number of formal provisions concerning human rights and democratic governance, the attention ... to these issues is growing. Despite a continued preference for discreet diplomatic action, donors appear increasingly inclined to try to influence the human rights and democratic governance practices ... through political conditionality. This trend is particularly advanced in relation to Africa.
>
> (Black *et al.* 1996: 277–8)

In 1990 Canada created the International Centre for Human Rights and Democratic Development – an institution which has gained a reputation for supporting 'organizations which challenge the status quo' (Keenleyside 1996: 253). Although it is widely recognized as an international leader on participatory development and good governance, Canada's guiding principles and norms conform closely to the policy approach of other donors. For instance, 'the upgrading of CIDA's human rights unit in 1992 to a good governance and human rights division directly parallel the evolution of thinking in the donor community' (Pratt 1996a: 253).

But again the rhetorical commitments were not always borne out in practice. When the cuts to Ethiopia were announced, many might have asked, as did the Ethiopian ambassador, 'does it look good for Canada to be cutting assistance to a country that is trying to establish democracy and to have given such big assistance [*sic*] to a country where [before 1991] there was military dictator?' (Morrison 1998: 373).

Though the SCJRCFP report gave less attention to human rights than either of the two preceding major reviews, it did urge that HRDGG be brought to the forefront of Canadian foreign policy and that aid termination or reduction be structured in such a way as to protect the most vulnerable groups in recipient states (e.g. through NGOs). At the same time it urged a multilateral rather than bilateral response to rights violations on the basis that bilateral approaches tend to be ineffective (and, it implied, therefore not worth the potential risks).

Good governance was defined further in the 2001 *Government of Canada Policy for CIDA on Human Rights, Democratization, and Good Governance*, described under 'Rights' below.

General social goals

Discussion of social goals has largely been subsumed in the discussions of human security, above, as well as the poverty-reduction agenda, also discussed above.

Environment

Assessments of the impact of environmental considerations on Canadian aid policy vary dramatically. On the one hand, Black *et al.* (1996: 277) call environmental protection and sustainability the 'archetypal issue on which the systemic logic of the aid regime reflects and complements the domestic economic interests of donors'. But in practice there have been many setbacks in recent history, such as the disruption of the implementation of the 1992 Policy of Environmental Sustainability. It did enjoy some elevation under Axworthy, who at least at the beginning of his tenure implied that environmental degradation was a threat to human security on a par with military conflict.

Rights

As with the British aid regime, rights have entered the CIDA lexicon both on their own terms and subsumed under the concepts of democracy and good governance.

There has been a clear tension between three strains in DFAIT thought:

1   the need to take human rights into account;
2   concern about the inconsistency of government application of human rights conditionality; and
3   skepticism about the effectiveness of unilateral responses to human rights abuses.

A September 1993 discussion paper tried to alleviate this tension by suggesting that CIDA support programming in these areas (i.e. employ positive incentives) rather than using aid as a rather blunt on-off switch. However, the paper noted that the pressure of quick fixes – i.e. to take *some* stand – when politically sensitive crises erupt – remains strong (Morrison 1998: 409–10).

As previously noted, certainly human rights have played a role in punitive aid measures against specific aid recipients, especially in the 1993 round of cuts (Zaire's was suspended and Kenya's and Rwanda's was curtailed) (Morrison 1998: 372). But the election of the Liberals in 1993 did not seem to bode particularly well for the status of rights on the foreign policy agenda or aid more specifically. While Liberal Foreign Affairs Minister Andre Ouellet's official statements, and the take reflected in *Canada in the World*, appeared to balance HRDGG concerns with commercial ones, many in the human rights community perceived him to be unsympathetic.

The publication in June 1994 of five 'interim programming priorities' included full participation of women, democracy/good governance/human rights, private-sector development, and environmental sustainability and 'reflected the Agency's major policy thrusts during the early 1990s, except for structural adjustment' (Morrison 1998: 382).

An area worthy of special mention here concerns the issue of women in development, in which Canada has been a global leader. While attention to it has of course waxed and waned, it garnered particular attention under CIDA President Huguette LaBelle, even in the face of continuing and severe budgetary constraints.

Meanwhile, a major step was taken in November 1995 when CIDA adopted an official policy on HRDGG. This committed the agency to strengthening the role and capacity of civil society in LDCs and taking concrete steps to increase participation, improve democratic institutions, and promote transparency and efficiency in public services.

Accordingly, attempts were made to mainstream this into all of CIDA's programming areas. Human rights and conflict resolution remained major foci of CIDA's activities in Sri Lanka, the Middle East and Central America. New programming in South Africa and Haiti was heavily reoriented to support the democratic transition. The Somalia and Rwanda crises of 1992–3 and 1994, respectively, 'were catalysts in promoting growing interest among internal aid donors for the use of aid for conflict prevention and peace building, as well as post disaster programming' (Morrison 1998: 409–10). HRDGG spending went up to 10 percent for 1995–6 (Morrison 1998: 410).

In 2001 CIDA issued a policy statement, *Government of Canada Policy for CIDA on Human Rights, Democratization and Good Governance*. It is a measure of the relative profile attained by this area of policy that this is one of only eight policy areas meriting a specific policy paper from CIDA in the last six years. The others are environmental sustainability, gender equality, meeting basic human needs, poverty reduction, private-sector development, aid effectiveness, and rural development. Note that none of these is dedicated to pursuing Canadian interests first and foremost, but rather all are clearly designed with the needs of development in poor countries in mind first and foremost. In fact, the *Human Rights, Democratization and Good Governance* document is explicit that this is today seen as CIDA's mission, deemed achievable alongside the pursuit of more particularly Canadian interests, but to be displaced by that pursuit. It says (CIDA 2001: 6) that

> The development perspective articulated by CIDA is not the only interest to be reflected in Canadian foreign policy; political and commercial interests are also important. CIDA is in a position, however, to effectively advocate development perspectives in the long-term interest of Canada, in keeping with the purpose of the official development assistance (ODA) program and the Agency's program and policy experience.
>
> (CIDA 2001: 6)

The wording of this statement clearly casts CIDA as an advocate for development among foreign policy players, rather than just an agency looking to promote more particularlistic Canadian interests through aid.

Rather like the DfID's *Realising Human Rights For Poor People* policy statement, CIDA's *Human Rights, Democratization and Good Governance* policy document defines these terms in an addendum.

Like the DfID document, the CIDA document defines rights with reference to the UDHR. However, while the DfID document addresses civil and political rights first, the CIDA document foregrounds economic and social rights. However, both clearly have their roots in internationally agreed, comprehensive standards. The document defines democratization as, among other things,

> strengthening popular participation in the exercise of power, building democratic institutions and practices, and deepening democratic values in society. Mechanisms for participation include formal processes such as elections and referenda [and] less formally through ... independent popular organizations which serve to articulate and channel people's concerns. Democratic institutions include federal and provincial/state legislatures and municipal councils, and institutions such as the judiciary that are responsible for the rule of law.
>
> (CIDA 2001: 21)

This is very similar to the wording laid out in the 2003 UK FCO White Paper discussed in the last chapter.

Good governance is defined in terms that are even more reminiscent of the 2003 FCO White Paper, using essentially identical language to that cited in the last chapter.

> By governance we mean that the manner in which power is exercised by governments in the management of a country's social and economic resources. Good governance is the exercise of power by various levels of government that is effective, honest, equitable, transparent and accountable. There is no internationally agreed definition as yet.'
>
> (CIDA 2001: 21–2)

Finally, the document clearly articulates the strategy for responding to rights concerns through the development assistance program. Specifically, while it says that HRDGG analysis will henceforth feature in assessment of all bilateral programs, including in Country Development Programming Frameworks (CDPFs), it advocates a mix of carrots and sticks, and specifically forswears withdrawing assistance solely because of a recipient's human rights record (CIDA 2001: 16).

Tensions

In British aid policy, it will be recalled, repeated attempts have been made to demonstrate that development, rights, security, trade promotion and most other foreign policy goals can not only coexist on the foreign policy agenda, but in fact to mutually reinforcing.

Acknowledgements of tensions between goals have been much more common in both the official and unofficial rhetoric in Ottawa around aid, as well as among CIDA-watchers. Traditionally many have perceived that assistance is given a low priority among policy tools for the same reason that the question of human rights is given a low profile among policy goals: because many in Ottawa 'perceive Canada's participation in the third world as essentially a matter of altruism and nothing in which Canada has a vital stake' (Lyon *et al*, cited in Morrison 1998: 410).

TRADE TENSIONS

We can see this acknowledgement of tension as far back as 1977 and the start of the Marcel Dupuy Presidency of CIDA, which is whence Pratt traces the explicit desire to exploit aid to promote trade (Pratta/b/c 1996: 5). Ten years later, the covering letter to *Canada in the World* explicitly indicated that a softer stance would be taken on rights. 'Our aim,' it said,

> is not to punish countries and innocent populations whose governments abuse human rights but rather to change behaviors and to induce govern-ments to respect their people's rights [an indication of a preference for carrots as well as sticks]. Responses to specific situations require careful *balancing* of many considerations.
>
> (cited in Morrison 1998: 395; emphasis mine)

Bilateral punishments, then, were not only seen as being ineffective but also as likely to hurt Canada more than to achieve their aim.

Meanwhile in May 1995, Ouellet confirmed many of the worst fears of the human rights community in a meeting with Association of South East Asian Nations (ASEAN) foreign ministers when he asserted that that Canada would vigorously pursue trade links to developing countries regardless of their human rights records (Morrison 1998: 409).

In Keenleyside and Taylor's and Scharfe's examinations of Canadian foreign policy toward regimes which systematically violated human rights in Argentina, Chile, Indonesia, South Africa, South Korea and Uganda, a 'general reluctance' was found 'to engage in economic sanctions against violators with which Canada has substantial and growing commercial interests' (Keenleyside and Taylor 1984: x). How accurate are these claims that human rights will only be taken into account when the Canadian government perceives it will not alienate commercial interests? How likely is it that commercial or other economic relations with a violator country would actually be disrupted by Canada's imposition of some sort of economic punishment – and how important is any one of these relationships likely to be to a wealthy donor the size of Canada? While Nossal concedes that 'the web of economic linkages between Canada and violators may affect human rights policy, since interruption in trade, investment, or development assistance affects some individual Canadians, and thus the Canadian economy', he objects that

> The economic argument is not as compelling as it may at first seem. Although based on rational notions of maximized self-interest, it makes little sense from a rational perspective, for it includes no assessment of the magnitude of the economic costs to Canada of measures used by Ottawa to further human rights.... Canada's economic links with any single state in the East or the South that violates human rights (indeed, all such violators combined) represents a tiny percentage of all external trade.
>
> (Nossal 1988: 49)

GEOPOLITICAL TENSIONS

Tensions existed between the geopolitical and rights, as well: for instance, Canada's criticisms of Eastern bloc human rights violations during the Cold War were much more vociferous than they were for comparable problems in Western donors, much as is the case in the US and Britain (Skilling 1988). And Nossal believes strategic interests generally receive greater priority, and concedes that there indeed appears to be an inverse link between Canada's perceived strategic stake in a state and the likelihood that it will take action to alleviate human rights violations in that state.

> In the major cases of violations in the past decade, where 'strategic concerns' have largely been absent, as in Uganda, Kampuchea, or Sri Lanka, Ottawa has taken a stiff stand against violations; where clearly identifiable strategic interests exist, it tended to play down violations. Canada's considerable ambivalence on South Africa, or its relatively muted concerns about Indonesia's political prisoners or its invasion of East Timor, or its quiet diplomacy on human rights violations in Central America, or its indifference to violations in Iran in the 1970s, can be linked to the strategic importance of the states involved.
>
> (Nossal 1988: 53)

Nossal does not define 'strategic interests' in this context, a testament to the extent to which economic and security interests are inseparable. In fact, at least one other author has cited these same cases as examples of the primacy not of geopolitical, but rather of economic interests (Scharfe 1996).

However, 'to those who hoped that an integrated review would examine the linkages between security and international development, and explore the trade-offs between defense and aid spending', it was disappointing that defense was able to secure a separate review and therefore that many of the real tradeoffs in foreign policy allocation resources, and relationships between different foreign policy tools, remained unexamined (Morrison 1998: 381).

In its final report, titled *Canada's Foreign Policy: Principles and Priorities for the Future*, the committee's evaluation of CIDA and its policy incoherence, possibly resulting from these tensions, was particularly harsh. (It was even more scathing in its first draft, though some of the criticisms were toned down by staffers.) But essentially, CIDA appeared to be trying to serve two contradictory masters, and therefore serving neither very successfully. It appeared to 'be promoting structural adjustment policies that seemed to hurt the poor; to be confusing development objectives with Canada's trade interests and to be straying far from the stated objectives of the aid program' (Morrison 1998: 387). The report urged six practical steps: clarify the mandate, distinguish between aid and trade, reform conditionality, target assistance, improve results and maintain support (Morrison 1998: 387).

On the other hand, some explanations of Canada's lack of firmer commitment to human rights focus on inefficacy rather than lack of will. For example, Nossal identifies four 'gloomy' themes in government statements about human rights in the 1970s and 1980s. First, he says, the very terms adopted to describe human rights as an issue imply intractability (i.e. officials' frequent use of the terms 'thorny' or 'complicated'). Some of this perceived intractability stems from the second theme Nossal identifies: that because there are no universally agreed-upon definitions of human rights, dealing with such rights in an international context is particularly difficult. Third, Canadian policy-makers tend to de-emphasize Canada's potential for affecting international politics unilaterally. Unlike their counterparts in the US, most Canadian policy-makers believe that too few recipients are dependent enough on Canada to allow it much leverage in influencing that state's domestic policy. Finally, Nossal cites the kinds of constraints on which we focus here: human rights targets are only one of many goals that Canada pursues, and often appear to be less vital to Canadian interests than are strategic or commercial concerns (Nossal 1988: 47–8). Therefore, though Canadian policy-makers believe citizens of other states deserve basic rights, many feel that effort in that direction would be wasted. Since there is little chance of effecting change, why not deploy resources in areas where they are more likely to have an impact?

Perhaps ironically, the commitment has been at least ostensibly bipartisan, as the Conservative governments of the late 1970s and mid-1980s (Clark and Mulroney) made public announcements to this effect as well (though with greater frequency regarding Eastern bloc states). In addition, 'senior cabinet members, most notably a number of secretaries of state for external affairs, have supported a significant role for human rights in foreign policy' (Nossal 1988: 47). Such pronouncements have even been formalized, especially in the area of overseas development assistance and other aid. Successive governments' commitment to linking aid to human rights is laid out in several major documents, two of which (the 1986 Hockin-Simard Report and the 1988 Winegard Report, *For Whose Benefit?*) were reports to special committees in Parliament. *Sharing Our Future* claimed that these new frameworks would 'help make it more feasible to take human rights under serious consideration in the formulation of our aid policy' (Nossal 1988: x). Whether or not these kinds of commitments have been kept is examined below.

How Canadian aid policy is made today

Parliament

Institutional arrangements in Canada are of course largely modeled on the British form (with important exceptions such as federalism and the Charter of Rights and Freedoms). Because of the fusion of powers between executive and legislature, and the model of responsible government, the same constraints on the independence of Parliament apply in the Canadian case and limit its potential to press for policy changes, except in the case of key ministers, addressed below. Another avenue of influence is the role of key committees. In the case of aid policy, these are the Foreign Affairs and International Development Committee, its Subcommittee on International Human Rights, and the Committee on International Trade. However, with the exception of the periodic reviews, CIDA's and DFAIT's technical responsibility to them over specific country-level policy decisions is limited. Importantly, Morrison concludes, in his exhaustive analysis of CIDA, that party has little impact – for instance CIDA's biggest gains and biggest cuts have come under the Liberals, while both parties have made firm rhetorical commitments to pursuing human rights in foreign policy. This stands in sharp contrast to the regular and massive structural changes in the British aid bureaucracy that have come with changes in government.

Civil service

Therefore, a great deal of responsibility devolves on the civil service and the ministers that are its elected heads. In fact, the way that Morrison's definitive history of CIDA (1998) is set up reflects this – the chapters mirror the tenure of key ministers and CIDA presidents. The impact of many of these figures has already been discussed – especially the impact of their personal views and past professional experience. CIDA has not experienced the same battles for impact on the FCO that the ODA/Overseas Development Ministry (ODM)/DfID has with the DTI in part because the role of trade has always been more acknowledgedly supreme in Canadian foreign policy.

Outside interests

Assessments of the attitudes of Canadian public opinion toward aid is mixed. While Rhoda Howard–Hassmann has documented the support of public and policy-makers alike for human rights generally, public knowledge about aid suffers from some of the same weaknesses it does in the US – most have no idea how much is spent on aid and most assume it is far higher than it is and therefore favor reductions (Black and Thiessen 2007). Some 31 of 50 participants in a 2002 study (Opoku-Dapaah 2002) did not even know which kind of agency CIDA was, believing it to be an NGO or an IGO. In the early 1990s both Pratt and Stokke concluded that public and official support of the values of 'humane internationalism' was weakening in major donors (Pratt 1990: 207–19, Stokke 1989). This has not been helped much by the fact that recent strategy papers such as *Canada in the World* have paid less attention to 'established forms of public outreach' (Morrison 1998: 398). Since the 1990s, public approval of overseas development assistance has improved somewhat (Black and Thiessen 2007).

As in so many other donor countries, of course, immigrant groups are often more engaged on foreign affairs issues than other groups. Matthews and Pratt (1988: 9) argue that, since Canada is home to so many recent immigrants, these effects are likely to be particularly strong and to reinforce existing commitments to taking rights into account in policy decisions.

More organized outsiders hold a huge amount of potential power in Canada.

Business interests in Canada have traditionally been very powerful, in part because of the traditionally high priority placed by the government on promoting business and commercial interests. Therefore leaders of the business community have long had what has been described as 'intimate access ... to government decision makers'. Pratt cites 'the responsiveness in general of Canadian public policy to the interests of the corporate sector' noting that, therefore 'it is hardly surprising that as CIDA's budget grew, Canadian exporters and investors were quick to urge that CIDA promote their interest through the aid program' (Pratt 1996b: 18).

If we can infer the benefits of this access from policy outcomes, they appear to be great. The Aid–Trade fund is a classic example of the measurable results of the aforementioned 'urging'. Canadian policy on tied aid, already briefly discussed, is one example, and

> CIDA has long reserved part of its bilateral program for richer developing countries of special interest to Canadian businesses. This portion, first fixed at 10 percent in 1975 grew to 20 percent in 1978 and to 25 percent in 1988. As well, CIDA successfully pursued joint financing of some major capital projects with the Arab development fund, to the distinct advantage of Canadian capital exporters.
>
> (Pratt 1996a/b/c: 18)

This attempt to create buy-in from business has been further institutionalized in the form of CIDA-INC.

It should be noted, however, that 'this emergence of programs catering to business was not easily accomplished. Many people in CIDA were clearly suspicious of it.' A 1991 report put it thus: 'historical consideration for Canadian economic interests abroad and the use of profits or benefits to motivate firms or individuals are looked at with suspicion if not contempt' (Pratt 1996a/b/c: 19).

But if the 'business lobby' and the 'development lobby' are often seen as countervailing and competing forces in their attempts to influence government, NGOs from the development and academic communities have enjoyed much greater pride of place in CIDA policy-making than has been the case in many other donor states.

This is in part due to constraints that CIDA's budgeting places on staff increases. These constraints have meant that a great deal of work that is done 'in-house' by other donors is contracted out to think tanks, academics, and private consultants and consulting firms from within CIDA. This has also meant that

> bilateral programs began in the 1980s through country focus programs to engage a limited number of NGOs and NGIs in activities that CIDA was anxious to have undertaken. In addition a few ... were invited to submit tenders for some regular bilateral contracts. These new forms of funding quickly became an important part of the CIDA/NGO/NGI relationship.
>
> (Pratt 1996a/b/c: 18)

In addition, the consulting process and attempt to create a stake in the development process has been much more extensive and systematic than is the case in some other donors.

The NGO relationship has of course waxed and waned in its importance as various ministers have come and gone. Ouellet was reported to be rather skeptical of NGOs, for instance but Axworthy enlisted their help with the landmines project (English 2001: 11, 100), as did Trudeau. Morrison (2000) concludes that the 1980s were the high-water mark for NGO influence, and that the relationship between NGOs and CIDA declined markedly during the budget cuts of the 1990s and CIDA's increasing reliance on for-profit consultants.

Two other contextual factors need to be noted, of rather different characters. One of these is what is often referred to in internal correspondence as the 'Elephant to the South' and the constant, if implicit, pressure to consider US preferences. Another concerns the extensive consultations that are conducted in donor countries, not just with DFAIT or CIDA posts but with members of the political, development, health, educational and other relevant communities in the recipient country.

It is, however, possible for the policy-making process to go too far. In one case, during consultations in Guatemala, a general who had been convicted of war crimes was mistakenly invited as one of 200 persons of note, on the Canadian government's dime, to consultations on development assistance during the 1990s (along with Rigoberta Menchu, the human rights activist and one of his alleged former victims).

Implications for hypothesis-testing

Not only can it be difficult to set clear priorities in aid policy, but there is often also a gap between rhetoric and its translation into specific decisions. Therefore it is crucial to actually look at the way that particular values are balanced in specific aid decisions, if they conflict, as so many have contended they do. If, as Pratt (1996a/b/c: 7) has said, 'CIDA's bilateral aid reflects both the importance that Canada attaches to each recipient country and CIDA's judgment on how these funds should be spent', then we should be able to draw some important conclusions not just by looking at decisions in the aggregate, but examining specific decisions to determine how often goals are seen as conflicting and, when they do, how choices are made.

Archival research

Openness

In his report to the Royal Commission on Bilingualism and Biculturalism, Gilles Laland wrote of the Department of External Affairs:

> not always without ill will, the authorities of the Department gave us numerous examples of their general distrust of outsiders, including researchers of good standing, who desire to consult official records, even the least confidential ones, dealing with Canadian foreign policy.
>
> (English 2001: 98)

While there does not seem to be as much widespread lament about the lack of openness in Canadian foreign policy-making as in British, CIDA served as an interesting contrast in this respect with the DfID. While documents earlier than the current Country Development Programming Frameworks are in many cases unclassified, the archival system of CIDA is less centralized than that of the DfID, and therefore much access depends on the good will and staff availability of particular geographic programs. There was no standard policy evident about access to these archived materials, especially in the case of internal (if unclassified) documents. In some cases, materials were sent directly to me through the mail without hesitation. Two geographical branches were extremely helpful during a visit in May 2006, allowing access to any non-classified documents as well as generous logistical support. Other branches were unwilling to grant this access, arguing that staff time was too limited.

Freedom of Information (FOI) legislation exists in Canada, but one must be a citizen or landed resident to take advantage of it.

Documents available

Throughout its history, CIDA has regularly produced some form of framework paper for its larger programs. The actual form and terms for these has varied widely and relatively frequently over time, especially as new assessment procedures and 'results-based management' have been instituted. These review progress to date in particular bilateral relationships and lay out the general aims and specific goals for that country in the coming three-to-five-year period. These play a large role in the allocation of the next round of funding as well, and the department always has the potential to move funds around on a more short-term basis as circumstances might dictate. However, I was able to examine all of what are now most often called 'Country Development Programming Frameworks' (CDPFs) that are current and public, as well as all for the time period of this study that still exist in the archives, for the countries of the Americas and of Central Europe, the Middle East and the Maghreb, as well as for a few select countries from Asia and Sub-Saharan Africa that were supplied by helpful individuals in particular country-level programs. There were a few cases in which earlier CDPFs – even their 'final' and therefore usually-for-public-consumption form, were classified at a high enough level that they were not provided.

As was the case with Britain, other bilateral assessments are produced under different names on an occasional basis. In addition, some more general (i.e. regional) or specific (a sector within a specific recipient country) documents are produced.

For the following content analyses, I have examined all available current and past bilateral CDPFs. Because I am interested in how priorities are weighed relevant to each other in particular bilateral instances, I have NOT included regional documents. And because I want to look at the overall weighing of all possible priorities vis-à-vis each other, I have not included specific sectoral strategies which will by definition be focused on some priorities over others.

I followed an identical content analytic process as that for Britain, with identical operationalization of variables. In the case of documents available only in French, I adopted the French term that most closely approximated the English.

Issue coverage

Table 7.1 presents the emphases of these strategy papers. As was the case with Britain, the vast majority of the references are to concepts dealing with development, followed by trade, rights and good governance. This is in line with the thrust of earlier policy papers such as *Canada in the World*, more than with the new *International Policy Statement*, which of course was not issued until just before these documents were examined in the summer of 2006. Whether these relative emphases are mirrored in actual aid amounts will be examined in the multivariate statistical analyses that follow.

Few differences actually exist between coverage of external and internal documents, with the exception of references to effectiveness of aid, which is significantly higher in the case of external documents. This seems less a case of repackaging in any substantive way for public consumption than it does one of attempting to build public support for the ODA program by affording the public a sense of return on investment.

The regional variation of the documents is rather truncated, as not all regions granted access to older documents. Again, significance of these differences is impossible to determine for certain without t-tests, but some interesting differences can be seen. There is less inter-region variation in proportion of references to development than was the case with Britain. Good governance is referred to much more frequently in CDPFs for Middle Eastern countries than those in other regions, as is the issue of rights, though this is a less marked difference. Notably, trade is referenced much less frequently in strategies about Africa or the Middle East than is the case with other regions. While this is not surprising in the case of Africa, it is more so in the case of oil-rich Middle Eastern countries.

Documents from before and after the end of the Cold War differ mainly in terms of the increased reference to effectiveness after the end of the Cold War. Presumably this results in part from the increased focus on effectiveness in the donor community generally, and in part from the end of the Cold War allowing for a shift away from strategic importance and toward effectiveness (though there is no difference in the frequency of references to strategic issues during the Cold War versus after).

The frequency of references to effectiveness is also the main thing that distinguishes Liberal from Conservative governments (though this may in part be a function of the fact that Liberal governments have been in power more often in recent years when the discussion has shifted toward effectiveness in the donor community more generally. Documents under Conservative governments have also referred far more to development per se than those prepared under Liberal governments, which is a bit more surprising, and perhaps reflects a desire on the part of Conservative administrations to demonstrate their commitment to development. Though we might expect to see those prepared under Axworthy reflect a higher proportion of attention to either rights or development, the only difference in documents during the Axworthy era is a lower proportion of references to trade and a lower proportion of references to emergency assistance. It is interesting that trade, as a self-interested aid goal, sinks into the background without being systematically replaced by more altruistic criteria for aid decisions, with the exception of emergency assistance, which we should expect to see provided regardless of political considerations.

Recipients around which a good deal of human rights activism has taken place have more references in their strategy papers to development (perhaps to justify the continued provision of aid to states in the face of human rights violations), emergency assistance (same rationale) and, unsurprisingly, rights. It is an interesting truism that in most donors' strategy papers, the issue of rights is

Table 7.1

	Development: proportion of references (%)	Good governance and democracy: proportion of references (%)	Rights: proportion of references (%)	Economic Management: proportion of references (%)	Security: proportion of references (%)	Trade: proportion of references (%)	Colonialism: proportion of references (%)	Emergency assistance (%)	Aid effectiveness: proportion of references (%)
Internal documents	49	7	10	1	1	40	1	2	0
External documents	63	8	5	91	1	11	1	1	1
P(T<=t)	0.10	0.92	0.22	0.53	0.83	0.14	0.91	0.47	0.01
Factors pertaining to geopolitical forces									
Africa	50	6	2	0	1	5	1	1	0
Americas	65	6	6	3	1	21	1	1	1
Asia and Pacific	64	7	8	1	1	22	1	4	1
Europe	50	14	11	2	1	24	2	2	0
Middle East	61	9	8	1	1	10	3	2	1
Cold War	45	4	4	1	2	39	1	4	0
Post-Cold War	60	8	7	1	1	13	1	1	1
P(T<=t)	0.39	0.32	0.21	0.23	0.35	0.18	0.82	0.51	0.00
Factors pertaining to donor's decision-making context									
Conservative	60	6	9	1	1	33	1	4	0
Liberal	1	8	6	1	1	12	1	1	1
P(T<=t)	0.00	0.37	0.50	0.28	0.49	0.06	0.89	0.23	0.00
Not Axworthy	60	8	6	1	1	16	1	1	0
Axworthy	47	5	1	1	1	4	1	0	0
P(T<=t)	0.53	0.51	0.47	0.57	0.39	0.01	0.74	0.00	0.94
High HR activism	71	11	12	1	1	27	5	5	0
Low HR activism	0	8	6	1	1	16	5	2	1
P(T<=t)	0.06	0.61	0.06	0.92	0.15	27^	0.13	0.06	0.00
High immigrant population	60	11	9	1	0	23	2	1	0

Low immigrant population	59	7	6	2	1	16	1	2	1
P(T<=t)	0.94	0.40	0.44	0.35	0.02	0.38	0.42	0.25	0.68
Factors pertaining to recipient									
LLDC	57	7	5	1	1	5	1	1	1
Not LLDC	60	8	7	2	1	20	1	2	0
P(T<=t)	0.69	0.74	0.49	0.08	0.26	0.01	0.15	0.01	0.50
Major importer	61	8	8	2	1	23	2	2	0
Not major importer	56	8	5	1	1	6	1	1	1
P(T<=t)	0.45	0.74	0.11	0.23	0.73	0.00	0.04	0.02	0.44
Oil exporter	59	8	8	2	1	21	2	3	1
Not oil exporter	61	7	4	1	1	11	1	0	1
P(T<=t)	0.79	0.49	0.03	0.35	0.48	0.16	0.20	0.00	0.68
Strategic importance	57	10	8	1	2	22	1	3	0
Nonstrategic importance	60	7	6	2	1	8	1	2	1
P(T<=t)	0.66	0.25	0.54	0.54	0.18	0.51	0.63	0.42	0.19
Humanitarian crisis	28	7	1	2	0	3	1	1	1
No humanitarian crisis	62	8	7	2	1	18	1	2	1
P(T<=t)	0.03	0.76	0.00	0.88	0.41	0.00	0.57	0.16	0.51
Nuclear	62	9	14	1	1	18	3	3	0
Nonnuclear	59	8	6	2	1	17	1	2	1
P(T<=t)	0.77	0.59	0.11	0.61	0.60	0.02	0.14	0.52	0.00
Large state	61	6	9	1	1	22	2	5	0
Small state	59	8	6	2	1	17	1	1	1
P(T<=t)	0.75	0.26	0.29	0.19	0.45	0.01	0.51	0.11	0.00

generally raised only when there are violations going on in the recipient, not when the recipient is performing well. Strategies for these recipients also include fewer references to aid effectiveness, perhaps because current problems over-shadow the concern with long-term outputs at the time. Then again, states with emergencies tend not only to need more emergency assistance but to attract more activism.

The only thing that distinguishes strategies for countries with large Canadian immigrant populations from those without is the lower occurrence of references to security. It is unclear why this would be.

Which characteristics of the recipient itself affect which criteria are applied in its strategies? There are few differences between strategies for LLDCs and strategies for less-poor countries, save lower attention to trade (LLDCs may be incapable of it) and emergency assistance (LLDCs already tend to be getting higher aid amounts).

But in line with hypotheses 2 and 6, coverage of major Canadian export destinations differs in important ways from coverage of other states. There is a much greater focus on trade (unsurprisingly), common history (which also tends to be associated with higher trade volumes), and emergency assistance – perhaps emergencies are of greater concern with major trading partners. This last distinguishes strategies for oil exporters from those of other states as well (and parallels the lower frequency of references to emergency assistance in LLDCs). Rights are also cited more frequently, challenging the notion that oil exporters 'get away' with more.

When we divide states into two groups based on the index measure of strategic importance, testing hypotheses 4 and 8, we find that there are actually few meaningful differences in what is taken into account in policy-planning toward more strategically important versus less strategically important states.

However, states that have experienced a humanitarian crisis in the last two years are definitely evaluated differently, unsurprisingly given the extent to which references to emergency assistance have varied among different classes of recipients. These states are less likely to see aid policies made with reference to development, rights or trade – three things that factor highly in nearly all reports. Short-term emergency assistance seems to outweigh all other considerations. Nuclear states are only treated differently in that there are literally no references to aid effectiveness in any of the strategies regarding them. Perhaps it is understood that their a) nuclear status or b) large size, in the case of for instance India, make the importance of aid obvious regardless of effectiveness? Since the same difference holds for large versus small states, that may very well be the reason for the difference.

Table 7.2 presents states that received versus those that did not receive aid in one sample year, the last in the study. It will be noted that, while this is a more limited list than Britain's, it is still very substantial given the massive budget cuts of the mid-1990s.

So, this tells us what the policy-makers consider rhetorically. How does this stack up to who actually gets what?

Table 7.2

Recipients, 2004	Nonrecipients, 2004
Afghanistan	Anguilla
Albania	Armenia
Algeria	Aruba
Angola	Azerbaijan
Antigua and Barbuda	Bahrain
Argentina	Belarus
Bahamas	Bermuda
Bangladesh	British Virgin Islands
Barbados	Brunei
Belize	Burma
Benin	Cayman Islands
Bhutan	Central African Republic
Bolivia	Cook Islands
Bosnia	Cyprus
Botswana	Dominica
Brazil	Estonia
Bulgaria	Falkland Islands
Burkina Faso	Federated States of Micronesia
Burundi	French Polynesia
Cambodia	Gibraltar
Cameroon	Greece
Cape Verde	Grenada
Chad	Hong Kong
Chile	Israel
China	Kuwait
Colombia	Kyrgyzstan
Comoros	Latvia
Congo (Republic of Congo)	Libya
Costa Rica	Lithuania
Croatia	Macau
Cuba	Macedonia
Czech Republic	Malta
Djibouti	Marshall Islands
Dominican Republic	Mauritius
DRC	Mayotte
Ecuador	Moldova
Egypt	Montserrat
El Salvador	Nauru
Equatorial Guinea	New Caledonia
Eritrea	Niue
Ethiopia	Northern Marianas
Fiji	Oman
Gabon	Palau
Gambia	Qatar
Georgia	Saudi Arabia
Ghana	Singapore
Guatemala	South Africa
Guinea	South Korea (Republic of Korea)
Guinea-Bissau	St Helena
Guyana	St Vincent and Grenadines

Table 7.2 continued

Recipients, 2004	Nonrecipients, 2004
Haiti	Syria
Honduras	Taiwan
Hungary	Tokelau
India	Tonga
Indonesia	Turkmenistan
Iran	Tuvalu
Iraq	United Arab Emirates
Ivory Coast/Côte D'Ivoire	US Virgin Islands
Jamaica	Wallis and Futuna
Jordan	
Kazakhstan	
Kenya	
Kiribati	
Laos	
Lebanon	
Lesotho	
Liberia	
Madagascar	
Malawi	
Malaysia	
Maldives	
Mali	
Mauritania	
Mexico	
Mongolia	
Morocco	
Mozambique	
Namibia	
Nepal	
Nicaragua	
Niger	
Nigeria	
North Korea (Democratic Republic of Korea)	
Pakistan	
Palestinian Territories	
Panama	
Papua New Guinea	
Paraguay	
Peru	
Philippines	
Poland	
Romania	
Russia	
Rwanda	
Samoa	
Sao Tome and Principe	
Senegal	
Serbia and Montenegro	
Seychelles	
Sierra Leone	

Table 7.2 continued

Recipients, 2004	Nonrecipients, 2004
Slovakia	
Slovenia	
Solomon Islands	
Somalia	
Sri Lanka	
St Kitts and Nevis	
St Lucia	
Sudan	
Suriname	
Swaziland	
Tajikistan	
Tanzania	
Thailand	
Timor (East Timor)	
Togo	
Trinidad and Tobago	
Tunisia	
Turkey	
Turks and Caicos	
Uganda	
Ukraine	
Uruguay	
Uzbekistan	
Vanuatu	
Venezuela	
Viet Nam	
Yemen	
Zambia	
Zimbabwe	

Aggregate statistical analyses

All recipients

Table 7.3 presents results of the analysis of the gatekeeping decision for Canada. This is clearly a complex decision that responds to a variety of considerations about the international and domestic arenas as well as about the recipient and its relationship with Canada. Fulfilling CIDA's increasing focus on development for its own sake rather than as a means to more self-interested ends, poor states and states experiencing humanitarian crises are more likely to get aid, as are large states. Interestingly, those at a trade intersection are less likely to get aid (suggesting that strategic concerns are not only less important than need, but also that perhaps these states are, by dint of their position, attracting aid from other states, so that Canada does not feel it needs to give to these states, or that its aid would be relatively redundant in these states). Those involved in international conflict are also less likely to receive aid (in contrast to British aid patterns, and suggesting that such areas are not seen as a good investment). This could also reflect the increased focus on aid effectiveness, however – states in conflict are of course often also unable to use aid effectively.

As with Britain, states are more likely to receive aid after the end of the Cold War as broader dispersement occurs, for similar reasons.

In terms of trade relations, states that have high levels of Canadian aid indeed are more likely to be granted aid, in keeping with hypothesis 1, but those that

Table 7.3

Variable	Gatekeeping decision	Allocation decision
	Coefficient (standard errors)	Coefficient (standard errors)
Year	0.20***	−531.91
General characteristics of recipient		
Recipient GDP	-6.72^{-12}***	-1.73^{-08}
Human rights measures		
Human rights change	−0.06	153.57
Recipient polity score	0.00	39.45
Economic value measures		
Canada exports to recipient	2.35^{-06}***	−0.00
Canada imports from recipient	-7.54^{-07}	0.00
Recipient oil exports	−0.00	8.94**
Recipient GDP growth	−0.00	−58.12
Recipient population	6.70^{-09}***	1.69^{-06}
Strategic value measures		
Recipient nuclear capabilities	−0.00	7171.19
Internal dispute	−0.42	41.90
External dispute	−0.93***	293.10
Distance from Canada	0.00	0.26
Post-Cold War	1.54***	121.66
Trade intersection	−1.29 ***	−2159.08
Need measures		
Humanitarian crisis	0.19 **	1009.78*
Domestic politics measures		
Human rights activism	0.01	−1737.90
Immigrants from recipient	-5.43^{-07}	0.02 (marg)
Canada GDP	-4.79^{-12}	2.38^{-08}
Canada GDP growth rate	−0.04	129.43
Liberal	0.34 (marg)	884.50
Colonial history measure		
Commonwealth	−4.72 ***	−3848.11
Policy history	006	39.50
Aid previous year?	0.00***	0.44***
Significance of model	0.00	0.00
N	2361	548
R^2		0.02, 0.87, 0.41

Notes
*** = significant at $p < 0.001$; ** = $p < 0.01$; * = $p < 0.05$; (marg) = $p < 0.075$ (one-tailed).

Canada has high levels of imports *from* are in fact less likely to receive aid. This may be because these states tend to be wealthier among the developed states. Commonwealth ties also make a difference, but large immigrant populations more specifically do not increase a state's chances of receiving aid. Perhaps this is because Canada is already such a multiethnic society, and without direct colonial ties to immigrant groups, that the impact of particular groups is muted. In fact few immigrant groups in Canada are as large proportional to overall population as is the case in Britain. Significantly, key Canadian export markets are more likely to receive aid.

Many of these considerations fall away at the allocation stage and we appear to be looking at a much more straightforward calculus, with the presence of a humanitarian crisis and oil exports driving nearly all the year-to-year variation, despite the fact that the model overall explains a great deal of the variance between groups. In this sense the actual aid fortunes of states are very much in keeping with the criteria emphasized in the rhetoric of the individual country strategies.

Does trade change the calculus?

The gatekeeping decision remains a complex one when we divide states into 'high' and 'low' Canadian importers (Table 7.4), to test hypothesis 3.

Even when we distinguish key trade relations from others, need is still a major motive for Canadian aid. Poorer states in both categories are still more likely to receive aid, as are more populous states. However, those in both groups involved in an international conflict are less likely to get aid, though internal conflict is taken into account only for the high importers – perhaps because it could interfere with trade flows. So this is one piece of evidence against a need based in and favor of a more pragmatic approach to aid, whether for self-interested reasons or because conflict decreases aid effectiveness. The end of the Cold War makes both categories of states more likely to receive aid, due to general dispersal patterns. The only difference based on which party controls the government is that Liberal governments are more inclined to give aid to states that are not important export markets for Canadian goods. So under Liberal administrations we are more likely to see selfless rationales overcome self-interested ones, regardless of the fact that country strategies reflect more rhetorical focus on development under Conservative administrations. Both parties give consistently to high importers, however. And geographical proximity matters for high importers, but not for low importers. Why this would be so is unclear, but again high importers are likely to be more geographically proximate in the first place.

When we turn to testing hypothesis 6, things are again more straightforward at the allocation stage, but here the calculus is more complex for low importers than for high ones, whose aid receipts (generally about 15 percent higher than low importers) appear to be driven mainly by trade relations. For both groups at this stage, large states get more. But for low importers, being at a trade intersec-

Table 7.4

Variable	Gatekeeping decision		Allocation decision	
	Coefficient (standard errors) low importers	Coefficient (standard errors) high importers	Coefficient (standard errors) low importers	Coefficient (standard errors) high importers
Year	0.22*	0.31**	−738.55	35.93
General characteristics of recipient				
Recipient GDP	−1.57^{-}***	−6.48^{-12}**	−1.46^{-07}	−1.45^{-08}
Human rights measures				
Human rights violations	−0.00	−0.35	1129.10	−2398.85
Recipient polity score	0.00	−0.00	44.20	20.17
Economic value measures				
Canada exports to recipient	0.00	6.41^{-08}	0.35***	−0.02
Canada imports from recipient	3.10^{-06}	−6.49^{-07}	−0.01	0.01
Recipient oil exports	−0.00	0.00	7.66	12.20*
Recipient GDP growth	−0.00	0.01	−120.94	146.39
Recipient population	5.69^{-08}**	6.73^{-09}***	0.00 (marg)	−3.58^{-06}*
Strategic value measures				
Recipient nuclear capabilities	−1.45	0.36	13,229.78	5953.98
Internal dispute	−0.18	−0.91	−379.44	−2136.37
External dispute	−0.77**	−1.17**	−446.71	−1582.81
Distance from Canada	0.00	−0.00**	−0.20	1.88***
Post-Cold War	1.34***	1.49**	1426.14	−3849.40
Trade intersection	−0.49	−1.29	−6920.56*	−6603.74
Need measures				
Humanitarian crisis	0.00	0.29**	−230.69	1302.49
Domestic politics measures				
Human rights activism	−0.33	0.52	−4776.87	−665.44
Immigrants from recipient	−7.85^{-06}	6.32^{-08}	0.02	0.02
Canada GDP	−4.06^{-12}	−9.18^{-12}*	3.36^{-08}	5.58^{-09}

Canada GDP growth rate	-0.01	-0.13*	92.89	334.74
Liberal	0.60*	0.01	309.58	149.79
Colonial history measure				
Commonwealth	1.13	-0.00	-6197.41	
Policy history	0.00	0.00*	44.20	20.20
Aid previous year?	7.51^{-06}	0.00	0.28***	0.37***
Significance of model	0.00	0.00	0.00	0.00
N	1551	8·0	348	200
R^2			0.02, 0.57, 0.23	0.05, 0.86, 0.51

Notes
*** = significant at $p < 0.001$; ** = $p < 0.01$; * = $p < 0.05$; (marg) = $p < 0.075$ (one-tailed).

tion also matters (it has a negative effect, perhaps for the reasons discussed above – that these states may be attracting higher levels of aid from other donors – though this is not an assertion I test) as does having a high level of exports back to Canada (which increases aid levels). For the high importers, being an oil exporter helps. Being an important export market improves aid amounts for even the lower category. Both of these observations indicated self-interested rationale for higher aid amounts.

Does strategic importance change the calculus?

Testing hypothesis 4, at the gatekeeping stage, we not only see more volatility year to year in 'nonstrategic' recipients but also an extremely complex calculus (Table 7.5).

For these states, nine of the variables in the model are significant predictors of whether the state will receive aid. Only six matter for the 'strategic' states. Among the strategically less important recipients, poor, large, nonnuclear states that are relatively stable and key trading partners do best, reflecting a mix of altruistic motives (the first three variables), concerns with effectiveness (reflected in the desire to give to stable states) and commercial interests. Oddly, being at a trade intersection has a negative effect. For the more strategically important states, the chances of receiving aid are helped by being populous non-nuclear, less democratic and having large numbers of immigrants in Canada. Why would less democratic states get more? This is a question that begs further investigation. It is unlikely it is a spurious observation, since human rights violations have a marginally positive relationship to aid chances as well. It is unlikely of course that Canada chooses to give to nondemocratic states explicitly, but this does end up being the case. If this is the case, aid discussions with less democratic states should emphasize the need for improvement, and should impose some sort of costs for failure to do so.

Testing hypothesis 8, at the allocation stage, we again see a much simpler calculus than at the gatekeeping stage. Again, more factors come into play for less strategically important states, namely whether they have had a humanitarian crisis, whether they are a nuclear state (which increases aid, demonstrating self-interest) and whether they are an oil exporter (which decreases it, demonstrating altruism). For more strategically important states, all that seems to matter is just that – being strategically important. We therefore see support for strategic importance as a key delineating characteristic between recipients, but we still see no effect on rights.

Though not all results could be reported here due to space constraints, these analyses were also rerun with the key measure of human rights in the recipient being change in human rights over the past year rather than overall human rights conditions. No substantive differences were observed. The same was true when the 'add' and 'drop' decisions at the gatekeeping stage were analyzed.

One possible interpretation of these non-results is that aid is responding to HR issues in partner states in exactly the way the 2001 policy paper on HRDGG says it will: with a mixture of carrots and sticks, and that therefore the net impact on aid is nil. Preliminary analyses designed to test this assumption, by running the analyses separately for states whose aid went up and those whose aid went down revealed tentative support for this possibility.

For all recipients pooled together, there was a marginally significant positive relationship between rights abuses and aid increases, but no relationship between rights abuses and aid decreases. This is an important caveat to taking overly pessimistic lessons from the foregoing discussions, and suggests that aid programs do respond to rights abuses by attempting to a) increase the stake of the recipient government in maintaining a positive relationship with Canada; and b) perhaps provide training and other capacity-building resources to nourish the institutions of civil society that create the preconditions for democratic participation. The analyses were not carried out in a manner that disaggregated by sector (to see, for instance, what kind of aid was being received by states with poor human rights performance and whether this was different than that being received by states with strong human rights performance), but that would be a fruitful avenue for future research.

So when do rights matter?

As in the British case, and given the complex mix of factors that come into play in Canadian aid policy, it seemed wise to test more comprehensively the extent to which the various other likely factors in the aid process might affect the role of rights. I therefore ran one final analysis, presented in Table 7.6, testing for interactive effects of human rights with each of the other key variables.

The results of this analysis were very interesting and confirmed some of our earlier results. While we saw that states which had been the subject of human rights activism were less likely to be granted aid, it is also the case that these are one of the few classes of states that actually have human rights taken into account. The similarity to the British case is striking because, taken together, the two cases imply that activism can be very effective in enhancing the role of rights in foreign policy decisions. This seems to confirm the increased role of NGOs in agenda-setting in recent years in the donor community at large.

This final analysis, then, provides a glimmer of hope for a role for human rights in aid considerations. Whether this will continue under the new Harper administration, especially as CIDA still struggles to define a focus, remains to be seen.

More evidence from the documentary record

As discussed in earlier chapters, in an area as complex as aid, it is very possible that considerations can have important effects that are not easily captured in aggregate analyses, as most analyses of aid tend to be. It would certainly be worthwhile to conduct further analyses that examined individual aid sectors separately, as well as distinguishing direct budget support, from program aid, from project aid. However, perhaps the most direct way of looking at the nuanced

Table 7.5

Variable	Gatekeeping decision		Allocation decision	
	Coefficient (standard errors) low strategic	Coefficient (standard errors) high strategic	Coefficient (standard errors) low strategic	Coefficient (standard errors) high strategic
Year	0.17**	1.41	−711.10	1348.56
General characteristics of recipient				
Recipient GDP	$−6.71^{-12}$**	$−1.54^{-11}$	$−2.32^{-08}$	1.08^{-08}
Human rights measures				
Human rights violations	−0.08	2.04 (marg)	106.58	297.59
Recipient polity score	0.01	−0.14	24.74	110.74
Economic value measures				
Canada exports to recipient	2.23^{-06}**	0.00	−0.00	0.01
Canada imports from recipient	$−5.89^{-07}$	0.00*	0.00	−0.01
Recipient oil exports	−0.00	−0.00	9.43**	−0.70
Recipient GDP growth	−0.00	−0.07	−38.47	−317.14
Recipient population	4.74^{-09} (marg)	1.24^{-07}*	7.99^{-06}	4.97^{-06}
Strategic value measures				
Recipient nuclear capabilities	−1.78*	−7.91*	12,912.18*	−3388.98
Internal dispute	−0.47*	0.60	28.60	−2528.87
External dispute	−1.22***	6.68	319.91	2394.47
Distance from Canada	5.08^{-06}	0.00	0.20	0.58
Post-Cold War	1.56***	58.22	655.21	−2,688,473.00
Trade intersection	−1.38**	−1.37	−4288.44	−3721.96
Need measures				
Humanitarian crisis	0.12	0.55	1103.93 (marg)	−927.30
Domestic politics measures				
Human rights activism	0.08	−0.58	−2087.82	−32.14
Immigrants from recipient	$−2.48^{-07}$	0.00*	0.01	0.03
Canada GDP	$−3.49^{-12}$	5.92^{-11} *	3.11^{-08}	$−1.80^{-08}$

Canada GDP growth rate	−0.04	0.17	103.63	1009.00
Liberal	0.35 (marg)	59.74	1258.36	111.88
Colonial history measure				
Commonwealth	0.36	48.53	−4113.84	
Policy history				
Aid previous year?	0.00**	−0.00	0.44***	0.60***
Significance of model	0.00	0.00	0.00	0.00
N	2141	220	500	48
R^2			0.02, 0.87, 0.40	0.16, 0.79, 0.69

Notes

*** = significant at $p < 0.001$; ** = $p < 0.01$; * = $p < 0.05$; (marg) = $p < 0.075$ (one-tailed).

Table 7.6

Variable	Gatekeeping	Allocation
Year	0.20***	−531.91
Year*HR	0.34***	−930.21
General characteristics of recipient		
Recipient GDP	-6.72^{-12}***	-1.73^{-08}
Recipient GDP*HR	-10.34^{-12}	-2.23^{-08}
Human rights measures		
Human rights violations	−0.06	153.57
Recipient polity score	0.00	39.45
Recipient polity score*HR	0.00	42.53
Economic value measures		
Canada exports to recipient	2.35^{-06}****	−0.00
Canada exports*HR	4.32^{-06}	0.00
Canada imports from recipient	-7.54^{-07}*	0.00
Canada imports*HR	-9.02^{-07}	0.00
Recipient oil exports	−0.00	8.94**
Oil exports*HR	−0.00	12.03
Recipient GDP growth	−0.00	−58.12
Recipient GDP growth*HR	−0.00	−34.09
Recipient population	6.70^{-09}***	1.69^{-06}
Recipient population*HR	7.23^{-09}	2.74^{-06}
Strategic value measures		
Recipient nuclear capabilities	−0.00	7171.19
Recipient nuclear capabilities*HR	−0.00	8993.04
Internal dispute	−0.42	41.90
Internal dispute*HR	−0.54	34.09
External dispute	−0.93***	293.10
External dispute*HR	−1.39	893.01
Distance from Canada	0.00	0.26
Distance from Canada*HR	0.00	0.84
Post-Cold War	1.54***	121.66
Post-Cold War*HR	2.03	300.93
Trade intersection	−1.29***	−2159.08
Trade intersection*HR	−2.22	−1930.31
Need measures		
Humanitarian crisis	0.19**	1009.78*
Humanitarian crisis*HR	0.24	894.09
Domestic politics measures		
Human rights activism	0.01	−1737.90
Human rights activism*HR	−0.00*	−450.09*
Immigrants from recipient	-5.43^{-07}	0.02 (marg)
Immigrants from recipient*HR	-7.24^{-07}	0.00
Canada GDP	-4.79^{-12}*	2.38^{-08}
Canada GDP*HR	-4.79^{-12}	5.49^{-08}
Canada GDP growth rate	−0.04	129.43
Canada GDP growth rate*HR	−0.00	92.94
Liberal	0.34 (marg)	884.50
Liberal*HR	0.43	993.09
Colonial history measure		
Commonwealth	−4.72***	−3848.11
Commonwealth*HR	−3.33	−2039.01

Table 7.6 continued

Variable	Gatekeeping	Allocation
Policy history		
Aid previous year?	0.00***	0.44***
Significance of model	0.00	0.00
N	2361	548
R²		0.02, 0.87, 0.41

ways that a consideration such as human rights can have an effect is by looking at individual decisions themselves.

In the thousands of pages of documentary evidence I examined from CIDA, I found no instances in which a bilateral aid program was terminated solely on the basis of human rights violations. As will be seen from a comparison of Table 7.1 in this chapter with Table 6.1 in the last chapter, rights as a concept emerges less frequently in Canadian programming frameworks. But I did find that human rights entered into strategies about recipient or 'partner' countries in two main types of ways.

The first of these is as part of the overall development challenge to be addressed in a country. Most CDPFs produced by CIDA today feature a section called '[Country]'s Development Challenge' that is positioned after the introduction and context sections of the paper. In cases where substantial rights violations exist, they have been in every case I have seen included in this section. Interestingly enough, comparing some analogous CDPFs with British CSPs or CAPs, such as the first ones prepared in this decade for Colombia, reveal substantially more overt attention to rights in the CDPFs than in the analogous DfID documents. While this does not mean that aid *per se* is cut or raised in a way that would be picked up by the aggregate analyses, it does mean that rights issues are acknowledged and that implicitly this may lead to more closely monitored programs, aid being given for specific projects rather than as direct budget support, or similar. This is especially the case since in many cases rights are acknowledged as being part and parcel of the 'Development Challenge' (which seems, to my reading, to imply a greater need to engage than if it is just considered as part of the 'context').

The second way is interesting in that it allows human rights to enter the policy dialogue and key policy documents without CIDA explicitly sanctioning it. CIDA regularly includes as part of CDPF annexes recommendations from Parliamentary committees and subcommittees, including the Standing Committee on Foreign Affairs and International Trade (SCFAIT) Subcommittee on Human Rights and International Development (for instance the most recent CDPF for Colombia involves such a recommendation. Unsurprisingly, these are often far more sanguine about the use of aid to pursue human rights than are the CDPFs themselves, which after all are supposed to represent a more holistic approach to development.

Interestingly, however, in some cases where one might expect to see it raised, such as in Cuba's more recent CDPF, it is not mentioned at all. This case may be something of an outlier, however, as Canadian foreign policy-makers have often prided themselves on having a far more engaged relationship with Cuba than is the case for the US.

Conclusion

Canadian foreign policy attempts to steer a middle course between many competing policy imperatives: between the Francophonie and the Commonwealth, between friendship and suspicion of America, between a self-image as a good global citizen and a budgetary reality that constrains its ability to lead. Historical trends suggest a certain amount of incoherence as a result of these disparate goals, but constants have remained trade prioritization and strategic position of recipients. Recent developments suggest new strategies forward are being attempted, especially since 2005. Both Liberal PM Jean Chretien and Liberal Finance Minister Paul Martin, Jr committed to grounding the aid program more explicitly in the MDGs, but it is unclear whether the new Harper government will follow through on this line, especially with defense spending on the rise and new commitments to rebuilding in Iraq and Afghanistan. As in the other donors, attention to effectiveness has been on the rise since the 2005 Paris declaration. In response to traditional criticisms from the DAC and others, there has been a new commitment to greater regional and sectoral concentration, though only time will tell to what extent this is borne out.

Besides the election of the Harper government, another major policy development that occurred after these statistical analyses end was the April 2005 release of the government's international policy statement. Unfortunately, because of the aforementioned broadness of the aims therein, as well as the competing impulses that continue to be a hallmark of Canadian foreign policy, it is as yet unclear that the policy statement will lead to any real changes. It features frequent references to development but also to Canada's commercial interests and economic security. Development is to be addressed through five strategies: doubling aid in real term; enhancing effectiveness through streamlining; enlisting public support; increasing proportional allocation to Africa; and enhancing partnership with recipient countries. Unfortunately, as of yet these goals appear to be broad enough that they have led to easy rhetorical changes rather than hard but substantive policy shifts. (For an excellent discussion of these weaknesses in the international policy statement see Black and Thiessen 2007).

As it nears the end of its sixth decade, Canada's aid program is still searching for a focus and a distinctive identity in the donor community.

8 Inherited from history and geography
Australian development assistance and human rights

Though of course sharing a common cultural origin with the preceding donors, Australia's geographical isolation and much smaller population and economy have been defining factors in its overall foreign policy and in its aid program Following Smith *et al.* (1996), three aspects of this bear a brief review before a more specific discussion of the role of human rights in Australian foreign policy:

1 Australian isolation, which has led it to seek 'great and powerful friends' (Menzies, cited in Smith *et al.* 1996: 25), and which has exacerbated;
2 its sense of constraint as a middle-power; and
3 the sometimes conflicting pull toward regionalism in its foreign policy.

Australia's sense of regional isolation and presumed indefensibility has had a profound impact on every part of its foreign policy. This has led to a sense of dependence, first on Britain and, after World War II, the United States. US progress in the Pacific, rather than British assistance, was widely seen as the decisive factor in sparing Australia almost certain Japanese invasion. This precipitated a marked reorientation toward the US in Australia's alliance strategy (especially as formalized through Australia New Zealand United States mutual defence treaty (ANZUS)).

Geographic and cultural isolation have led to some of the most infamous aspects of Australia's foreign and domestic policy such as the 'White Australia' initiatives. Defensiveness about these policies has bred both suspicion of international laws, and reluctance to speak out about human rights violations is other states. For instance, postwar Foreign Minister Herbert Vere Evatt made strenuous efforts to include a provision in the UN charter that would prevent the new organizations from intervening in 'internal affairs'. This was based in large part on a desire to maintain Australia's trusteeship of Papua New Guinea, to retain the 'White Australia' immigration policy, and to shield Australia's treatment of Aborigines from criticism. The inclusion of noninterventionism in Article 2(7) of the UN Charter was largely the result of Evatt's efforts (Smith *et al.* 1996: 208). (Evatt would later go on to attempt to block the 1952 condemnation of apartheid in the UN, the first violation of the nonintervention principle in the name of human rights (Smith *et al.* 1996: 208)).

Australia's policy-makers regularly use the term 'middle-power' to describe the country. As mentioned above, Australian experiences in World War II did much to cement this status as a defining force behind Australian foreign policy choices. Having had little experience with the development of an independent foreign policy before the war, the sudden threat from Japan and the clear vulnerability of Britain at the time imbued Australian foreign policy-makers with a kind of collective post-traumatic stress. This formative experience has led both to its pursuit of 'great and powerful friends' and a nagging sense of its own vulnerability.

> Every country has its foreign policy difficulties and dilemmas, problems inherited from history or geography or imposed by contemporary events. So it is with Australia, an outpost of European culture permanently located alongside Asia, remote from her friends (except New Zealand) and major markets, with a wealthy economy still substantially dependent on oil brought long distances across the open seas.
>
> (Millar 1968: xv)

Finally, the regionalism that this combination of isolation and middle-power status has engendered[1] has been seen as crucial to safeguarding Australia's geopolitical and economic interests.[2] It has increased even more in response to the increase in regional agreements in other areas of the world (Smith *et al.* 1996: 17–18). As we will see, this regionalism has had profound effects on Australia's aid patterns. A recent DAC report called Australia's 'proximity and interrelatedness to developing countries almost unique among DAC countries' (OECD 1996: 7).

Moreover these three attributes – isolation, vulnerability and middle-power status – have led Australia to feel that many of its national interests are quite fixed, especially its need for export promotion. This need dominates nearly every aspect of its foreign policy-making. As Smith *et al.* have put it, 'concerns about environmental crisis, political repression, violent conflict and human rights – both close at hand and far away – are subordinated in the search for trade and investment opportunities' (Smith *et al.* 1996: 127). This has been a more dominant aim of its aid program than is the case for either Canada or Great Britain.

Human rights in Australian foreign policy thinking and practice

Human rights defined

Members of the Australian NGO community have criticized an implicit prioritization of civil and political rights over economic, cultural and social ones (HRCA 1995). While the most recent National Action Plan (NAP) (see below) offers no explicit definition of rights, there are certain aspects that it officially highlights in specific bilateral relations. For instance, in the NAP discussion of the current dialogue with China, the issues emphasized include

> freedom of association, expression, and religion; the human rights situation ... affecting other ethnic and religious minorities ... the treatment of dissidents; legal reform; ... the death penalty; the use of torture and other degrading practices; and reports of coercion in ... China's family planning policies.
>
> (DFAT 2004: 6)

This reflects an emphasis on first-generation civil and political rights. Similar issues arise in the case of Vietnam: 'freedom of expression; the plight of ethnic and religious minorities in the central highlands; restrictions on the use of the internet; religious freedoms; and the death penalty' (DFAT 2004: 6). And the Iran dialogue bears out many of the same themes; discussions focused on 'our respective constitutional, judicial and legal systems, the position of minorities, the position of women, freedom of expression and ... national human rights institutions, and the death penalty' (DFAT 2004: 6).

These emphases are borne out in the programmatic foci of, for instance, the China dialogue: 'legal reform and capacity building, education, police ethics, women and children's rights, the role of civil society, and the implementation of international human rights instruments' (DFAT 2004: 6). The same is true of the Iran dialogue: 'Iran visited Australia in 2003 to study the ... Australian Human Rights and Equal Opportunity Commission' (DFAT 2004: 6).

The evolution of the role of human rights in Australian foreign policy rhetoric and practice

Because of its internal record, Australia has historically had to tread a bit more lightly than some democratic states in its human rights foreign policy stands and activities, lest it be accused of hypocrisy. Today policy-makers are willing to include strong rhetorical stands on human rights in official policy statements. But a strong restraint of another sort remains: the imperative not to impinge upon commercial interests.[3]

We have seen in the cases of the other two donor countries that key ministerial appointments have been very important for the status of human rights on the foreign policy agenda. In the case of Australia, the most important of these was probably the appointment of Gareth Evans as Foreign Minister in September 1988 by Bob Hawke. Evans's concept of Good International Citizenship (GIC) seemed to promise to bring issues of rights and good governance to the fore. Even these, however, were often justified in terms of Australia's interests (Smith *et al.* 1996: 219). As Evans put it, 'we can be faithful to humanitarian concerns and in the process also acquire for Australia human resources and skills which strengthen our economy and enrich our society' (cited in Smith *et al.* 1996: x).[4]

Human rights issues have been institutionalized in the larger DFAT bureaucracy in the form of a Human Rights and Indigenous Issues Section, which occupies a position analogous to that occupied by human rights at the FCO in Britain during the early days of John Coles's career – it is part of the UN unit with a host of other only marginally functionally related units. Human rights concerns have been instituted more explicitly within aid policy following the release in August 2001 of a Parliamentary report by the Joint Standing Committee on Foreign Affairs, Defense and Trade, *The Link between Aid and Human Rights*.

In multilateral settings, Australia has actually been something of a leader in drawing attention to human rights issues. For instance, at the UN Conference on Human Rights in Vienna in 1993, Australia proposed that UN member states prepare national plans of action regarding human rights, outlining the status and future goals of domestic and international policies and activities in the field of human rights. This proposal was adopted as part of the Vienna Program of Action, and the following year Australia became the first country to complete one. This was updated in 1995 and again in 1996–7, and an entirely new NAP was begun in 1998 and launched in late 2004 (DFAT 2007 www.dfat.gov.au/hr/nap/natact_plan.html). The NAP is a rather extensive document, and the section on bilateral strategies is especially relevant in the context of this investigation. It explicitly refutes the nonintervention principle (DFAT 2004: 5) but also takes care to say that 'in our bilateral dealings, we do not presume to hold other nations to standards that we do not apply to ourselves'.

At the very start of its discussion, the NAP lays out the tensions between human rights and other goals of foreign policy, and these will be discussed in greater detail below. But the proposed approach to addressing these tensions reveals a gàp between a reasonably strong official rhetoric around rights and an extremely soft-pedal approach toward the choice of bilateral tools for addressing these violations in other states. The best way to ameliorate any 'difficulties' other states may have in implementing human rights protections, it says, is to understand these difficulties in the context of the overall relationship and to offer 'practical assistance' (DFAT 2004: 5) to these countries. This approach suggests a reluctance to take high-level, public, or punitive action against violator states. While higher-level dialog is listed as a possibility, there is little in the report to suggest that this is an option that will be pursued on a regular basis. Low-level, discreet diplomatic action is emphasized: 'Representations are normally made through the Australian diplomatic mission in ... the country concerned, as this is considered the most effective channel to register Australian views with the relevant authorities' (DFAT 2004: 6).

This light-touch approach characterizes the pursuit of human rights as a goal in foreign policy. Here is one example. In August 2001, Senator Hill, who represents the External Affairs Minister, was asked about the government's response to Zimbabwean human rights abuses. He responded:

There is no doubt that all Commonwealth countries are increasingly disturbed by what is occurring in Zimbabwe – the lack of respect for the rule of law and the violence, which appears to be at least in part state sanctioned – and we share a desire to see a different standard of behavior as soon as possible.

(Australia Parliament 2001: x)

But is any action taken in support of these stances? On this point the senator became a bit more equivocal. He dismissed one suggested diplomatic action, that of disinviting President Mugabe (of Zimbabwe) to an upcoming Commonwealth Heads of Government Meeting on the basis that confronting Mugabe in person regarding human rights would be more beneficial. But he assured his fellow senators that the government 'is seeking to use all opportunities that are available to Australia – in diplomatic terms or in other ways – to influence a better behavior in the shortest possible term in Zimbabwe' *(Australia Parliament* 2001: x). He declined to be more specific.

The NAP also makes it clear that the very provision of development assistance is something it sees as addressing basic human rights. This is a highly problematic assertion since aid generally serves to support governments to which it goes, especially as direct budgetary support. And even project and program aid is likely to reinforce the power of recipient governments because of the fungibility of aid: when it helps do something on which the government would otherwise have had to spend money, the government can spend that money elsewhere (Boone, cited in HRCA 1995: 60).

Other than the NAP, at least two other key recent foreign policy documents merit examination as we try to establish a working definition of human rights in the context of Australian foreign policy and a sense of where they fit into the hierarchy of goals, and which tools are seen as most appropriate for pursuing them.

The first of these is the 1997 Foreign and Trade Policy White Paper. Australian interests are unambiguously the focus of the 1997 White Paper, *Charting Australia's Regional Future* (DFAT 1997). As the joint statement issued (by the Minister for Foreign Affairs and the Deputy Prime Minister and Minister for Trade) upon its release said,

Its fundamental message is that in all that it does in foreign and trade policy the Government will apply a basic test of national interest: how does it advance the security of Australia and the jobs and standard of living of the Australian people.

(DFAT 1997: 1)

In terms of priorities, 'The White Paper identifies globalization and the continuing economic rise of East Asia as the two most profound influences on Australian foreign and trade policy over the next fifteen years' (DFAT 1997: 2). So though both security and economic interests are identified as 'tests', the two most important trends are predominantly defined in economic terms (though globalization cannot be reduced to this). The paper also reasserts Australia's regional orientation, its need to emphasize bilateral relations over multilateral ones (something that would change dramatically in the subsequent White Paper), and the importance of the US alliance. While the issue of human rights are mentioned, it is again justified as a means to pursue Australia's national interests rather than as an end in themselves: 'national interests cannot be pursued without regard to the values of the Australian community, including its support for fundamental human rights' (DFAT 1997: 3). In fact, human rights concerns are cast essentially as an afterthought.

The 2003 foreign policy White Paper, *Advancing the National Interest*, begins with a definition of Australia's values; notably first among these is 'tolerance' suggesting, perhaps, a libertarian or *laissez-faire* approach to human rights, followed by 'perseverance' and finally 'mateship'. It goes on to discuss Australia's heritage as a liberal democracy and to link that to economic freedom, significantly to freedom from want of basic needs. It then connects economic freedoms to political freedoms including 'the freedom of individuals to speak, to think, to believe and to associate – or not to associate – as they see fit. It is also the freedom to appoint and dismiss a government freely and fairly through the ballot box' (DFAT 2003 www.dfat.gov.au/ani/overview.html). So, as in the NAP, basic civil/political freedoms and democratic governance are the context for the rest of the discussion. They are, again, first justified however not as ends unto themselves but because 'these freedoms produce a more stable and prosperous Australia. And ... they also produce a more stable and prosperous international community, which is both an important end in itself and benefits Australia's own stability and prosperity' (DFAT 2003). A similar justification is evident a few paragraphs later: 'it is essential that we continue to promote economic and political freedom abroad. Our security depends, in part, upon it.' The document goes on to list a series of 'core challenges' which include

- maintaining security and prosperity;
- confronting terrorism and global threats to our security;
- building prosperity through market liberalization[5;]
- regional cooperation;[6]
- advancing wider global interests;
- projecting Australia and its values;
- promoting good governance, human rights and development.

(DFAT 2003)

In this section the goal of human rights is primarily dealt with as part of the now familiar HRDGG triad, as well as subsumed under the rubric the rule of law and sustainability. Again including rights as a foreign policy goal is justified in terms of its contribution to the prosperity and security of Australia. The 'practical approach' to human rights is again embraced and the executive summary of the report explicitly claims to 'eschew the soap box' (DFAT 2003). It also refers to taking action on 'human rights issues that make a difference' (DFAT 2003). This seems an odd turn of phrase, and implies that not all rights issues meet that standard. Good governance is most emphasized of any specific subset of rights – though in fact, as has been discussed in detail by others (HRCA 1995) and in earlier chapters, there are arguments to make against the inclusion of GG as subsuming fundamental universal rights at all. And the GG focus is certainly not justified primarily in HR terms.

> The help we give other nations to improve their governance covers a wide range of areas, including legislative, administrative and judicial institutional capacity building. Australia also contributes to strengthening policy formulation and implementation. For example, Australia supports efforts to enhance the trade policy skills of developing countries, to enable them to reap the benefits of trade liberalization.
>
> (DFAT 2003)

(Aid, notably, is mentioned only in one very brief paragraph.) Like *Charting Australia's Regional Future*, the 2003 strategy paper emphasizes multilateral avenues.

Do these policy statements and the actions that have followed from them acknowledge the potential tensions between pursuing human rights and pursuing other goals? Certainly other observers have admitted such tensions, as well as the result that human rights concerns are subsumed to commercial interests.[7] But it is less clear that the government acknowledges them. The NAP notes that: 'on occasion, support for human rights will create difficulties in Australia's bilateral relationships' (DFAT 2004: 6). But, as noted above, it goes on to imply that quiet diplomacy and 'practical assistance on the ground' are the best ways to resolve such tensions.[8] Carrots then, not sticks. As discussed earlier, a combination of these techniques offers donors the best chance of affecting human rights abroad, while overreliance on carrots is likely to create a moral hazard. On the other hand, some would argue that in fact little tension has existed between HR and other goals because Australia's overwhelming concern for its own security and economy has outweighed any others.[9]

Australian aid

In 2005 Australia gave a little less than $USD 1.7 billion in aid, 25 percent of its GNI. Some 85 percent of this was bilateral. Nearly two-thirds, $USD 954 million, went to Asia and Oceania.

The play of priorities in Australian aid

Brief institutional history

Though an aid program existed under a variety of departmental aegises prior to the 1970s, a dedicated aid organization dates to 1974, when Edward Gough

Whitlam's Labour government established the Australian Development Assistance Agency (ADAA). In 1976 it became Australian Development Assistance Bureau (ADAB), when it was brought into the Department of Foreign Affairs under the Liberal government), and, in 1987, the name changed again to Australian International Development Assistance Bureau (AIDAB). In February 1991, ministerial responsibility was transferred from the Minister for Foreign Affairs and Trade to the Minister for Trade and Overseas Development, and later to the Minister for Development Cooperation and Pacific Island Affairs, a move that was intended to raise the visibility of the aid program (OECD 1996: 14). The portfolio was finally renamed Australian Agency for International Development (AusAID) in March 1995 when, under the new government, the ministerial position for development assistance was done away with and responsibility handed back to the Minister for Foreign Affairs. Out of the three main donors in this study, AusAID is the only one of the aid agencies that is directly governed by a department that is also explicitly responsible for trade. Discussions of the other donors have illustrated the conflicts this kind of arrangement can cause in cabinet and civil service: it makes it difficult for the aid program to have an independent voice, and it means that it must share control over aid policies and priorities with organs of government whose primary missions are not international development. NGOs have been consistently critical of this aspect of AusAID's institutional position. 'Delivering aid through a "national interest" lens ... remains a major distraction from focusing on alleviating poverty' (AidWatch 2006: 6).

Real and steady cuts in aid budgets as a percentage of GNP have been a defining reality for the Australian aid program over the course of its history, until very recently. Other distinguishing figures (relative to the rest of the donor community) have included a very high degree of tying, especially to Australian or New Zealand firms. In part because of persistent budgetary cuts, staff numbers have remained very small and this has led some to question the capacity for the kind of in-depth strategic research and policy formulation that would be ideal (OECD 1996: 14).

Unlike the DfID or CIDA, AusAID does not coordinate Australia's multilateral development efforts, which instead take place elsewhere in DFAT.

The first White Paper (WP) ever to explicitly focus on the aid program was launched in June 2006, following the announcement in September 2005 that the aid budget would be doubled (in absolute, not real terms) by 2010 to about A$4 billion, the first ever multiyear increase in the aid budget. Titled, *Australian Aid: Promoting Growth and Stability*, it claims to focus (in order) on poverty reduction, sustainable development, and progress toward the MDGs; and to be underpinned by Australian values, including 'economic and political freedom and our humanitarian spirit' (DFAT 2006: 3). It also justifies aid in terms of the need to support stability in the region to foster Australia's own security. The key to poverty reduction is clearly economic growth (the first of the 'development lessons' to which the WP says it is responding), and that economic growth is seen to be fostered by trade openness. Notably the WP redefines the objective of

Australia's aid program from 'To assist developing countries to reduce poverty and achieve sustainable development' to 'To assist developing countries to reduce poverty and achieve sustainable development, *in line with Australia's national interest*' (DFAT 2006: 5; emphasis mine). Accordingly, the framework is organized around four basic themes:

1   accelerating economic growth;
2   fostering functioning and effective states;
3   investing in people;
4   promoting regional stability and cooperation.

(DFAT 2006: 5)

What this means for the balance of rights with other goals is as yet unclear. However, many NGOs have criticized AusAID's focus on growth as the primary route to economic development, arguing that the uneven distribution of its effects exacerbate already large gaps in developing countries between rich and poor, while encouragement of outward-oriented economic strategies often undermines the existing social-welfare system that protects the most vulnerable in poor states (see for instance HRCA 1995). The fact that the WP proposes to encourage growth largely by improving the 'policy environment for private sector growth' and encouraging more trade (DFAT 2006: 7) seems to bear out these fears that the focus is too much on supporting the growth of a middle class, with the assumption that benefits will trickle down, rather than focusing on the poorest in society as the DfID and CIDA have done. The governance section primarily involves programs for training leaders and rewarding good performance and efforts to reduce corruption. 'Investing in people' subsumes support for health and education, but not in the language of rights – justified instead as a means to a more productive workforce and a more accountable government. Other traditional factors guiding aid strategy such as regionalism remain intact.

Several of the key priorities of the British and Canadian aid programs are evident in AusAID commitments, but there are also significant differences, which result directly from these unique characteristics of the Australian foreign policy-making context.

Commonwealth

Though of course itself a member of the Commonwealth, the Commonwealth status of recipients has remained a minor consideration in Australian aid decisions and is not a stated factor in any current country strategies. Australia's own former trustee relationship with Papua New Guinea (which formally ended in the 1960s), however, has created a unique and definitive relationship with that country, as well as creating tensions with Indonesia.

Commercial interests

As has been noted, commercial interests are more unambiguously a goal in the Australian aid program than is the case for the other two donors. Australian aid is seen as part of a coherent strategy that places export promotion and good trading relations, especially trade liberalization, above all else in almost all foreign policy decisions (save when a vital geopolitical interest with a key ally is clearly at stake).[10] There has long been an official emphasis on tying (OECD 1996: 8–9), and 'Australian aid is seen as a helping hand for businesses to diversify trade and ... gain access to potential markets – [and yet the DAC reviewers caution] pressures for subsidization are felt and distinctions have to be drawn between short and long term benefits.' At the time of the 1996 DAC review, Australia's share of ODA that was going to directly financing imports by developing countries was 20 percent compared to the DAC average of 12 percent (OECD 1996: 29).

An important tool for export promotion in the 1980s and 1990s was the Development Import Finance Facility (DIFF) program, which was a form of mixed credits, combining ODA and export credits. Like ATP in Britain it was very controversial but DAC reports commended it for evolving over the course of its lifetime (it was abolished in 1996) to the point that it caused remarkably little distortion to the development aims of aid (OECD 1996: 29).

Australian aid watchdog organizations continue to document on a yearly basis the huge proportion of related contracts that go to a 'small number of aid delivery companies' (AidWatch 2006: 6). This practice is so common that it has earned a nickname among critics: 'boomerang aid' (see for instance AidWatch 2006: 6; HRCA 1995).

Geopolitics

What the OECD rejoices in, aid watchdog organizations might lament: strong coordination between the DFAT and DoD, and between AusAID and Australian defense forces, including a great deal of attention to the links between development cooperation, peacekeeping and peacebuilding (OECD 1996: 9). On the one hand, AidWatch cautions:

> [a]n increase in funding for security programs with Australian aid money in 2005 continues a worrying trend. Military interventions in the Solomon Islands, planned police interventions in PNG, defence projects in the Philippines and many other defence or security projects continued to be allocated out of aid funds. Furthermore, Australia's security is continually emphasized as a cornerstone of the aid program [as noted above] which we argue detracts from the need to be more acutely focused on poverty reduction and alleviation in our region.
>
> (AidWatch 2006: 6)

Aid Watch is concerned that this is a sign of a 'newly interventionist' Australian aid policy borne out by recent events in Papua New Guinea, the Solomons and Indonesia (AidWatch 2006: 9).

The ongoing importance of security considerations in aid decisions and the high security content in country-level aid packages has been evident recently in that

> of the $800 million budgeted for the program [in Papua New Guinea] the majority was dedicated to salaries and accommodation for Australian offi-cers ($324 million) and logistics for Australian officers ($394 million)....
> Publication of this information made front page headlines in PNG and raised much concern amongst local PNG police who used the information to stage mass rallies in the capital of PNG.
>
> (AidWatch 2006: 6)

Aside from these concerns, the main effect of geopolitical considerations on the aid program is an extremely strong regional focus, with 30 of its 33 current bilateral programs being located in Asia or Oceania.

Poverty reduction

As the 2006 WP exemplifies, the official line taken by AusAID and DFAT more generally has been that trade promotion, especially through economic liberaliza-tion, and the (kind of) economic growth that is assumed to accompany it, is the best way for LDCs to develop. As noted above, there has for just as long been skepticism in the NGO community about those links (e.g. HRCA 1995; Oxfam 2005). Paired with the emerging consensus in the donor community around poverty elimination (and the MDGs), this appears to some extent to be shifting the dialog within AusAID and to a lesser extent, within DFAT more broadly.

Beginning in the early 1990s, AusAID began to give more attention to basic services that would serve poverty-alleviation goals such as health care and rural development with a view to addressing poverty's root causes (OECD 1995: 7). In 1997 this consensus was crystallized in the report, 'One Clear Objective: poverty reduction through sustainable development', released by the Committee to Review the Australian Overseas Aid Program.[11] However, the most recent DAC peer review (2004) expressed concern about AusAID's lack of poverty focus (cited in AidWatch 2006: 6). The general consensus is that the lack of progress can be chalked up to the continuing commitment to development models that focus too narrowly on macroeconomic growth indicators (OECD 2004).

Good governance

The NAP (6) specifically cites the development cooperation program as one where the government seeks to address GG and HR as 'linked' to development, and both the NAP and the 2003 and 2006 White Papers focus on promoting democratic institutions and transparency. Earlier I reviewed the theoretical and practical problems with equating these with a universal and indivisible set of human rights. The specific focus on civil and political rights to the exclusion of economic, social and cultural rights in the Australian setting is reviewed substantially in the HRCA's *The Rights Way to Development*. AusAID, too, did not define GG in the detailed terms that the DfID has until the most recent WP, which made for a great deal of latitude in the application of the term.

The evaluations of AusAID in this area are mixed. While critics point out that good governance can in its narrowest form mean little more than a set of technical regulations aimed at assuring efficiency, and in its broader form suggest that civil and political rights are the most important of human rights, some critics have gone further to say that focus on good governance in AusAID practice has been not just insufficient but actually detrimental to the protection of rights in partner countries. For instance, AidWatch claimed that 'the ECP imposed [in Papua New Guinea] in the name of "good governance" was found to be unconstitutional and seemingly not a "good governance" program at all' (AidWatch 2006: 6). However, the DAC chose to cite this area of AusAID's planning in its most recent (OECD 2004a, cited in AidWatch 2006) peer review.

The DAC did note in an earlier report, however, the Australian government's very specific definition of what good governance means ('management of a country's resources in an equitable and accountable manner') but also the extent to which AusAID focuses on carrots and 'dialogue' rather than on more aggressive or punitive measures (OECD 1996: 42).

General social goals

While these were addressed to some extent above, there has been an improvement in recent years in the focus on women in development (OECD 1996: 25), which began with a policy 'turnaround' in 1989–90 that included more focus on health aid, marked by the presentation of the first ever health-sector strategy and the establishment of an advisory group for international health. Health spending had increased from about 2 to about 5 percent over the first part of the 1990s. It is accorded high profile, along with education, under the 'Investing in People' focus of the most recent White Paper.

Environment

This is a stated goal of the aid program, and was a major component of the 1990s foreign policy statement *Toward a Sustainable Future* as well as of the 1997 report of the Committee of Review. It has been at least a partial influence on some high-profile country-specific decisions as well. For instance in the Solomon Islands, assistance to the forestry sector was withdrawn in 1995 when the government of the Solomons failed to introduce sustainable forestry practices (OECD 1996: 25). Renewable energy funding, however, was at an all-time low by 2005 (AidWatch 2006: 6).

Rights

Observers have criticized aid policy in particular for being bereft of responsiveness to human rights in the recipients. The lower status that rights concerns have enjoyed as a foreign policy goal in Australia, both relative to other donors, and relative to security and commercial goals, has led to a reluctance to condition aid decisions on rights or other domestic policy issues in the recipient (OECD 1996: 11).

> Australia explicitly does not accept that aid to *any* given country should be made conditional on political reforms by recipient governments. A policy of dialogue and practical support for capacity building has been adopted with activities selected so as to reach the most constructive outcome feasible within a given context.
>
> (OECD 1996: 42; emphasis mine)

Aid is explicitly tailored to work within contexts rather than to change them. This approach also clearly excludes political conditionality, even as part of say a poverty-reduction strategy (the only reason it is allowed for the DfID for instance).

However, in some extreme cases, the DFAT and the aid program have responded by withdrawal or withholding of aid. These cases include Burma currently, China after Tiananmen, Fiji after the 1989 coup and South Africa during apartheid (OECD 1996: 42). These cases all share the characteristics of being very high profile, and all but one were in Asia or the Pacific.

In some cases, as well, rights have entered the equation through the back door, as a component of other goals that are given higher profile. For instance, *Toward a Sustainable Future* states that 'Australia believes that environmentally sustainable development must embrace support of universal human rights, including the right of all people to participate in and share the benefits of development' and 'all development cooperation activities should be supportive of fundamental human rights while recognizing there is no single model for the management of a country's social and economic resources' (DFAT 1999: 5).

In 2001 Parliament's Joint Standing Committee on Foreign Affairs, defense and Trade conducted, on Downer's request, an inquiry into 'the link between aid and human rights', as the final report would be titled. Submissions came in from the HRCA, Oxfam and other development NGOs as well as government agencies and individuals. The committee has in fact long been interested in both issues and had actually issued its first report on various focus issues as they related to the aid program as far back as 1973. Unfortunately, the terms of reference for the inquiry were called 'very limited' (Parliament of Australia 2001: 2) by the committee itself, to the point that they felt, after the single public hearing held, that it was inappropriate to make specific recommendations based on the report. The report lays out not only the official government position on a rights-based approach to aid, but also reviews and evaluates current and potential choices of tools for pursuing human rights. The DFAT/AusAID position reflected in the report (which detailed the stances of all seminar participants) was that a rights-based approach to aid was undesirable because human rights meant different things to different people; because such an approach would detract from a focus based on poverty alleviation; because AusAID felt that the obligation of respecting these rights rested with the governments of the countries where those rights were in jeopardy; and because a rights-based approach would limit the forms and delivery of aid (which is in and of itself a very interesting assertion). AusAID also claimed that it saw rights as indivisible, though its sub-mission clearly centered on political and civil rights. While the committee was quick to emphasize what it saw as the substantial common ground between AusAID and participants from civil society, it also noted that AusAID at several points seemed 'dismissive' (Parliament of Australia 2001: 62) of the arguments of the other participants and recommended a formal, ongoing series of discus-sions between AusAID and relevant NGOs.

Tensions

Some tensions have been noted in the foregoing discussion, and these have been consistently reflected in DAC evaluations. In 1992 a DAC report asked

> whether there was an over-emphasis on strategic, short term commercial, and humanitarian aspects at the expense of the importance of sustainable development ... and whether this ... emphasis in turn contributed to the apparently limited degree of public support for the aid effort.
>
> (cited in OECD 1996: 12)

The 1996 review concluded that little real headway had been made. The 1992 review had also noted that the reason for this lack of focus on development was clear: because the 'current official ... approach argues that sustainable and open economic growth in developing countries is essential to development, at the same time allowing Australia's economy to benefit' (OECD 1996: 7). And then the most recent DAC peer review in 2004, reflecting on the 2003 White Paper, cautioned in almost identical language:

> Reference to the national interest requires clarification. Even if, in a long-term perspective, development interests and national interests coincide, in the short term, these interests can diverge and therefore due attention should be given to the long-term development interests of partner countries. AusAID has a key role to play to ensure ... that Australia's national interest does not override that of its partner countries...
>
> (DAC 2004: 24)

Of course these tensions, or the lack thereof, have not escaped the eyes of human rights and aid NGOs, many of whom have been cited above and who decry 'the moral and ethical compromises which were being extended through our aid program such as boomerang aid and good governance before poverty alleviation' (AidWatch 2006: 6).

How Australian aid policy is made today

Parliament

There is mixed evidence about the role of Parliament in aid decisions in Australia. On the one hand, the Australian Parliament shares all the aspects of the Westminster system that limit the scope of Parliamentary action in Canada and Britain.[12] In foreign policy MPs are likely to have a particularly small role for all of the usual reasons that the executive tends to dominate these kinds of issue areas more than others. The Senate has, however, because it is unelected, been quite outspoken on a number of foreign policy issues (such as participation in the Vietnam War and going so far as to censure the government over the war in Iraq). It has also initiated regular investigations into foreign affairs issues. But the main ways that Parliament can hope to have an impact on aid policy specifically is through the work of committees (as demonstrated to some extent by the 'Link between Human Rights and Aid' inquiry. DFAT 'liaises on a regular basis with Parliamentary representatives, particularly with the Parliamentary Group of Amnesty International, and with NGOs and individuals on human rights issues and cases of interest.' (Commonwealth of Australia 2004: 7–8). DFAT also regularly appears before the Human Rights Sub-Committee of the Parliamentary Joint Standing Committee on Foreign Affairs, Defense and Trade. Since 1992, the department has also occasionally reported to the Human Rights Sub-Committee on human rights policy and activities (Commonwealth of Australia 2004: 7–8).

According to the OECD,

> both the public and Parliament show significant levels of interest in the overseas aid program and its underlying rationale ... Parliament, which receives annual ministerial reports on the programme and detailed budget proposals for approval, appears well informed by comparative DAC standards, [and] *recognizes the programme's contribution to Australia's economic and security interests....*
>
> (OECD 1996: 7;emphasis mine)

Australian aid policy is not governed by specific legislation but the DAC sees Parliament's role as being quite large, anyway, by comparative standards (OECD 1996: 11). Parliament does of course have to approve the aid budget and has also received annual reports on the aid program's performance from the minister in charge (OECD 1996: 11).

Civil service

Bureaucratic politics is, as suggested above, a very cohesive (some might even say closed – but more on that later) – affair. There is a clear line to take, mainly that 'good relations with important governments, such as Indonesia's, are so crucial that the maintenance of good will is paramount – even when this means relative silence on the issue of East Timor, for instance' (Smith *et al.* 1996: x). The Prime Minister can, of course, when he wills it, seize control of the depart-mental stance in ways that belie the 'Yes Minister' façade. For instance,

> the departmental line in DFAT in favor of signing the Antarctic Minerals Convention was dramatically overturned by the then-Prime Minister, Bob Hawke, without informing either the department or the Minister, in order to shore up the Environmental vote in the 1990 election.
>
> (Smith *et al.* 1996: x)

Prime Minister

Again, as in any Westminster system, the Prime Minister possesses a great deal of structural and normative power, including his appointment power and his impact on cabinet discussions. Examples of reorganization as part of rationaliza-tion under particular prime ministers has been discussed in some detail above, but none in recent history have made the aid program one of their top priorities.

Outside interests

Australian public opinion on foreign affairs has been accused of being unusually apathetic for reasons of isolation and perceived dependency (Mackie 1975: 69; Millar 1968: xii; Smith *et al.* 1996: ix). However, relative to other donors, the public possesses relatively high levels of awareness of the most sizeable com-ponents of Australia's aid program. Surveys in 1987 and 1994 on what Aus-tralians thought of aid found that three-quarters of people interviewed could identify at least one country that received Australian assistance (of course, with fewer countries in the portfolio, this may not be surprising). Overall approval was very high for aid, mainly based on the idea that aid benefited Australians (OECD 1996: 14). A government-commissioned poll in 1998 found that 85 percent of Australians supported Australia's overseas aid program. And further, fully 50 percent of Australians claimed to have contributed money or time to an overseas aid agency in the past 12 months, a figure that must sound remarkable to American observers. A second wave of the same poll, conducted in 2001, found that attitudes towards ODA were even more positive then than in 1998, and that 51 percent of Australians believe aid should emphasize long-term development. (The issue of human rights, notably, receives little mention.[13]) In addition, the three main reasons Australians believe Australia should have an overseas aid program are: 1) to look after those who are less fortunate, 2) for humanitarian and moral reasons, and 3) because Australia is wealthy and can afford it. If these attitudes are taken into account, need should matter in aid-disbursement decisions.

In a society where so much foreign policy debate has centered around immigration, the impact of immigrant groups or 'ethnic lobbies' is likely to be particularly large. But Australia is a very multiethnic society and immigrant groups have in most cases assimilated quite smoothly.[14] This is particularly important for the larger issue of human rights in foreign policy because so many conflicts that have led to increased immigration have involved substantial abuses of human rights.

For all the trade orientation of Australia's aid program and its foreign policy more generally, the impact of the business community seems to result more from government commitment to commercial interests, than from the existence of a business lobby that is somehow better organized or more powerful than in Britain or Canada. In cases where government has created formal advisory groups to coordinate input from different lobbies, many of the best known of these have been trade-oriented, but again there is little evidence that this springs from a disproportionate amount of power held by the business lobby in Australia *vis-à-vis* other donors. They do however, possess all the usual advantages *vis-à-vis* issue-oriented interest groups and NGOs.

While the 'development lobby' has not enjoyed the pride of place it has in Canadian foreign policy, it has had a say, as demonstrated, for instance, in the dialog that has been initiated by the Joint Committee on Foreign Affairs, Defense and Trade. Many NGOs of course see themselves as watchdogs. Therefore many of them were, for instance, vociferous critics of DIFF.[15] In terms of rights in foreign policy more generally, the 2004 NAP (DFAT 2004: 8) noted that

> [t]he department conducts formal consultations twice a year with representatives of Australian human rights NGOs on issues of current interest. The agenda for these talks is jointly set by the Department and NGO representatives. Subjects discussed include the annual sessions of the Third Committee of the UN General Assembly and the Commission on Human Rights, human rights in specific countries and thematic issues. Whenever possible the Minister for Foreign Affairs attends these consultations.

However, whether these are true consultations or more disseminations of information is contested, as reflected in the committee's report on the 'Link between Human Rights and Aid' already described.

Furthermore, the backdrop of Australia's immigration policies has made for a stormy relationship, historically, between many rights and development NGOs and the government. For example, in 1998, the Australian government threatened Amnesty International with 'serious consequences' should it continue to name or publish information identifying a Somali asylum-seeker whom the government had repeatedly tried to deport to Mogadishu, where he could be tortured or killed. The man himself had agreed to be named. AI representatives claimed that the move 'effectively amount[ed] to censorship. It is completely unacceptable ... [and] not for governments to decide whether reporting the case of someone facing torture or death upon deportation is in that person's interest' (Amnesty International 1998). Given the adversarial relationship that has existed between advocacy groups and the government, it is possible that the NGO efforts might be somewhat discounted by policy-makers, and that human rights activism in Australia around rights issues in recipients would have an accordingly diminished effect (though, since activism works largely by drawing public attention to an issue, rather than by direct appeals to policy-makers, that can continue to be an effective avenue of influence, regardless).

There are other ways that Australian aid patterns have been argued to differ from those of other donors. In her study of Australian aid over six years in the 1980s, Gounder found 'some support for the view that Australian bilateral aid discriminates against the more populous countries in some years'. The regional focus, as well, has been borne out in the aid program in both policy and practice and was institutionalized in the form of the 'Jackson Report', a report issued by the aforementioned National Committee to Review the Australian Overseas Aid Program, which recommended that AIDAB concentrate ODA on regionally proximate recipients.

Implications for hypothesis-testing

While there appear to be fewer gaps between rhetoric and practice in Australia than in the other donor cases, this may be increasing due to the pressure to incorporate HRDGG into aid discussions. The (tentative) institutionalization of human rights within DFAT over time is a hopeful sign – has it had results in practice?

Archival research

OECD describes the main documentary evidence thus.

> For its main partner countries AusAID has developed medium-term country strategies. These ... are developed jointly with the partner countries, after consulting governmental and nongovernmental institutions in Australia. They provide the basis for annual country programmes within the framework of budgetary allocations. But the strategy and annual programmes are useful planning instruments for AusAID and the recipient government and figure prominently in the policy dialogue at all levels between donor and recipient...
>
> (OECD 1996: 7)

So, as with CDPFs in Canada or CSPs/CAPs in Britain, the Development Corporation Strategies (DCSs) and Development Cooperation Papers (DCPs) in Australia are the central documentary evidence of the factors that are weighed in considering specific aid decisions. To the best of my knowledge I am the only researcher to have attempted extensive analysis of past and present internal DCSs and DCPs.

Openness

Openness is enough of an issue in Australian government that it has been a focus of at least two books in recent years (Terriu 2000; Uhr 2005). Gaining access to AusAID's archived policy documents was more arduous than was the case for either CIDA or DfID. One issue is lack of staff, referenced above. In one of the rounds of budgetary cuts the AusAID library was essentially decimated; archives moved offsite and the facility closed to anyone not on staff at AusAID. Person-hours are tight. But the sense of closedness seems to go deeper than that as well, for I was offered few alternatives for pursuing the documents (*vis-à-vis* experiences with CIDA and DfID). Sources at AusAID and in the NGO community suggested that this was due to a combination of ingrained, if subconscious, internal and external defensiveness. Australia's foreign policy has been, as noted, sensitive to criticism and while at the same time AusAID enjoys a lower profile and less autonomy in Canberra than is the case for CIDA or DFID in their respective institutional contexts. That said, once in Canberra, I found AusAID staff universally patient and extremely generous with their time and effort.

Documents available

Australia's aid program is, of course, much smaller than that of the other two donors. I have examined all publicly available DCSs and DCPs that were accessible either electronically or through interlibrary loan, or at AusAID (about 30). In addition I have also viewed a limited number of internal drafts, which I have used on background only.

Content analysis

Table 8.1 describes the limited number of publicly available documents. Development concepts constitute an absolute majority of the references in all cases, followed by good governance and trade, and then rights.

Several of the distinctions made in the examination of the Canadian and British documents cannot be made for the Australian documents because the range is rather more restricted. There is, for instance, no real variation on region, and all documents are from the post-Cold War period.

Only two of the factors examined seem to have an impact on the relative profile of concepts considered in the country strategies. These were whether the recipient was an LLDC and whether it was an oil exporter. LLDCs are more likely to be cited for good governance issues. This could be interpreted as evidence that poorer countries (which are less likely to be key trade partners) are

Table 8.1

	Development (%)	Good governance and democracy (%)	Rights (%)	Economic management (%)	Security (%)	Trade (%)	Colonialism (%)	Emergency assistance (%)	Aid effectiveness (%)
Factors pertaining to donor's decision-making context									
High media attention/HR activism (only Vanuatu in 2000)									
Low imm. pop	79	73	2	1	1	7	1	0	2
High imm. pop	77	9	3	1	3	4	1	1	1
P(T<=t)	0.37	0.34	0.20	0.16	0.18	0.12	0.50	0.21	0.23
Factors pertaining to recipient									
Not LLDC	8	8	2	1	2	5	1	1	1
LLDC	10	13	1	0	2	7	1	1	1
P(T<=t)	0.31	0.03	0.10	0.05	0.49	0.20	0.23	0.45	0.25
Not major importer	77	8	3	1	3	6	1	1	1
Major importer	79	8	2	1	1	5	1	0	2
P(T<=t)	0.36	0.48	0.22	0.16	0.15	0.50	0.41	0.23	0.17
Not oil exporter	81	6	1	1	3	5	1	1	1
Oil exporter	74	12	35	1	1	5	1	0	2
P(T<=t)	0.10	0.07	0.07	0.49	0.13	0.46	0.46	0.20	0.28
Not strategic	79	7	2	1	3	5	1	1	1
Strategic	76	11	2	1	1	6	1	0	1
P(T<=t)	0.27	0.20	0.36	0.31	0.18	0.43	0.41	0.28	0.45
Humanitarian crisis – no variance									
Nuclear = only China									
Large state	79	7	2	1	3	5	1	1	1
Small state	76	11	2	1	1	6	1	0	1
P(T<=t)	0.27	0.20	0.36	0.31	0.18	0.43	0.41	0.28	0.45

held accountable for GG issues more often than more well-off countries. However, it is also quite possible that these countries actually suffer more from GG problems than do more well-off countries. LLDCs are, however, less likely to be encouraged to engage in economic reforms, which suggests the former interpretation may be the correct one.

However, oil exporters are more likely to have both good governance and rights mentioned. This rather undercuts the idea of states 'getting away' with more rights violations when they are important trade partners (expressed in hypotheses 2 and 4).

Aggregate statistical analyses

Overall patterns

Table 8.2 first shows us a sample of the dependent variable, demonstrating the selection of Australian aid recipients in a sample year – the last in the study. It will be noted that this list is both far smaller and more regionally concentrated than is the case for the other two donors, as we would expect.

Table 8.3 (column 1) presents the determinants of which Australian states receive aid in any given year. In terms of recipient characteristics, larger states get more aid as do those in conflict. Both of these observations potentially support a needs-driven or altruistic aid-disbursement approach. While large states could also be getting aid because they represent larger potential markets, states in conflict are generally not going to be fruitful trading partners. Interestingly, more states receive aid when the Australian economy is experiencing slower growth as was the case with Canada. Why this would be is unclear, unless it reflects a desire to reach out to neighbors to stimulate trade. Reflecting Australia's regionalism, closer states are more likely to get aid, as are those with more immigrants in Australia. As expected, rights make no difference.

Table 8.3 (column 2) presents those factors associated with aid levels. Here we see a more complex set of factors come into play – so it appears a closer examination of states occurs once they make it onto the recipient list. First, in terms of characteristics of the recipient, geographically proximate states, fellow members of the Commonwealth, and those experiencing a humanitarian crisis are more likely to get aid, as are those at a trade intersection. At this stage, internal conflict suppresses aid amounts, suggesting a desire not to direct aid where it is unlikely to be used efficiently. Basic poverty makes no difference. But one result is truly surprising given Australia's foreign policy record.

First, states with worse human rights records actually get more aid. This suggests a 'carrot' approach that we would expect, but a rights approach that we might not, given the accusations that have been made about the amorality of Australia's aid program. An alternate and less generous interpretation is that this bears out the fears of critics that Australian aid is serving to prop up violator regimes because of the prioritization of other goals. Second, the volume of Australian trade with a recipient does not affect aid disbursements at either stage.

Table 8.2

Non-recipients, 2004	Recipients, 2004
Albania	Afghanistan
Algeria	Antigua and Barbuda
Angola	Bangladesh
Anguilla	Barbados
Argentina	Bhutan
Armenia	Botswana
Aruba	Brazil
Azerbaijan	Burma
Bahamas	Cambodia
Bahrain	Chad
Belarus	Chile
Belize	China
Benin	Colombia
Bermuda	Cook Islands
Bolivia	Croatia
Bosnia	Cyprus
British Virgin Islands	Dominica
Brunei	Egypt
Bulgaria	Estonia
Burkina Faso	Ethiopia
Burundi	Federated States of Micronesia
Cameroon	Fiji
Cape Verde	Ghana
Cayman Islands	Grenada
Central African Republic	Guatemala
Comoros	Guinea
Congo (Republic of Congo)	Guyana
Costa Rica	Haiti
Cuba	Hong Kong
Czech Republic	Hungary
Democratic Republic of Congo (1998)	India
Djibouti	Indonesia
Dominican Republic	Iran
Ecuador	Iraq
El Salvador	Jamaica
Equatorial Guinea	Jordan
Eritrea	Kenya
Falkland Islands	Kiribati
French Polynesia	Laos
Gabon	Lebanon
Gambia	Lesotho
Georgia	Malawi
Gibraltar	Malaysia
Greece	Maldives
Guinea-Bissau	Marshall Islands
Honduras	Mongolia
Israel	Mozambique
Ivory Coast/Cote D'Ivoire	Namibia
Kazakhstan	Nauru
Kuwait	Nepal
Kyrgyzstan	Nicaragua

Table 8.2 continued

Non-recipients, 2004	Recipients, 2004
Latvia	Niger
Liberia	Nigeria
Libya	Niue
Lithuania	North Korea (Democratic
Macau	Republic of Korea)
Macedonia	Oman
Madagascar	Pakistan
Mali	Palau
Malta	Palestinian Territories
Mauritania	Papua New Guinea
Mauritius	Peru
Mayotte	Philippines
Mexico	Rwanda
Moldova	Samoa (1997)
Montserrat	Senegal
Morocco	Sierra Leone
New Caledonia	Slovenia
Northern Marianas	Solomon Islands
Panama	Somalia
Paraguay	South Africa
Poland	South Korea (Republic of Korea)
Qatar	Sri Lanka
Romania	St Kitts and Nevis
Russia	St Lucia
Sao Tome and Principe	St Vincent and Grenadines
Saudi Arabia	Swaziland
Serbia and Montenegro	Tanzania
Seychelles	Thailand
Singapore	Tokelau
Slovakia	Tonga
St Helena	Trinidad and Tobago
Sudan	Tuvalu
Suriname	Uganda
Syria	Vanuatu
Taiwan	Viet Nam
Tajikistan	Zambia
Timor (East Timor)	Zimbabwe
Togo	
Tunisia	
Turkey	
Turkmenistan	
Turks and Caicos	
Ukraine	
United Arab Emirates	
Uruguay	
US Virgin Islands	
Uzbekistan	
Venezuela	
Wallis and Futuna	
Yemen	

Table 8.3

Variable	Gatekeeping decision coefficient	Allocation decision coefficient
Year	0.22***	−1570.10*
General characteristics of recipient		
Recipient GDP	3.46^{-13}	−1.41-09
Human rights measures		
Human rights violations	0.10	2378.30*
Recipient polity score	0.00	−50.02
Economic value measures		
Australia exports to recipient	-1.75^{-07}	0.01
Australia imports from recipient	6.52^{-07}	−0.00
Recipient oil exports	0.00	−9.02
Recipient GDP growth	−0.00	−154.35
Recipient population	1.94^{-08} (marg)	0.00
Strategic value measures		
Recipient nuclear capabilities	−0.98	−10,306.83
Internal dispute	−0.42	−10,338.45**
External dispute	0.75*	2422.86
Distance from Australia	−0.00***	−2.22***
Post-Cold War	−0.24	4471.08
Trade intersection	−0.76	8419.15*
Need measures		
Humanitarian crisis	0.10	2128.65*
Domestic politics measures		
Human rights activism	−0.19	−565.47
Immigrants from recipient	0.00***	0.06
Australian GDP (marg)	-9.03^{-12}***	5.97^{-08}
Australian GDP growth rate	−0.11*	−130.67
ALP	−0.18	−5353.40
Colonial history measure		
Commonwealth	41.03	190,321.20***
Policy history		
Aid previous year?	0.00***	−0.01
Significance of model		0.00
N	2134	648
R^2		0.02, 0.85, 0.61

Notes
*** = significant at $p < 0.001$; ** = $p < 0.01$; * = $p < 0.05$; (marg) = $p < 0.075$ (one-tailed).

Does trade make a difference to the aid calculus?

As surprising as the non-effect of trade is, perhaps it is the case that trade does not have a direct effect on aid but rather serves as a sorting criterion for potential recipients with the indirect effect of affecting the calculus applied to them. Certainly Australia's position in the world and general foreign policy orientation would lead us to expect so.

At the gatekeeping stage (Table 8.4), the most notable result is that states with higher levels of violations are more likely to receive aid. This result is discussed further below. Larger states are more likely to be granted aid as are those in conflict (for both groups) and those that are close (for both groups), while those that are at a trade intersection are still less likely to receive aid. Taken together this again suggests a mix of self-interest and altruism: helping close states definitely serves Australian interests, and helping larger states may do the same. Helping those in conflict and those that are not located at a trade intersection suggests a willingness to help those that need it the most regardless of locale. Trade actually has an odd effect across the groups. Within the low-importing group, higher importers get less aid. We know that high importers do receive more than low importers – on average about 40 percent more. But low importers are actually less likely to receive aid depending on their import amount. These may be poorer states, but it is still a puzzling result. On the other hand high importers are more likely to receive aid based on how much they export *to* Australia. This demonstrates the importance of trade, certainly, but not the primacy of export promotion that we would expect. It may reflect Australia's geographic isolation and dependence on imports. The presence of an Australian Labour Party (ALP) government in Australia somewhat suppresses the likelihood of getting aid for high importers. So ALP governments are less likely to condition decisions on trade than are others. States that are high importers and have large diasporas in Australia are also more likely to be granted aid – this latter finding suggesting an impact that could be read three ways: shared interest, domestic lobby pressure, or desire to keep more immigration from occurring. While looking at all potential recipients together revealed no impact of rights, when we disaggregate by trade status, we see that in fact rights violations are associated with a lower likelihood of getting aid for those states are key markets for Australia. Is it possible that these states are in fact given more public attention by virtue of their trade relationship, and therefore aid decisions regarding them have to be made with an eye to public disapproval? One would like to think so, but results for the allocation stage challenge this interpretation.

At the allocation stage, we again see several similarities across the two groups. Nearby states get more regardless of their status as an importer. Changes in rights violations again only matter for the top group, but this time violator states benefit from more aid. So rights do interact with trade concerns, and it is the case that important trade partners 'get away with' more than states that are not key trade partners. But rather than unimportant states getting punished for violations, while violations are ignored in more important states, in fact violations get ignored in the economically unimportant states while the trade partners are given inducements presumably to improve their HR performance. Large, poor states get more in the bottom group, as do those at a trade intersection, but neither of these things matters for the top group. Having internal conflict depresses aid for the top group (presumably having a negative effect on trade patterns), while being an oil exporter increases it.

Table 8.4

Variable	Gatekeeping decision		Allocation decision	
	Coefficient low importers	Coefficient high importers	Coefficient low importers	Coefficient high importers
Year	0.23***	0.18 (marg)	−76.72	−2088.63
General characteristics of recipient				
Recipient GDP	2.23^{-11} (marg)	1.36^{-12}	$−1.38^{-07}$**	6.15^{-09}
Human rights measures				
Human rights violations	−0.00	0.42**	606.60	4081.84*
Recipient polity score	−0.01	0.01	−0.19	−45.85
Economic value measures				
Australia exports to recipient	−0.00*	$−3.58^{-07}$	0.17	0.01
Australia imports from recipient	0.00	1.05^{-06}*	−0.00	−0.01
Recipient oil exports	−0.00	−0.00	6.78	31.23**
Recipient GDP growth	−0.01	−0.00	−140.92	−393.43
Recipient population	4.69^{-08}*	5.85^{-09}	0.00***	$−1.33^{-06}$
Strategic value measures				
Recipient nuclear capabilities	−15.59	−0.37	−2050.76	−5916.61
Internal dispute	0.56	−1.22*	−1070.89	−20,457.26**
External dispute	0.73 (marg)	1.16*	1653.13	2017.26
Distance from Australia	−0.00***	−0.00***	−1.49***	−4.39***
Post-Cold War	−0.15	−0.26	−5382.60	11,612.73
Trade intersection	1.52*	−0.13	9747.03*	12,575.36
Need measures				
Humanitarian crisis	0.07	0.11	98.45	1551.26
Domestic politics measures				
Human rights activism	0.22	−0.00	−1270.57	1009.35
Immigrants from recipient	$−1.44^{-06}$	0.00***	−0.02	0.02
Australian GDP	$−8.59^{-12}$**	$−1.05^{-11}$**	3.47^{-08}	6.70^{-08}

Australian GDP growth rate	−0.06	−0.19 (marg)	589.46
ALP	0.66	−1.27 (marg)	−8198.54
Colonial history measure			
Commonwealth	−461.03***	31.38	187,638.70***
Policy history			
Aid previous year?	0.00***	0.00**	−0.07
Significance of model		0.0000	0.0000
N	1337	797	308
R^2		0.06, 0.66, 0.28	0.06, 0.90, 0.64

Notes
*** = significant at $p < 0.001$; ** = $p < 0.01$; * = $p < 0.05$; (marg) = $p < 0.075$ (one-tailed).

Do strategic considerations make a difference to the aid calculus?

At the gatekeeping stage, there are some dramatic differences between the two groups (Table 8.5).

Most markedly, those states that are strategically positioned appear to be judged based almost solely on that fact. Besides their strategic characteristics, the only factors that have a significant association with the likelihood of receiving aid are its distance from the donor and the presence of immigrants within the donor state. Meanwhile, a much more complex set of factors is taken into consideration with the less strategically positioned states, for whom there is far more volatility across time and apparently far more conditionality overall. Large, close states with more immigrants are unsurprisingly more likely to be granted aid, but those at key trade intersections get less, so that we see Australia is not trying to woo states at key intersections. Those involved in external conflict receive more.

At the allocation stage, we see a similar pattern emerge –strategically positioned states appear to be judged essentially on that fact and on few other things save their Commonwealth membership. In contrast the 'low-strategic' states are judged on their nuclear capabilities (nuclear ones get less, but of course as ever the distribution on this variable is very skewed), their status as an oil exporter (oil exporters get less, which may be altruistic as well as demonstrating a consideration of need) and trade (importers of Australian goods get more, while exporters *to* Australia, the NICs, receive less, as well as distance (in the expected direction).

What this shows us is a mixed bag of motives: need comes into play, but so does self-interest. However, it is nowhere near as overtly trade-driven as official policy or outside evaluations would lead us to believe. We must therefore be careful about generalizing too broadly about the single-mindedness of Australian aid motives. While trade matters in some cases, it is matched in importance by regionalism and, one suspects, increasingly by the poverty focus of the rest of the donor community.

Though not all results could be reported here, these analyses were also rerun with the key measure of human rights in the recipient being change in human rights over the past year rather than overall human rights conditions. The results were similar with minor exceptions. The same was true when the 'add' and 'drop' decisions at the gatekeeping stage were analyzed.

So when do rights matter?

So far, we see the impact of rights is indeed mitigated by trade concerns, but not strategic ones. But the complex nature of the way that trade seems to condition the effect of human rights begs us to look further. Once again, the effect of each of the key independent variables on the impact of rights was examined, and the results are presented in Table 8.6.

Here we see that in fact the only thing to condition the effect of human rights is once again the trade relationship with Australia. Again human rights violators are less likely to receive aid, but receive more when they do get it. This confirms the results shown in Table 8.4.

It is probable that this is being driven by the fact that Australia's universe of recipients is rather small, and there are many states with severe human rights violations that fall outside its more limited aid program. However, given that it has strong aid and trade ties with Indonesia, a large country with severe rights violations, it is probable that the Indonesian case is driving these contradictory results. Analyses run without the inclusion of Indonesia did not turn up a significant interaction effect of Australian exports and violations at the allocation phase, but the negative effect at the gatekeeping phase remained. This suggests that personal integrity rights do have some effect on the basic calculus, but clearly this is an important area for further research.

More evidence from the documentary record

As discussed in earlier chapters, in an area as complex as aid, it is very possible that considerations can have important effects that are not easily captured in aggregate analyses, as most analyses of aid tend to be. It would certainly be worthwhile to conduct further analyses that examined individual aid sectors separately, as well as distinguishing direct budget support, from program aid, from project aid. However, perhaps the most direct way of looking at the nuanced ways that a consideration such as human rights can have an effect is by looking at individual decisions themselves.

In the hundreds of thousands of pages of documentary evidence I examined from AusAID, as was the case with the DfID and CIDA, I found no instances in which a bilateral aid program was terminated solely on the basis of human rights violations. As will be seen from a comparison of Table 8.1 in this chapter with Tables 6.1 and 7.1 in the last two, rights as a concept emerges less frequently in Australian Development Cooperation Strategies and Papers. Rights concerns are very rarely mentioned generally speaking (sometimes four or five times in a document of dozens of pages), and the issue is not accorded its own section, nor does it merit inclusion as a target unto itself.

One other aspect of the inclusion of rights in Australian country strategies is worth mentioning here, and that regards the nature of rights. In the strategy papers I examined the overwhelming majority of the references was to rights to land, to property more generally, and to natural resources. There was little consideration of broader human rights or even broader civil and political rights. This minimalist approach is, of course, not surprising given the ambivalent status of rights historically in Australia's foreign policy approach and what some might call the individualist nature of its cultural orientation (a way in which it is often said to be similar to the United States).

Notably in some cases where both other countries' discussions take rights

Table 8.5

Variable	Gatekeeping decision		Allocation decision	
	Coefficient low strategic	Coefficient high strategic	Coefficient low strategic	Coefficient high strategic
Year	0.23***	0.21	1583.34	−347.57
General characteristics of recipient				
Recipient GDP	-9.13^{-14}	-4.46^{-12}	-2.38^{-08}	6.01^{-08}
Human rights measures				
Human rights violations	0.10	−0.02	4545.31	3291.75
Recipient polity score	0.00	−0.01	117.05	−118.70
Economic value measures				
Australia exports to recipient	-1.69^{-07}	-2.67^{-08}	0.08**	−0.01
Australia imports from recipient	6.63^{-07}	1.99^{-06}	−0.10**	0.02
Recipient oil exports	0.00	−0.00	−33.45**	−11.35
Recipient GDP growth	−0.00	−0.00	190.73	−381.59
Recipient population	2.31^{-08}*	1.59^{-08}	8.09^{-06}	−0.00
Strategic value measures				
Recipient nuclear capabilities	−1.46	−0.85	−43,799.33***	−7235.96
Internal dispute	−0.72 (marg)	1.02		−979.63
External dispute	0.79**	0.77	−4161.59	8206.87
Distance from Australia	−0.00***	−0.00***	−7.51	−2.57
Post-Cold War	−0.36	−0.12	−14,634.09***	5425.88
Trade intersection	−1.14*	Dropped		
Need measures				
Humanitarian crisis	0.10	0.24	2492.12	−362.21
Domestic politics measures				
Human rights activism	−0.21	20.71		−1859.03
Immigrants from recipient	0.00*	0.00***	0.06	−0.10
Australian GDP	-9.81^{-12}***	-8.06^{-12}	6.33^{-08}	7.64^{-08}

Australian GDP growth rate	-0.12*	0.02	94.44	1749.98
ALP	-0.19	-0.48	10,077.51	
Colonial history measure				
Commonwealth	42.08***	23.81		48,620.17*
Policy history				
Aid previous year?	0.00***	0.00 (marg)	-0.30	0.71***
Significance of model	0.0000	0.0000	0.0000	0.0000
N	2046	307	50	89
R²			0.34, 0.90, 0.88	0.46, 0.91, 0.74

Notes

*** = significant at $p < 0.001$; ** = $p < 0.01$; * = $p < 0.05$; (marg) = $p < 0.075$ (one-tailed).

Table 8.6

Variable	Gatekeeping	Allocation
Year	0.23***	0.21
Year*HR	0.19	0.27
General characteristics of recipient		
Recipient GDP	-10.02^{-14}	-4.46^{-12}
Recipient GDP*HR	-9.13^{-14}	-4.63^{-12}
Human rights measures		
Human rights	0.10	-0.02
Recipient polity score	0.12	-0.01
Recipient polity score*HR	0.00	-0.23
Economic value measures		
Australia exports to recipient	-1.69^{-07}	-2.67^{-08}
Australia exports*HR	-2.02^{-07}*	3.23^{-08}*
Australia imports from recipient	6.63^{-07}	1.99^{-06}
Australia imports*HR	7.72^{-07}	2.06^{-06}
Recipient oil exports	0.00	-0.00
Oil exports*HR	0.00	-0.00
Recipient GDP growth	-0.00	-0.00
Recipient GDP growth*HR	-0.00	-0.00
Recipient population	2.31^{-08}*	1.59^{-08}
Recipient population*HR	3.23^{-08}	2.33^{-08}
Strategic value measures		
Recipient nuclear capabilities	-1.46	-0.85
Recipient nuclear capabilities*HR	-3.24	-0.87
Internal dispute	-0.72 (marg)	1.02
Internal dispute*HR	-1.02	1.04
External dispute	0.79**	0.77
External dispute*HR	0.62	0.54
Distance from Australia	-0.00***	-0.00***
Distance from Australia*HR	-0.23	-0.00
Post-Cold War	-0.36	-0.12
Post-Cold War*HR	-0.44	-0.32
Trade intersection	-1.14*	**Dropped**
Trade intersection*HR	-2.00	-9.93
Need measures		
Humanitarian crisis	0.10	0.24
Humanitarian crisis*HR	0.12	0.32
Domestic politics measures		
Human rights activism	-0.21	20.71
Human rights activism*HR	-0.33	34.02
Immigrants from recipient	0.00*	0.00***
Immigrants from recipient*HR	0.00	0.00
Australian GDP	-9.81^{-12}***	-8.06^{-12}
Australian GDP*HR	-11.38	-9.32
Australian GDP growth rate	-0.12*	0.02
Australian GDP growth rate*HR	-0.14	0.00
ALP	-0.19	-0.48
ALP*HR	-0.17	-1.33
Colonial history measure		
Commonwealth	42.08***	23.81
Commonwealth*HR	36.05	50.21

Table 8.6 continued

Variable	Gatekeeping	Allocation
Policy history		
Aid previous year? (marg)	0.00***	0.00
Significance of model	0.0000	0.0000
N	2046	307
R^2		

Notes
*** = significant at $p < 0.001$; ** = $p < 0.01$; * – $p < 0.05$; (marg) = $p < 0.075$ (one-tailed).

heavily into account, Australia's does not do so. For instance, I compared the strategy papers closest to 1996 from all three donors for a large Asian country which is generally recognized to have substantial human rights problems.[16] The Canadian document made no fewer than 20 references to rights; the British document, though only about half the length of the Canadian, made 15. The Australian DCP made – none. It may be relevant to the key hypotheses of this study to note that the recipient in question is a particularly important trade partner for Australia.

Conclusion

Australian aid policy faces a much different set of constraints than is the case for either of the other two donors. This may account for the desire to use carrots rather than sticks, and to remain focused on priorities and partners that are clearly and traditionally important. This sets Australia apart from the wide disbursement of the DfID and the somewhat incoherent patterns of concentration by CIDA. Much of the rhetorical focus is borne out in the analysis above: the regional concentration and the importance of trade and strategic variables. But there is also a surprising omission – need – and a surprising factor present – the impact of respect for personal integrity rights. Given the small size of Australia's aid program, we must treat these results with caution, but they clearly suggest that, while there are some consistent aims of Australia's very coherent approach to foreign policy, the process and the results are more complex than they first appear.

9 Context and consideration
Three other donor states

The three donors thus far considered differ in some important ways but share some obvious similarities in their aid programs. All are members of the Commonwealth and products of a shared colonial history; they share a common head of state; and they are all English-speaking. Additionally, while being cautious about invoking the word 'culture', they can arguably be assumed to share some basic understandings about the way international relations work, the proper role of aid, and the meaning of 'human rights'. Is it possible that these similarities are driving some of the tendencies seen thus far? How generalizeable are these findings?

In order to shed some light on this question, this chapter briefly considers some trends in human rights considerations in foreign aid in three other donors. While not providing a comprehensive test of the central hypotheses of this study, this gives us at least a sense of whether or not similar kinds of goals take precedence in other donor states. They include donors smaller and larger than the three we have just examined, ones that are more or less generous, and ones from very different historical backgrounds and geographic regions.

Norway

Norway is widely recognized as being a leader in aid policy. It is both the most generous in many years (in terms of its GNI (0.87 and 0.94 in 2004 and 2005, respectively) and also – as one of the 'like-minded countries' – one of the more willing to support structural changes in the international system that are in line with LDC priorities, such as those that were advocated in the 1970s under the New International Economic Order (NIEO) rubric. While being a small state can certainly constrain some policy choices, it also allows Norway to be 'choosier' in who benefits from its aid. Norway does not have large-scale trade or investment with or in the developing world and no real colonial ties. It has therefore always focused on economic and social rights and targeted its aid at the poorest in the poorest countries.

Human rights in Norway's foreign policy

Norway's status as one of the 'like-minded states' has meant that it has been more likely than some other donors to approach aid from what some observers (most notably Stokke 1989, 2005) have liked to call 'humane internationalism', which they distinguish from 'realist internationalism' or even 'liberal internationalism' though the latter phrase came into play increasingly in the recessive economic environment of the 1980s. Stokke, Egeland and others have traced a particular commitment to the strong welfare policies and clear statism of Norwegian domestic policy, as well as to the orientation of its domestic political parties and the strength of the church in Norway.

Definitions of human rights

These factors have, for one thing, had an impact on the kinds of rights that have been prioritized in Norwegian foreign policy as well. While other Western donor countries like the US and to a lesser extent the UK, Australia and Canada, have tended to allow rights definitions to reduce to the civil and political, or more narrowly to 'good governance' and its attendant political structures, Norwegian aid has had a clear focus, certainly in its relationships with the developing world, on economic, social and cultural rights over civil and political ones.

This orientation has been borne out in foreign policy generally but in aid more than most other tools. In addition, aid is seen as more important in the range of tools in Norway than in some other states. More on this follows below.

Pursuit of human rights

Norway's very constitution is marked by its struggle for national independence (Egeland 1988) and as such has a clear orientation toward civil and political rights as well as self-determination. Norway, like many small states, has sought to pursue rights largely in the context of peace and multilateralism, working with the UN as closely as possible to pursue multilateral approaches to rights, trade regimes and global stability. During the Cold War this also seemed a safe middle position to take between the US and Soviet stances. Its strong support was both signaled by and represented in the election of Foreign Minister Trygvie Lie as the first UN Secretary General. While Norwegian policy-makers were optimistic after the war about the UN's potential to make peace and serve as a global mediator, and in fact saw this as largely a reflection of their own self-image and perceived place in the world, the Cold War would quickly prove that it was very difficult, and in fact sometimes dangerous, to attempt to stake out a middle ground. Therefore it was not until the late Cold War era and more markedly the post-Cold War era, that domestic impulses toward human rights advocacy could be more fully expressed. In the 1970s and 1980s, for instance, these included the following: strong support for the NEIO as a solution to economic and social problems in the developing world and to global poverty more generally, willingness to condition aid decisions on local socioeconomic policies, giving more in foreign aid and to the UN than any other nation in relative terms (in support of the aforementioned goals), supporting all possible international human rights mechanisms, and making public statements in international forums and bilateral settings condemning extreme cases of abuse (Egeland 1988).

A brief overview of Norwegian aid

The main impulses behind Norwegian aid at the inception of the program included most prominently

1   a natural extension of domestic social-welfare policies;
2   the view that this was an area where Norway could be a leader, commensurate with its orientation toward and interest in international peace; and
3   the general left-leaning orientation of politics in the country. In fact the aid programme stems from the immediate postwar era, when the Social Democrats (Labour) were in office. In part as a balance to the controversial step of joining NATO, Labour felt the need to support aid efforts and the aid program attracted early and enthusiastic support from many components of society (Stokke 1989b).

However, Norway's party structure includes a mix whereby all main parties have an ideological orientation that is likely to support aid. The main opposition to Labour are the Christian People's Party and the Centre Party, both of which have been strongly supportive of welfare-state policies at home and abroad. This has led to important White Papers dealing with rights and aid to be issued under both parties. One of the most important of these was White Paper 36 in 1986 which codified many of these impulses into official policy stances. Among other things it allowed for the suspension or cessation of aid for rights violators and the explicit consideration of ILO standards specifically when making determinations of who was and was not a violator. Again here is a specific instance where promoting economic/social rights abroad was seen as supporting Norway's commercial interests as well.

As with the donor states encountered earlier, responsibility for aid has shifted rather frequently in terms of the independence of the aid agency, now called NORAD (Norwegian Agency for Development Cooperation), and which parts of aid policy it controls. NORAD first became an independent directorate of the Ministry of Foreign Affairs (MFA) in 1968, and was given responsibility for bilateral but not multilateral aid. The MFA would actually consolidate its power over other aspects of development over time, while keeping many of these new responsibilities out of NORAD. From 1976 on this even included the overall planning function for bilateral aid. In February 2004, NORAD was reorganized and further absorbed into the MFA. As of the most recent DAC peer review in 2004 (OECD 2004b), the effect of this change on the shape and priorities of aid policy was unclear.

What has been the role of other domestic actors, outside of government? Public opinion on Norwegian aid has traditionally been strongly supportive. As of the most recent DAC report cited above, it continued to be; the public are aware that Norway is a leader in its field. Development and rights NGOs in Norway have a more powerful voice than is the case in the other donors considered thus far (in fact the DAC considers the large amount of aid disbursed through NGOs – 22 percent in 2004 – to be a unique feature of NORAD's disbursement practice). In fact, Egeland identifies the 'ad hoc' rights lobby, consisting of a mix of socialist and Christian organizations, 'the most effective' of all the foreign aid lobbies (Egeland 1988: 114). Reflecting this, White Paper 38 also pledged to work directly with domestic and recipient country NGOs as much as possible because it recognized their effectiveness in getting to some of the areas hardest hit by political strife, open conflict or endemic underdevelopment. The business lobby has had a relatively weaker position. However, as Norway's open economy and small size make for a traditionally commercial orientation, the impact of the business lobby cannot be discounted completely.

The play of priorities in Norway's aid program

Traditionally Norway's aid has been driven by what was seen as a mutually reinforcing mix of commitments: to peace, to a stable international environment for trade, to development, and to the economic/social/cultural rights abroad of the kind supported in its own welfare state. This has largely continued, bolstered by Norway's status as an incredibly important aid-giver.

In the field of rights, Norway has actually endorsed – formally – and in fact gone on to put into practice, a rights-based approach to aid of the sort advocated by the 'Rights Way to Development' referenced in the Australian chapter. DAC has commended NORAD on this, but says that this has led to at least one negative externality along with the positives. This is the wide disbursement of Norwegian aid, which in 2004 spanned 120 countries. Aid has become even more dispersed in recent years, with smaller and smaller proportions of aid going to the partner countries that Norway has identified as its prime areas of interest.

One additional aspect of the commitment to a rights-based approach is that Norway has become a leader in provision of humanitarian assistance. Disbursements clearly demonstrate this, but the DAC cautions that invariably humanitarian interventions take place in settings where data-gathering is difficult and therefore assessment of effects – which more and more aid agencies want to be able to do effectively – is quite hard. The DAC peer review cautioned that as the public has increasingly become interested in the specific 'return' on their aid investment, this kind of information will become increasingly important.

Japan

Japan's foreign policy – including on human rights and foreign assistance – has been marked indelibly by its experiences in World War II. It was thus an aid recipient until 1989 but quickly transitioned into being in fact the single largest donor by 1991. It continues to be an incredibly important donor, second only to the United States in absolute volume. However, Japan's aid program has also been one of the most roundly criticized on several quite different grounds.

Human rights in Japan's foreign policy

Definitions of human rights

Definitions of rights have been difficult to find in Japanese foreign policy statements historically. Observers have speculated that due to its own human rights abuses against Koreans and Chinese (among others) during the course of World War II, Japan has been loathe to take a strong stance vis-à-vis human rights abuses in other nations lest it draw accusations of hypocrisy.

Pursuit of human rights

The new PM, Abe, has taken the potentially significant step of establishing a human rights desk for the first time within the Foreign Ministry, but this has been criticized by HR watchdog groups such as HRW for its near-exclusive focus on the abduction of Japanese citizens by North Korea.

This desk is the only dedicated human rights organization in the Japanese foreign policy structure, though Japan does take into account severe HR violations in decisions about the application of specific foreign policy tools, such as ODA. It generally believes that HR violations in partner states are best dealt with using 'quiet and continuous demarches' (HRW 2007 hrw.org/ english/docs/2007/01/08/japan15098.htm) along the lines of the Australian model.

A brief overview of Japanese aid

Japan's ODA administration has attracted a great deal of attention from the policy and scholarly communities, because it is unique in so many ways. The first of these has already been mentioned: Japan's rapid turnaround from recipient to not only donor but incredibly important donor. Its emergence in the donor community coincided with a period of global recession that caused many other donors, such as Canada, to make severe cuts in their aid budgets, allowing Japan to quickly become a dominant donor force in many developing countries. Japan, however, has made its own cuts in recent years in response to its own recent recessionary woes, and looks unlikely to regain the top spot any time soon. In addition, Japan's ODA as a proportion of GNI is one of the lowest in the DAC (0.19 and 0.28 in 2004 and 2005, respectively), and its proportion of loans to grants the highest in the DAC.

Legislation governing Japanese aid goes back only to 1992, when its Overseas Development Act was passed. It set up a relatively weak role for the Diet and a structure of aid policy-making and implementation that is widely considered to be uniquely complex among donors. Policy-making in fact is vested in four different ministries (the Ministry of Finance, the Ministry of Foreign Affairs, the Ministry of International Trade and Industry, and then the relevant 'line ministry' for a given project (Foerster 1995), and implementation is vested in another two. For most of the 1990s these were the Overseas Economic Cooperation Fund (OECF) and the Japanese International Cooperation Agency (JICA); after reorganizations in 1999 and 2003 they are the JICA and the Japanese International Bank for Cooperation (JIBC), which merged the OECF and the Japanese Import–Export Bank. To make matters even more interesting these two implementing agencies do not report to the same ministries. The OECF for instance was formally housed under yet another ministry, the Economic Planning Agency or EPA. This has led, predictably, to a lack of coherence and 'vision' behind the Japanese ODA program, to which I return in a moment.

As might be guessed from the disbursement of much Japanese aid through 'banks', ODA from Japan is also much higher in its loan element than any other DAC donor – 55 percent in 2002 according to the most recent DAC peer review in 2003 (OECD 2003). In addition, the terms of its loans are less generous than those of many other donors and, with the increasingly high profile of debt relief efforts since 2005 and the takeoff of the HIPC initiative, this component of the Japanese aid program is likely to come under even further scrutiny.

Another unique feature of the Japanese aid program has been its ostensible 'request basis', which refers to the fact that all new projects are supposed to originate with a proposal and formal request from the recipient country. While this may seem to put the reins of development clearly in the hands of recipient-country decision-makers and therefore assure a more efficient and appropriate use of aid, in fact the proposal process has largely been driven by members of the Japanese business community in-country. This can be beneficial for the recipient because these Japanese nationals are likely to be able to help recipients craft proposals in a manner that is likely to get funded, but it also means that these members of the business community can often have a substantial impact on the form of the project, and can make sure that it will benefit them as well. There have been some high-profile examples of projects that were written in such a way that *only* a particular Japanese firm would be able to fulfill it – this was the case with a particular Thai university that wrote a proposal for printers that could only be filled by a single Japanese company, NEC. ODA policy requires that the principal consultant on any Japanese aid project be a Japanese national (Ensign 1992).

So among domestic constituencies that have an interest in and an impact on ODA, the business community plays a role in the Japanese process that is uniquely privileged among current DAC donor policy. This relationship is further strengthened by the high degree of overlap in personnel between the business community and the highest levels of government. The very strong propensity of high-ranking officials to take on a second career (driven in part by early retirement ages) in business has even been given a poetic term, *amakudari*, that literally means 'descended from heaven' (Foerster 1995). However, this has strong potential to create vested interests among government officials in supporting the business community generally and sometimes certain firms in particular, if they anticipate a likely and lucrative position awaiting them there. The conflict of interest arising from these arrangements was deemed to be great enough and frequent enough that recently regulations were put in place prohibiting retired senior government officials from taking another job until two years after their retirement.

In terms of the role of other domestic interests, the NGO community has traditionally been relatively weak and often either been cast or cast itself in an adversarial position vis-à-vis the aid ministries, in part because, some have argued, they tend to promote humanitarian and poverty-alleviation goals that are out of keeping with the traditional aims of Japanese foreign aid (Foerster 1995). Public opinion on foreign aid seems to be increasingly skeptical (OECD 2003) and most Japanese have misconceptions about the amount of aid given. They increasingly want to know what exactly they are getting for the large amounts of aid disbursed.

The play of priorities in Japan's aid program

The 1992 ODA Charter was revised in 2003 and defines the goal of Japanese ODA as 'to contribute to the peace and development of the international community, and thereby to help ensure Japan's own security and prosperity'.

There are two sets of claims that are traditionally made about Japan's foreign aid program that are pretty clearly at odds with each other:

a   that there *is* no real focus or philosophical impulse behind Japan's ODA, owing to the institutional lines upon which aid policy-making is fractured and perhaps to the youth of the program; and
b   that Japanese aid serves almost entirely to further its commercial agenda, with the exception of cases of extreme humanitarian need.

To these two claims we can add another, that Japan actually uses its aid to pursue the interests and preferences of the US instead. This tendency, known as *gaiatsu*, implies that the US has brought its economic and military might to bear in order to pressure Japan to employ its large aid program to also pursue US security interests and its global economic aims. Observers have argued that there are three primary ways Japan might do this: support for regimes that were seen as bulwarks against communism during the Cold War; support for allies in the current war on terror (or reprisals against state sponsors of terror); and support for market reforms in formerly protectionist economies (Katada 1997; Miyashita 1999; Tuman *et al.* 2006). Recent evidence suggests, however, that the impact of neither *gaiatsu* nor trade is statistically significant in the aggregate, and that in fact the frequent accusations about Japan's commercially oriented ODA are based on official policy rhetoric and a few high-profile cases, rather than a pervasive tendency in all ODA disbursements (Tuman *et al.* 2006).

A clearer strategic orientation can be seen in the regional focus of the ODA program, with between 60 and 70 percent of aid going to Asian nations in most years (aid officials generally practice a 70–10–10–10 rule of thumb, with the 10s being Latin America, Africa and the Middle East.

Development on its own terms has had a rather low profile, even though Japan's aid has traditionally gone to the poorest of poor countries. The most recent DAC peer review urged Japan to clarify its policies on aid to the poorest.

Human rights considerations have entered the game rather late, and Japan has been roundly criticized by human rights watchdogs for, among other things, its ongoing relations with some of the world's worst rights abusers such as Burma, with whom nearly every other DAC donor has disengaged. Critics also cite its failure to take advantage of its powerful position as the most important aid donor for many states (such as China and India) to press for human rights improvement. In fact Japan has clearly shied away from doing this, lauding Clinton's delinking of human rights from MFN for China, and only expressing concern to India about its nuclear program, while maintaining a deafening silence about human rights abuses being perpetrated in Kashmir (HRW 1995). However, recent evidence suggests that at least the language of HR is starting to enter the foreign policy debate – the establishment of an HR desk (albeit with an extremely narrow mandate) was noted above, and a 2006 study found the civil, political and personal integrity rights in recipient states to be a significant predictor of ODA amounts (Tuman *et al.* 2006). Some speculate that this might be due to a reorientation of aid made necessary by Japan's recent recession (i.e. Tuman *et al.* 2006), though other donors have often placed *more* emphasis on commercial gains through aid during periods of recession. It's more likely that the emerging focus in the donor community on HRDGG has led this focus.

United States

The United States is an outlier in many ways – including the role of human rights in its foreign policy and its approach to development assistance. Indeed, many aspects of both reflect a self-awareness of this exceptional status, and observers have commented that this leads to an inconsistency between the standards it applies to itself and others (e.g. Mertus 2004). A wealth of rich descriptive and analytic work exists on both topics.

Human rights in United States foreign policy

Since independence the United States has essentially seen itself as a leader in the rights and freedoms of the individual. However, due to an erstwhile but persistent strain of isolationism in its foreign policy, it has been inconsistent in its willingness to apply these standards to others via this foreign policy.

Definitions of human rights

The US Constitution presents a relatively accurate portrayal of the kind of rights and liberties that are privileged in US foreign policy (Donnelly 2004; Forsythe 1987: 204; Mertus 2004). For those who see all rights as indivisible and mutually necessary, this privileging of civil and political rights over economic, social and cultural rights is highly problematic. Civil and political rights of course also tend to be individually rather than collectively based, which is consonant with an American ethos of 'rugged individualism' that valorizes self-made men on the model of Horatio Alger. These kinds of rights are also commensurate with liberal rather than social democracy, as they require merely that the government refrain from repressing. They oblige the government to do little to promote economic welfare or equality beyond basic equality before the law. While other views of rights have been asserted by individual members of government and by the NGO community, US legislation dealing with either domestic or foreign affairs is generally oriented in a strictly political and civil way (as exemplified in much of the legislation below).

Pursuit of human rights

While rights goals have been present in the guise of support for self-determination and freedom from outside interference through most periods of US foreign policy history, the inclusion of human rights norms as a policy goal is usually dated to the Carter administration. This is not to say however that it was only Carter that was responsible for this, as Congress played a more important role in getting HR on the policy agenda in the first place than is often realized (see e.g. Forsythe 1987; Mertus 2004). The US Congress, since it is elected separately from the chief executive, has greater freedom of action than its counterparts in most Parliamentary systems and the US system often divides government between the two major parties, creating what has famously been called 'an invitation to struggle' (Crabb 1992). While Carter did form the Bureau of Human Rights within the State Department, thus taking the crucial step of providing an institutional home for the issue within the executive branch bureaucracy, this followed rather than led important actions on the part of Congress in the 1970s, in part emboldened by an executive that was substantially weakened after the scandals and foreign policy defeats of the early 1970s. Many of the most important issues where Congress stood up to the president were over human rights, and HR arguments were invoked when Congress opposed the president over VN war funding, passed the War Powers Act, censured Turkey over its involvement with Cyprus, and forbade CIA activities in Angola (Forsythe 1987).

Reagan came into office determined to re-center US foreign policy on strategic interests, but ended up justifying much of his renewed vision of containment in human rights terms (Forsythe 2004; Mertus 2004), a testimony to the stickiness of the issue in the hearts, minds, and bureaucratic structures of US foreign policy-makers. This gained further traction as US support to many repressive regimes in Latin America began to be revealed.

Bush I and Clinton after him were quick to try to link post-Cold War pushes for trade liberalization with other kinds of freedoms, though it became clear that both would in important cases choose the former over the latter. China was a telling test case for both administrations; Bush I granted China MFN status the year following the brutal crushing of the students' movement in Tiananmen Square, and in the next round of MFN negotiations Clinton would explicitly delink MFN status from human rights considerations.

Bush II's 'war' on terror has, too, largely been fought in the name of human rights in Afghanistan and related democratic norms and institutions in Iraq, but the fact that such things existed long before the war on terror and were not acted on until after 9/11 leads many to be suspicious of this rationale, while prisoner abuses abroad and certain elements of domestic security legislation at home have spawned accusations that the Bush regime is becoming one of the world's worst human rights abusers itself.

In terms of the policy tools that have been marshaled in the name of human rights, the record is strong, but it does not hold up so well when we look to actual policy outcomes. US legislation in the form of the Harkin Amendment to the International Development Act prohibits ODA except emergency assistance to the worst HR abusing regimes, but the record on whether this is implemented in practice is mixed, as will be seen below. Militarily, even before the war on terror, there was a mixed record in terms of the use of force for human rights or even simply humanitarian intervention. Certainly military action has never been taken *solely* for such reasons, and in fact even in cases where there were legitimate HR concerns, recent administrations have been careful never to couch intervention rationale solely in HR terms, lest a dangerous precedent be set (Mertus 2004). The US has even been cautious about committing troops to multilateral endeavours in the name of human rights, as the slow responses in Rwanda, Somalia and Darfur bear out.

A brief overview of United States aid

The US has the peculiar distinction of being both the largest donor in absolute terms by virtue of the size of its economy, and consistently one of the smallest in the proportion of its GNI that it gives in aid, in 2004 giving only 0.17 GNI in ODA (this improved slightly to 0.22 in 2005). Its aid is highly bilateral, with 82 percent of aid being given through bilateral measures in 2005.

The US aid system is similar to the Japanese in other ways as well in that it is highly fragmented. While USAID is the main foreign assistance agency, there are also foreign aid programs within the Department of State, the Department of the Treasury, the Department of Agriculture, the Peace Corps, the new Millennium challenge corporation, the InterAmerican Foundation, the African Development Corporation and the White House. This fragmentation might create greater buy-in but it can also lead to lack of coordination, turf wars and vehement differences of opinion, as these organizations have different goals and measure success by different standards.

The influence of Congress on specific allocations is perhaps greater than that of any other donor's legislature, owing to its independence (Lancaster and Van Dusen 2006). The effects of this in its impact on the role of human rights on the foreign policy agenda was noted above, and in aid policy there exist many possibilities for impacting both the general priorities of aid, and aid amounts to particular countries, including earmarks, directives, the requirement of notifications if an agency wants to use money in a way not originally proposed.

The role of Congress and members' potential independence in their voting choices enhances the potential impact that organized interests or members of the public generally can have on aid decisions. While business interests can have an impact, there has been little evidence to suggest this is substantially out of line with other donor countries. Nor is the development lobby particularly strong. Of organized interests, the most high profile in aid decisions, and the ones whose role is most hotly debated, is that of country-specific interest groups, largely made up of immigrants, coethnics or sympathizers with recipient countries. This impact, as in other donors, is particularly likely to be strong when these groups are well organized. It has been argued that the Cuban-American population in Florida, for instance, influences US (non)policy toward Cuba. Probably the most famous interest group in this debate is AIPAC, the American-Israel Public Affairs Committee, which some have argued to be instrumental in keeping Congressional support high for aid to Israel. However, Organski (1990) has rather convincingly refuted this claim.

The general public tend to be less supportive of foreign aid in the US than in other donors, and regularly overestimate the amount of money that goes to foreign aid. This is the product of at least three things. First, the American public are more disposed to isolationism than is the extent in many other donors. Second, they tend to have lower levels of knowledge about international affairs than is the case for their counterparts in other donors. Third, they lack a social-democratic tradition that the publics in most other donor countries share.

The play of priorities in the United States' aid program

The US aid program suffers from some of the same sorts of ironies that the US approach to HR does: the US sees itself as a leader and a do-gooder in the world, but often policies do not bear this out. Former USAID officials suggest that while there is always a mix of motives, strategic political ones, in part due to the US's superpower status, have predominated.

Fortunately there has been a wealth of sound empirical studies weighing the relative roles of different recipient characteristics as they are actually borne out. Among those that bear directly on this discussion are Cingranelli and Pasquarello (1985), Poe (1992), who examines the Carter and Reagan presidencies and Apodaca and Stohl (1999), who look at all presidencies from Carter through Clinton.

Cingranelli and Pasquarello's study was one of the first to examine this general question and sparked a host of research attempting to verify or refute its authors' claims.

Most of these proved that strategic interests matter, but that is not always the case. Cingranelli and Pasquarello found that these actually do not signify in determining a state's likelihood of receiving economic aid. But taking US military presence in a country as a proxy for strategic interest, both the Poe and Apodaca and Stohl studies found that strategic interest does not affect whether aid is given, but does affect the amount of aid.

Cingranelli and Pasquarello revealed that indeed states enjoying high levels of trade with the US were more likely to receive aid. Apodaca and Stohl also constructed an 'economic interest measure' that is a bit different from the one in the present study and showed that this affected the gatekeeping decision only under the Clinton administration, and then not in the direction predicted. In Poe's study, under both administrations states that have more trade with the US are more likely to receive aid (the variable is not included for the allocation phase).

Cingranelli and Pasquarello also showed that needier states were more likely to receive aid. In terms of developmental goals, both Poe and Apodaca and Stohl also found that in fact states with higher need are less likely to get aid, likely to get *less* aid, and that need does not matter at the allocation stage, suggesting that either developmental issues do not matter, states that are less needy are more likely to be strategically important (if the 'strategy first' arguments are correct), or that (more optimistically) aid is given to less needy states as they are the ones more likely to be able to absorb the aid. Poe's study indicated that under both administrations needy states are less likely to get aid, and under Reagan they are likely to get lower amounts on average as well.

Finally, in terms of human rights (measured with the PTS scale, as does this study), Poe saw no impact at the gatekeeping phase for either the Carter or Reagan administrations. However, he did discover that violators get less at the allocation phase under both administrations. Applying the same measure, Apodaca and Stohl (1999) found that, under Carter, Reagan and Bush, states with worse human rights records were less likely to get economic assistance but, when they did so, received more. Note that this is even the case for Reagan who claimed that human rights considerations would no longer have a role in foreign policy because they distracted the US from its more appropriate foreign policy goals. They attribute this to pressure from the Democratic Congress as well as to heightened sensitization in interest groups and the public regarding human rights abuses due to the increasing regularity and professionalization of the State Department's human rights reports.

US policy-makers have been more likely than those in many other donor states to recognize that the various aims of aid often conflict, and that, where the emphasis has been put when they do has varied with the presidential administration and the relative power and ideological position of Congress. The Bush administration, while taking positive steps toward development with the

Millennium Challenge Fund (MCF),[1] has made it very clear that aid is primarily a means to an end – presumably, of securing prosperity, free markets and the other freedoms that are presumed to come with them.

Considering these other donor states suggests that they share some important similarities with the three donors considered in previous chapters. They all exhibit a mix of motives in pursuing aid. National self-image and a perceived role in the international system is important in shaping aid approaches. If Britain's aid program has its roots in colonial obligation, America's has its roots in post-World War II superpower obligations, as the industrialized country least affected by the ravages of war and the one most clearly conscious of its role as preserver of peace and a particular conception of freedom. In Japan, a self-image that has been built in the postwar era almost entirely around economic might and regaining international prestige has driven an aid program that, while very young, is both very large and very much influenced in form and content by the *shosha* or business network. Norway's interest in peace and stability as a small country with a very open economy has led it to be both generous and multilateralist in its aid tendencies.

These cases also provide some variation on the key intervening variables that mitigate between recipient HR violations and donor response to them. For instance, the US's presidential system affords through Congress an avenue for goals like human rights to make it onto the foreign policy agenda even when the chief executive does not favor them. Congress also furnishes an avenue for interest groups and other 'interested publics' to shape the system in very meaningful ways because American politics increasingly rewards elected officials for responding to constituents and interest groups rather than to party.

Some further conclusions are drawn in the next chapter.

10 Developing a 'rights way'

Conclusions, implications and possibilities

When I began this research I suspected that one of the major stories that would emerge would be one of relatively stark contrasts between policy-makers at the top, pursuing primarily the national interest, and the implementing staff below them. I suspected I would find the latter would function in the manner of a classic agent, with pressure from NGOs and the interested public sometimes compelling the injection of human rights concerns into the conversation. What I have found is that the norms and realities of rights, especially of social and economic rights, have penetrated the foreign policy-making process in some very real ways, and through some unique avenues. They have done so through international NGOs and their real two-way dialog with major donor states through the G8, UN, OECD and more informal processes of global civil society. The impact of these norms can be seen to a greater extent in states like Britain than it can in either the US or Australia. Policy-makers in the US are too constrained by the US's global position (and by recent foreign policy choices, including the global 'war' on terror). And those in Australia are too constrained by the opposite set of circumstances: so much sense of their own budgetary and military limitations that they must maintain focus on economic security and regional peace. Among other domestic factors that lead to different foreign policy foci, donors' attitudes to global citizenship, which itself stems from their relative positions in global society, is paramount.

Directions for future research

Assumptions

I assume things about the way politics works both internationally and domestically and the way that decisions are made.

Tradeoffs

Governments make tradeoffs between goals. Certainly, most foreign policy-makers would like to simultaneously pursue and reach both strategic and economic goals, while working to make the world a safer place for the forms of governance they believe are best, and a less violent and more just environment for its inhabitants. On rare, serendipitous occasions, all these goals can be pursued and met simultaneously. But more often, the most efficient way to achieve a goal in one arena will not also be the most efficient way to achieve goals in others. There are few Pareto-optimal solutions. And governments have limited resources for pursuing foreign policy goals. This means that, when not all goals can be pursued in tandem, policy-makers must make choices about which goals will be given top priority.

Revealed preferences

The preferences of policy-makers are revealed by choices governments make about resource allocation. This assumption is especially important since much important policy dialog takes place out of the public eye, and rhetorical commitments must be treated with caution. Therefore preferences must be induced from the outcome of aid patterns. This makes it especially important to account for alternate explanations that could lead to the outcomes I observe – something I attempt to do throughout these chapters – and to test these alternative explanations as thoroughly as possible.

The importance of aid as policy tool

To draw conclusions about broader questions of foreign policy from this research, we must also keep in mind the place of development assistance in the overall arsenal of policy tools a government has at its disposal. While direct action in recipient countries would certainly be a quicker and sometimes more straightforward avenue for pursuing policy preferences, such actions violate Westphalian principles of sovereignty and risk international outrage at unjustified meddling. Therefore, aid becomes for donors a more subtle and hence more practicable and acceptable policy tool, while conveniently promoting the appearance of altruism. Development assistance, too, is only one form of aid, and Blanton (2005), Cingranelli and Pasquarello (1985), and others have demonstrated sometimes very different determinants of ODA and military assistance.

Which kinds of recipients appear to be good investments

While it is possible to question nearly any assumption, I believe most of mine are plausible to the point that these results yield meaningful insights into the nature and rationale of aid disbursement, and into the broader role of human rights in foreign policy.

Strengths of the project

This book contributes to the growing body of knowledge on aid motivations by presenting some results of the first systematic archival research at three major

OECD donors, including one clear leader in the aid community, the DfID. I move beyond models derived from studies that exclusively focus on the US, a very atypical donor. In so doing I also pit strategic and economic explanations of aid against one another.

This is especially important because other donors have much more severely constrained resources than does the US for pursuing foreign policy goals. This is true of budgetary, military, diplomatic or any other kind of resource – and it means that these states face important tradeoffs among policy goals.

Future directions

As I was completing this project I read Carol Lancaster and Ann Van Dusen's nice monograph (Lancaster and Van Dusen 2005) on the emerging challenges facing USAID. Their careful consideration of the issues of implementation reminded me of another set of issues that needs to be considered here: the recipient side of the relationship and the increasing focus on aid effectiveness, largely left aside in the statistical analyses here. Aid effectiveness is of course notoriously hard to measure, which is perhaps why aid agencies did not expend many precious resources trying until the relatively recent past.

In addition, ongoing qualitative research is needed to tease out the way that donors respond to the various relevant events and activities within recipients. In many cases they may switch from less to more restrictive forms of aid, for instance, when human rights situations turn sour or governments fail to make adequate progress in meeting the needs of their citizens. This is something that is rather tricky to capture in aggregate analyses of the kind conducted here.

A related question is whether all aid *types* are the same in terms of which factors are taken into account in their commitment and disbursal. While I distinguish between tied and untied aid, and explore differences in the way each is distributed for aggregate OECD aid, I do not examine whether differences persist between each of these and overall aid for the individual donor states included in this study. And while tying status is one of the most important distinctions between different kinds of aid, there is a plethora of other nuances that could significantly affect the calculi of its disbursal decision. One of the most important of these is whether the aid is specifically tagged for emergency or humanitarian assistance; we expect aid so designated to have an explicit humanitarian (though not necessarily 'human rights') component. On the other hand, security assistance, which in general strengthens the policing capacity of the regime receiving it, should be the *most* responsive to human rights concerns, as it is likely to increase recipient regimes' repressive capacity and worsen any existing human rights abuses.

An entirely different aid category is comprised of assistance that is not monetary in nature at all, but comprised of direct military assistance in the form of materiel, weaponry or advice (as is a large proportion of US aid to several high-profile and controversial aid recipients, such as Israel). This entire category of assistance is excluded from the present investigation. To analyze it quantitatively would be somewhat more complex than is the case with monetary assistance, but not impossible, and clearly important. Past studies of US military assistance reveal conflicting evidence on this question (e.g. Blanton 2005; Cingranelli and Pasquarello 1985), and replicating these studies in the context of other donors would be an important step in expanding our understanding of these relationships.

More nuanced measures of domestic politics would also be an important contribution to studies that continue to wed quantitative and qualitative research methods. For example, the electoral and financial importance of immigrant groups in donors, the extent of organization of that group, and media coverage of the source country would require assembling these data from archival research on each donor country individually, a task beyond the scope of the present project.

In addition, without conducting interviews (and perhaps even with them) there is no certain way to determine the nature of specific policy-makers' rationale for making particular policy recommendations or decisions. Further analysis of the internal discourse surrounding specific aid decisions is an important next step in our understanding of the rationale behind them.

Further, aid clearly takes even less obvious forms than these, and the questions that have been asked here about the role of human rights in foreign policy deserve to be examined in the context of all manner of foreign policy vehicles: diplomatic processes, military action, and support for international initiatives and institutions such as the new International Court of Justice.

Further implications and conclusions

The analyses presented here have implications on several levels. Most importantly, they reveal how the internal state of affairs in the recipient competes with other factors in the donor's aid-decision process, and they provide evidence about the conditions under which human rights considerations have the greatest effect.

These results also provide evidence on current debates about whether democracies are more pacific than states with other forms of government. Because my research examines, as do Palmer and Regan (1999), policy and priority differences between established democracies, my results have implications for whether differences in the foreign policies of democracies are due to shared norms: since my research demonstrates variation in the extent to which democratic donors maintain a commitment to human rights in making aid decisions, it is therefore possible that variance exists on *other* norms as well in their application to foreign policy.

Although the issue human rights is theoretically at the heart of democratic government, is it something for which donors are willing to sacrifice potential gains in other arenas? A number of analysts speculate that democracies only pursue human rights goals abroad when it is not costly to do so, and go so far as to claim that these are often invoked as a rationalization for actions policy-makers wish to follow for other reasons (Chomsky and Hermann 1979). If it turns out that countries pursue policies for less altruistic reasons than they claim, what can – or should – be expected of the continued popular support for those policies? These are all critical questions in a post-Cold War world, where policy-makers and academics alike celebrate the spread of democratic governance.

Notes

1 Introduction: the 'rights way' in foreign policy?

1 This phrase is taken from a wonderful booklet by Andre Frankovits and Patrick Earle of the Human Rights Council of Australia entitled *The Rights Way to Development*. It is discussed further in later chapters.

2 For instance, on the field of aid a classic example is Olav Stokke's 1989 *Middle Powers and Global Poverty* or Cranford Pratt's 1990 *Western Middle Power Internationalism*.

2 The role of human rights in foreign policy

1 In the statistical analyses, there are practical as well as substantive reasons for focusing on personal integrity rights (the rights not to be tortured, disappeared, held without due process, or extrajudicially executed). Since these represent one of the most widely accepted sets of rights they should be accorded at least a basic level of respect in each of our donor states (and in fact they are). Fortunately, these also happen to be the rights which are most consistently documented by donor states and NGOs alike. I discuss these measures in greater detail in the chapter on research methodology. I measure subsistence rights (access to basic means for survival) in other ways in the same analyses, but exclude from the statistical analyses a consideration of a number of very important categories such as cultural and reproductive rights. These are documented with much less reliability, and have enjoyed less consistent support in donor states as well. Perfect measures of respect for rights are nearly impossible, though substantial strides are being made in that direction in recent scholarship.

2 Matthews and Pratt include a similar list, but also make the point that many actions are primarily symbolic and largely costless,

> designed to communicate to various publics disapproval of certain policies and practices, and identification with, and sympathy for, victims. Beyond such steps are reduction or severance of all ties (diplomatic, cultural, and economic). Although such actions have symbolic value their main thrust is punitive – to hurt the target country by denying it some benefit previously extended. However, the initiating state is bound to suffer as well. Any state that wishes to press a violator country will likely have to pay a cost, forgo a benefit, possibly sacrifice another interest. Steps adopted will therefore depend on circumstance, on where particular measures are likely to be effective and on the importance of promoting basic human rights relative to other foreign policy objectives.
>
> (Matthews and Pratt 1988: 16)

3 Morality was not entirely absent from many key realist arguments in the early twentieth century, such as that of Morgenthau. However, in the aftermath of fascism and the

looming shadow of the Iron Curtain, realist writers were concerned about the horrific potential of war waged in the name of universal principles (a fear that is no less relevant today) (Chandler 2004: 13).

4 In terms of aid, law in many democracies, as we will see, stipulates that foreign aid decisions must be made with some consideration of the human rights record of the recipient government, unless exceptional conditions apply, such as the existence of extraordinarily dire humanitarian need, or assurances that aid will make it to the needy.

5 There have been several studies of this tendency in US foreign policy. For example, Chomsky and Hermann (1979) find that US trading volume with Latin American countries is far more important than human rights records in predicting the amount of economic assistance given those countries. Scharfe (1996) found that changes in Canadian foreign policy towards Indonesia were more often both implicitly and explicitly linked to Indonesia's trade value to Canada than to Indonesia's record on human rights.

6 That any one relationship can certainly raise public awareness and condemnation is well established. For instance, there has been significant concern that increased investment in Indonesia will cost Canadian jobs. Scharfe cites the cases of two companies, Inco Ltd (in the mid-1990s) and Bata Shoes (since 1979), which have been engaged in expansion of their labor-intensive production activities in Indonesia while simultaneously scaling down such operations in Canada. In both cases, the companies have been accused of labor practices in Indonesia which fall well outside the boundaries of Canadian labor law. In the case of Inco, Indonesian workers had to strike just to receive the national minimum wage of $2 a day (Scharfe 1996: 189). This dynamic is comparable to the perception in the US of the loss of American jobs to cheaper Mexican labor under the North American Free Trade Agreement (NAFTA)).

3 Development assistance: from means to end

1 An exception to this was, for some time, Sweden. Riddell cites the official Swedish government defence of its aid program circa 1962 as claiming that 'no other kind of motive is needed for extension of assistance by Sweden to underdeveloped countries' (Riddell 1987: 6).

2 For instance, a White Paper in 1975 signified an important shift in aid thinking for the British government because 'it indicates the shift in policy to an acceptance that development assistance should be provided not only for counties for which Britain had colonial responsibility but also for independent poor countries' (Riddell 1987: 6).

3 A 1965 UK White Paper, for instance, was significant because it spelled out the two key driving moral forces behind the UK aid program over time: poverty and inequality (Riddell 1987).

4 This was reflected for instance in both the title and content of the 1975 White Paper *The Changing Emphasis in British Aid Policies: More Help for the Poorest*.

5 Tomasevski suggests at least one potential approach:

> In order to be able to incorporate human rights into development aid one would need to adopt a different approach from that pursued today by donors. The starting point would be to focus on aid itself – at the policy as well as the project level – and assess it by human rights criteria.
>
> (Tomasevski 1993: 154).

6 The OECD says that tied aid,

> which includes loans, grants or associated financing packages with a concessionality level greater than zero per cent, is defined as aid which is in effect (in law or in fact) tied to the procurement of goods and/or services from the donor country and/or a restricted number of countries. This definition applies whether the 'tying' is by formal agreement or by any form of informal understanding between the recipient and the donor country, or whether a package includes components from

the list in Article 32 ... that are not freely and fully available to finance procurement from the recipient country, substantially all other developing countries and from the Participants, or if it involves practices that the DAC [Development Assistance Committee] or Participants consider equivalent to such tying. (OECD, www.oecd.org//ech/act/XCRED/arrangement/anglais/chapitre3-en.htm, last accessed 23 March 2006). Tied aid can take the form of, among other things, Official Development Assistance (ODA) loans, ODA grants, and Other Official Flows (OOF).

7 They claim that their independent variables have different relative effects on each decision, though it is difficult to assess this claim as significance levels are not reported.

8 I exclude from this analysis all states with economies which are larger than or roughly equal to that of the donor state.

9 Reed (2000) has suggested that a unified model such as censored probit provides an effective alternative way to model two separate but related decision. While I do not take this approach in the present study, it offers a potentially interesting lens through which to examine this dual process in the future.

4 Methodology: means, not end

1 When conflicts have arisen in the ANZUS alliance, for instance, Australia has often sided with the US over New Zealand (though the importance of the alliance since the end of the Cold War has weakened substantially).

2 Furthermore, 'it should be noted that economic aid relations with a recipient state have never been suspended solely as a result of human rights violations' (Cunliffe and Hill 1989: 116).

3 That this was indeed a deliberate strategy is supported by the public stance taken by Foreign Minister Bill Hayden in 1984:

> There is as you know a large gap off East Timor in the sea-bed boundary. In that gap are positioned natural gas fields and probably oil fields. We would not be regarded with great public celebration if we were to make a mess of these negotiations, and yet the implication of the negotiations is that as the area open or undefined at this point is off East Timor, a certain recognition must be established to East Timor. For some people in my party who have expressed concern about the pressure of Indonesia on East Timor, this is a cold, hard, sobering reality that must also be addressed in respect of those other interests we must attend to.
>
> (*Canberra Times*, 18 April 1984, quoting a speech made by
> Foreign Minister Bill Hayden in a speech to the Joint Services
> Staff College in April 1984 and cited in Scharfe by Taylor 1991: 171)

4 This price was utter silence from the government, despite international outcry, after the murder of four Australian journalists on 16 October 1975 by Indonesian troops in Balibo.

5 The 'selection effects' problem is that, in some situations, it is difficult to measure the impact of a given independent variable because there is a correlation between that independent variable and the process through which observations are selected into one's sample. For example, Gartner and Siverson (1996) examine the phenomenon that states that initiate wars are more likely to win them than are the *targets* of initiation, especially when the target receives no help. Gartner and Siverson explain that this finding is a biased one. This is due to the fact that we can only observe a certain subset of wars that could potentially happen – those that are *selected* by the initiator based on their estimation of their chances of winning.

6 In another instance of this reverse-need prioritization, until the release of *Sharing Our Future* in 1988, Canada's aid disbursement was based in part on a 'Categories of Eli-

gibility' list. It ranked recipients according to the nature and intensity of Canada's interests in the country, as well as by the mechanism of aid disbursement, and so relegated 'some of the poorest LDCs to marginal status as Canadian aid recipients' (Gillies and Brecher 1989) *Sharing Our Future: Canadian International Development Assistance* was an aid-policy document released by the Canadian International Development Agency (CIDA) which underlined support for human rights as a key consideration in foreign policy decisions.

7 Another potential selection effect results from the fact that aid recipients might anticipate the donor's terminating of aid and hence move to improve their human rights performance because they fear their aid getting cut off. I am currently considering how to address this problem.

8 It might be suggested that instead change be measured as an ordinal variable, subtracting the status of aid (0, 1) in year t-1 from the status of aid (0, 1) in year t, to create three possibilities with –1 = aid withdrawn, 0 = no change, and 1 = aid initiated. This creates two problems.

First, it would code the maintenance of an aid relationship identically to the maintenance of a nonaid relationship – two states of the world which are fundamentally different. Specifically, maintaining an aid relationship with a human rights violator is likely to indicate that the donor state is to some extent turning a blind eye to the violations. Not aiding a state one year that was not aided in the previous year is less likely to indicate anything about the donor's evaluation of the state it is not aiding. However, because of bureaucratic inertia, both of these 'not change' sorts of observations are far less significant than a change in either direction.

Second, the decision to halt aid is unlikely to be simply the inverse of the decision to begin aid. That is, there is not a constant threshold of human rights respect, or economic value, for that matter, above which states grant aid and below which they do not. Terminating aid is seen as being the most dramatic of measures, and is rarely done. In the case of Britain, it has happened only twice on human rights grounds. (Decreases in aid or suspension of aid are more common). (*Human Rights in United Kingdom and United States Foreign Policy*, 1979). Initiating aid to a state that has not received it before is more common overall and its ostensible motives more diverse. It is expected that the human rights variable will have a greater effect in decisions to cease aid to a country currently being aided than on any other kinds of decisions made at the gatekeeping phase.

9 It might seem easier to simply divide the sample according to these criteria and conduct analyses on the three subsets rather than the complete set. However, this is likely to present a serious degrees-of-freedom problem.

10 Control variables not included. There are three forms of this model as discussed in the hypotheses. The fully specified form of the model for IIIa is the probit function: *Aid given (0 = no, 1 = yes) = b1 human rights record + b2 potential economic importance of recipient + b3 vulnerability of donor state ruling party + b4 potential economic importance * human rights record + b5 vulnerability * human rights record + b6 strategic value of recipient + b7 strategic value * human rights record + b8 end of Cold War + b9 ideological congruence + b10 similar degrees of democracy + b11 immigrants from recipient state in donor state + b12 past aid + b13 human rights interest groups + b14 mass-mediated humanitarian crises.*

11 Control variables not included. The fully specified form of this model is the regression function: *Aid given = b1 human rights record + b2 potential economic importance of recipient + b3 vulnerability of donor state ruling party + b4 potential economic importance * human rights record + b5 vulnerability * human rights record + b6 strategic value of recipient + b7 strategic value * human rights record + b8 end of Cold War + b9 ideological congruence + b10 similar degrees of democracy + b11 immigrants from recipient state in donor state + b12 past aid + b13 human rights interest groups + b14 mass-mediated humanitarian crises.*

12 Sensitivity analyses were performed using the newer Cingranelli and Richards Human Rights Index (CIRI) data (Cingranelli and Richards 2007). Results were similar, as might be expected since the two data sets are based on the same two sets of reports.

13 For instance, touting (among other things) the growth rate of Indonesia's economy, Indonesia's Minister for Investment has established – with the Canadian Exporter's Association – the Canada–Indonesia Business Development Corporation, which has received $1.5 million in funding from CIDA.

14 Another reasonable measure would include trade agreements between the two states, though this is not a measure currently incorporated in these analyses.

15 Additionally, in the future it may be desirable to include a measure of the total number of current trading partners of each donor and recipient as this may be a measure of how important any one potential export market is likely to be.

16 Data on military alliances are available from the Correlates of War data set, particularly the alliance subset compiled by Singer and Small.

17 There may be some collinearity between this and the other salience measure. These data can be compiled from headline counts of major national newspapers or nightly national news broadcasts, as summarized in the Kansas Events Data Set, www.wcfia.harvard.edu/ponsacs/, last accessed 3 June 2003).

5 The global context: cross-national aid patterns 1980–2004

1 The standard estimation procedure consisted of calculating the percentage of listed trade partners that were OECD members and using this as a proxy for OECD trade percentage.

2 The 75 percent cutoff point is effective theoretically because it clearly identifies those states with the highest annual imports and thus those seen as economically most critical. Empirically, a higher cut off point might result in too few observations to conduct effective analyses – especially given the interests in fixed effects (discussed later). Again, however, I show in the diagnostic section that the criteria are extremely robust to alternative specifications and indeed to both higher and lower cutoff points.

3 Bivariate regression results (*High OECD Imports* on *Untied Aid*): coefficient of 260,256, significant at the 0.001 level, $p < 0.000$, $t = 9.12$, 1,301 observations, F of 83.19 significant at the 0.001 level – $p < 0.000$ an R^2 of 0.06, constant = 109,594, $p < 0.000$, $t = 7.31$.

4 One might be concerned that population drives these results. But the state population and recipient imports from the OECD correlate at only 0.13 and in a multivariate regression of *Population* and *High OECD Import* on aid both variables have estimates that are strongly statistically significant (results not shown).

5 In only 187 out of 2375 cases was a state receiving aid the year before was it terminated.

6 As interesting as these results are, and despite the fact that the model overall is highly significant, the model does not offer any proportional reduction in error, suggesting the need for a certain amount of respecification.

6 Leadership out of obligation: British development assistance and human rights

1 It can be argued, of course, that this risks legitimizing the particular set of rights the donor happens to espouse, but can one really expect a donor government to espouse any others?

2 By 1970 ... British policy makers and observers had alike accepted that Britain could no longer aspire to world status, but was rather a 'major power of the

second order'. Their perception of the national interest which foreign policy should pursue reflected the more commercial orientation appropriate to a middle power.

(Wallace 1975: 4)

3 Notably, however, the actual list of four priorities listed in Cook's first Mission Statement reads as follows:

Security. We shall ensure the security of the United Kingdom and the Dependent Territories, and peace for our people, by promoting international stability, fostering our defence alliances, and promoting arms control effectively.

Prosperity. We shall make maximum use of our overseas posts to promote trade abroad and boost jobs at home.

Quality of life. We shall work with others to protect the world's environment and to counter the menace of drugs, terrorism and crime.

Mutual respect. We shall work through our international forums and bilateral relationships to spread the values of human rights, civil liberties and democracy which we demand for ourselves.

(Dickie 2004: 83)

Security and prosperity still rate first mention.

4 Cook's critics scorned him and this resulted in a *Daily Telegraph* headline the next day saying 'Cook to lead the FO on moral crusade' (Dickie 2004: 117). Several times Cook's colleagues in Parliament accused him of double standards, especially on arms sales cases regarding Indonesia, Zimbabwe and Morocco (Dickie 2004: 118–19, 150).

5 This was probably at least in part a response to the perception that British foreign policy in the postwar era has continually suffered from an inability to set priorities, an especially serious problem when government budgets and global influence are on the wane. For instance, Coles (Coles 2000: 47) notes that

they [critics] see a failure to decide rationally how much effort to devote to various components of overseas policy   to diplomacy, the armed forces and foreign aid – and to decide which international issues are worth taxpayers' money and which are not.

In fact, he notes that from the end of World War II to the turn of the millennium the FCO produced no clear foreign strategy document. This was not a problem conquered right away by the New Labour government, which Dickie (2004: 48) notes has aimed to have a diplomatic mission in any country of concern to British interests.

6 These were actually begun under the Conservatives and have been maintained by Labour.

7 The optimistic commentator might observe, however, that at least this *is* a tightrope now – times were that human rights would not have proved a necessary complicant to cultivating good relations with such a valuable market and emerging military power.

8 There was a similar dilemma for government in its attitude toward the fierce conflict between the Russians and the Chechnyans. Because there were political reasons for having some sort of partnership with Russia and NATO, as well as for persuading Russia to accept the enlargement of NATO with Eastern European countries, critical comments in Downing Street were muted about the Russians bombing Grozny. Therefore Putin was feted by Blair despite evidence presented at the EU regarding human rights abuses in Chechnya (Dickie 2004: 120–1).

9   Given the British aid budget situation … there may be more priorities than resources to deal with them. There are other claims on resources … such as emergency and humanitarian assistance. If the British bilateral programme is squeezed in the years to come, the problem of priorities will become more acute.

(OECD 1994b: 34)

10 Exceptions include aid to UK overseas territories, humanitarian assistance and contributions to multilateral development banks (FCO 2003).

11   Where there is good governance, even scarce resources are more likely to be well managed to ensure that maximum sustainable benefit is obtained from them, and equitably enjoyed. Where there is poor governance, even abundant resources are more likely to be misused, often causing lasting damage to the social, environmental, economic and political fabric of society.

(FCO 2003: 2)

12 He does caution that this is not necessarily the case when dealing with Europe or a crisis situation.

13 Coles suggests just such a strategy when he says that

the starting point for an assessment [of policy priorities] could well be the FO's annual reports to Parliament ... [which] contain not only a clear statement of objectives but also five pages describing the specific areas in which those objectives are regarded as having been achieved.

(Coles 2000: 77)

14 'The reason for keeping the country strategy internal, while of a slightly different nature, is apparently part of the same policy' (OECD 1994: 35).

15 Coles suggests almost this exact strategy when he says that the annual process by which funds are allocated to Whitehall departments could only be fully understood after 'a detailed analysis of this material ... which I have not undertaken...' (Coles 2000: 183).

16 Country name redacted because of classification level of material.

17 Country name redacted because of classification level of material.

7 Neither here nor there? Canadian development assistance and human rights

1 The most well-known examples of this more idealistic orientation to foreign affairs include opposition to cases of American interventionism (in Vietnam among other locales), leadership in the international effort to sanction Apartheid-era South Africa, and substantial commitment of troops and materiel by Canada to UN peacekeeping operations.

2 Its ambivalence in doing so led Dean Acheson to call Canadian foreign policy 'moralistic, hypocritical and harmful to Canada's longer term security interests' (Acheson 1966: 134–47).

3 Prior to the below-mentioned reports, discussion of the motives behind Canada's foreign aid did not even touch on human rights as a consideration. Dobell (1972) notes the following motives behind Canada's aid program to Francophone Africa: finding an outlet for Francophone Canadians, the desire to preempt a Quebecois aid program in Africa, and the desire to outflank Quebec in its attempts to heighten its international presence. He bemoans the failure of Canada to join European and US in involvement with 'far east'ern development efforts and the economic benefits they could render (Dobell 1972: 103).

4 'Even so, human security will outlive Axworthy, mainly because it was not just his idea and agenda' (Hampson *et al.* 2001: 15).

5 This is the Talisman Energy case, in which the company was allowed to engage in massive investment in Sudan despite Parliamentary evidence that this investment was allowing the Sudanese government to engage in further repression. Reportedly Axworthy wanted to take tougher action against Talisman, but the PM and other ministers disagreed.

8 Inherited from history and geography: Australian development assistance and human rights

1   This has increased since the end of the Cold War, partially in response to increasing transnational interaction.

2   In the 1980s and 1990s Australian foreign ministers presented an image of Australia as a nation enmeshed in the dynamism of the fastest growing economic region of the world. It was implied that this growth would re-enforce peace as well as prosperity in the region.

(Smith *et al.* 1996: 17)

3   This has not, however, stopped portions of the government objecting vociferously to aspects of Australia's cooperation with other states, such as calling American actions in Vietnam 'mass murder' or censuring the cabinet for participation in the current war in Iraq.

4   Evans also expressed the fear of being perceived a hypocrite that has been endemic in Australian foreign policy. 'Our opportunity,' he said,

> to influence events depends in this arena more than anywhere else, on keeping our domestic house absolutely in order. Our ability to secure advances in the areas of human rights [and] refugees, rests on our being and continuing to be seen to be ... a country which articulates and applies human rights and similar principles with absolute consistency and impartiality ... hypocrites are not merely disliked, in international relations as elsewhere. If they are our size, they are ignored.
>
> (Evans and Grant 1995: 37–8, cited in Smith *et al.* 1996: 220)

5   It here notes that the developed world spends six times as much per year supporting its own agricultural sector as it does on aid; whether this is meant to imply an argument for aid, or free trade, or both, is unclear.

6   Several regions are dealt with and rights and development both come under discussion. The focus is on people-smuggling and democracy, with an emphasis on multilateral responses.

7   For instance, 'While it may seem unfair,' notes Hewott (Hewett 1996: 1), 'to judge a government so early in its term, there are a number of worrying signs. The single-minded pursuit of Australia's commercial interests has already led to a conflict with important social, human rights and environmental concerns.'

8   The best means of managing such difficulties is generally to address human rights concerns in the context of a sound overall bilateral relationship through dialogue, and, as appropriate, by offering practical assistance to these countries to improve the human rights situation on the ground.

(DFAT 2004: 6)

9   For instance, Smith *et al.* (1996: 181) argue that, whether the threat was the 'Yellow Peril' or the 'Red Menace', the perception of threat that has haunted Australian foreign policy-makers has meant that any friend was a good friend, no matter how repressive domestically. In the Post-Cold War era, this may be more true of economic concerns than security fears. As ever, institutional arrangements can be powerful clues to policy priorities, as Smith *et al.* observe that the merger of the former separate Departments of Foreign Affairs and Overseas Trade institutionally enshrined 'the increasingly blurred lines between diplomacy and international economic policy' (Smith *et al.* 1996: 9).

10 As a recent DAC review put it:

> At first sight the rationale for the aid program with its compelling combination of humanitarian, foreign, and trade policy objectives, seems to ensure policy coherence almost automatically ... there is usually a powerful consensus on the importance of country-relationships themselves.
>
> (OECD 1996: 15)

11 This consisted of H. Paul Simons, Gaye Hart and Cliff Walsh. Notably, Simons, the chair, is the former Executive Chairman of Woolworths. The others are respectively the director of the Hunter Institute of Technology and the Executive Director of the S. A. Centre for Economic Studies.

12 This is reflected in, for instance, the media's general dissatisfaction with the ability of Members of Parliament to hold political executives accountable for their actions (Cook 2004: 159).

13 'Reducing poverty' is regarded as one of the most important issues facing the world today, as are 'ensuring peace' (which is in many ways related to human rights), 'improving health' and 'safe-guarding the environment'.

14 One example of this was the assumed impact of the 'Greek lobby' over debates about recognition of Macedonia upon its declaration of sovereignty after the breakup of Yugoslavia.

15 As discussed above, it encouraged firms to undertake capital intensive infrastructure projects that did not provide direct benefit to the poorest in developing countries (OECD 1996: 29–30).

16 Name redacted due to classification status.

9 Context and consideration: three other donor states

1 Some see even the form of the MCF as reflecting a US emphasis on reward based on individual achievement rather than on the presumption that equality is an end in itself.

References

Acheson, Dean (1966) *Power and Diplomacy*, New York: Atheneum.

AidWatch (2006) *Australian Aid: Promoting Insecurity?*, Canberra: AidWatch. Online. Available at: www.aidwatch.org.au/index.php?current=24&display=aw00991&display _item=1 (accessed 12 May 2007).

Amnesty International (various years) *Amnesty International Report: Various Countries*, New York: Amnesty International. Online. Available www.amnesty. org/ailib/aireport/ (accessed 30 March 2006).

Amnesty International (1998) *Amnesty International Annual Report: Australia 1998*, Canberra: Amnesty International Australia. Online. Available at: www.amnesty.org/ ailib/aireport/ar98/asa12.htm (accessed 12 May 2007).

Amnesty International (2001) *UK Foreign and Asylum Policy Human Rights Audit 2001*, London: Amnesty International UK.

Apodaca, Clair and Michael Stohl (1999) 'United States human rights policy and foreign assistance', *International Studies Quarterly* 43(1): 185–98.

Australia Parliament (2002) *Foreign and Trade Issues in the Parliament*, Canberra: Department of Foreign Affairs and Trade. Online. Available at: www.dfat.gov.au/ qwon/ (accessed 9 July 2002).

Axelrod, Robert and Robert O. Keohane (1993) 'Achieving cooperation under anarchy: strategies and institutions', in David A. Baldwin (ed.) *Neorealism and Neoliberalism: The Contemporary Debate*, New York: Columbia University Press.

Axworthy, Lloyd (2004) *Navigating a New World: Canada's Global Future*, Toronto: Vintage Canada.

Baehr, Peter and Monique Castermans-Holleman (2004) *The Role of Human Rights in Foreign Policy,* 3rd edn), Basingstoke: Palgrave Macmillan.

Barder, Owen (2005) 'Reforming development assistance: lessons from the UK experience (Center for Global Development Working Paper #70)', Washington, DC: Center for Global Development.

Barratt, Bethany (2004) 'Aiding or abetting: British aid and recipient human rights violations', in Carey, Sabine and Stephen C. Poe (2004) *Understanding Human Rights: New Systematic Studies*, London: Ashgate.

Beitz, Charles R. (1979) *Political Theory and International Relations*, Princeton, NJ: Princeton University Press.

Berry, Victoria and Allan McChesney (1988) 'Human rights and foreign policy-making', in Robert O. Matthews and Cranford Pratt (eds) *Human Rights in Canadian Foreign Policy*, Kingston: McGill-Queen's University Press.

Bissett, James (2000) 'Kosovo and human rights', Toronto: Center for Balkans Peace.

Online. Available at: www.balkanpeace.org/rs/archive/aug00/rs72.shtml (accessed 23 June 2006).

Black, David and Rebecca Thiessen (forthcoming) 'The Canadian International Development Agency: new policies, old problems', *Canadian Journal of Development Studies*, June 2007.

Black, David, Jean-Philippe Therien and Andrew Clark (1996) 'Moving with the crowd: Canadian aid to Africa', *International Journal*, spring.

Blanton, Shannon (2005) 'Foreign policy in transition? human rights, democracy, and U.S. arms exports', *International Studies Quarterly* 49(4): 647–67.

Bond, Doug, Joe Bond, Churl Oh, J. Craig Jenkins and Charles Lewis Taylor (2003) 'Integrated data for events analysis', *Journal of Peace Research* 40(6): 733–45.

Bose, Anuradha and Peter Burnell (eds) (1991) *Britain's Overseas Aid since 1979: Between Idealism and Self-interest*, New York: Manchester University Press.

Breuning, Marijke (1995) 'Words and deeds: foreign assistance rhetoric and policy behaviour in the Netherlands, Belgium, and the United Kingdom, *International Studies Quarterly* 39(2) (June): 35–54.

Breuning, Marijke (2004) 'Global sisterhood? women's representation and the priorities of development assistance', paper presented at the annual meeting of the International Studies Association, Montreal, Quebec, March. Online. Available at: www.allacademic.com/meta/p72734_index.html (accessed 12 May 2007).

Breuning, Marijke (2005) 'Women's policy priorities: does gender make a difference in the allocation of development assistance?', paper presented at the annual meeting of the International Studies Association, Honolulu, HI, March.

Brewin, Christopher (1986) 'Europe', in R. J. Vincent (ed.) *Foreign Policy and Human Rights: Issues and Responses*, Cambridge: Cambridge University Press.

Brodhead, Tim (1996) 'Paying the piper: CIDA and Canadian NGOs', in Cranford Pratt (ed.) *Canadian International Development Policies: An Appraisal*, Montreal and Kingston: McGill-Queen's University Press.

Brooks, C. and D. Brady (1999) 'Income, economic voting, and long-term political change in the United States: 1952–1996', *Social Forces* 77(4): 1339–74.

Brown, Stephen (forthcoming) '"Creating the world's best development agency"?: Confusion and contradictions in CIDA's new policy blueprint', *Canadian Journal of Development Studies*, June 2007.

Bueno de Mesquita, Bruce and David Lalman (1990) 'Domestic opposition and foreign war', *American Political Science Review* 84(3): 747–65.

Bueno de Mesquita, Bruce and Randolph M. Siverson (1995) 'War and the survival of political leaders: a comparative study of regime types and political accountability', *American Political Science Review* 89(4): 841–55.

Cable News Network online (1999) 'British PM urges China to ease Tibetan policy', Atlanta: CNN. Online. Available at: asia.cnn.com/WORLD/europe/9910/21/china.britain.02/ (accessed 8 July 2002).

Canada. Parliament, House of Commons, Standing Committee on External Affairs and International Trade (1987) *For Whose Benefit?: A Report of the Standing Committee on External Affairs and International Trade on Canada's Official Development Assistance Policies and Programs*, Ottawa: Queen's Printer for Canada, available from the Canadian Government Publication Centre, Supply and Services, Canada.

Canadian International Development Agency (1987) *Sharing Our Future: Canadian International Development Assistance*, Hull, Quebec: Canadian International Development Agency.

Canadian International Development Agency (2001) *Government of Canada Policy for*

CIDA on Human Rights, Democratization, and Good Governance, Hull, Quebec: Canadian International Development Agency.

Canadian International Development Agency (2002) *Canada Making a Difference in the World: A Policy Statement on Aid Effectiveness*, Hull, Quebec: Canadian International Development Agency.

Canadian International Development Agency (2003) 'Aid to Developing Countries', Hull, Quebec: Canadian International Development Agency. Online. Available at: dsp-psd.pwgsc.gc.ca/Collection-R/LoPBdP/CIR/7916-e.htm (accessed 15 May 2007).

Cardoso, Fernando H. and Enzo Faletto (1979) *Dependency and Development in Latin America*, Berkeley: University of California Press.

Carey, Sabine and Stephen C. Poe (2004) *Understanding Human Rights Violations: New Systematic Studies*, London: Ashgate.

Central Intelligence Agency (various years) *CIA World Factbook*, Washington, DC: US Government Printing Office.

Chandler, David (2004) *Constructing Global Civil Society: Morality and Power in International Relations*, Basingstoke: Palgrave Macmillan.

Chomsky, Noam and Edward S. Hermann (1979) *The Political Economy of Human Rights: The Washington Connection and Third World Fascism*, Boston, MA: South End Press.

Cingranelli, David L. and Thomas E. Pasquarello (1985) 'Human rights practices and the distribution of US foreign aid to Latin American countries', *American Journal of Political Science* 29(3): 539–63.

Cingranelli, David L. and David L. Richards (2007) *The Cingranelli–Richards (CIRI) Human Rights Database*. Online. Available at: www.humanrightsddata. org// (accessed 15 August 2007).

Coles, John (2000) *Making Foreign Policy: A Certain Idea of Britain*, London: John Murray.

Commonwealth of Australia (2004) *Australia's National Framework for Human Rights: National Action Plan*, Canberra: Commonwealth of Australia.

Cook, Ian (2004) *Government and Democracy in Australia*, Oxford and New York: Oxford University Press.

Crabb, Cecil V. (1992) *Invitation to Struggle: Congress, the President and Foreign Policy*, Washington DC: CQ Press.

Cunliffe, S. Alex (1985) 'British economic aid policy and international human rights: a comparative analysis of Conservative and Labour policies in the 1970s', *Political Studies XXXIII*: 112.

Cunliffe, S. Alex (1989) 'Economic aid as an instrument for the promotion of international human rights', in Dilys M. Hill (ed.) *Human Rights and Foreign Policy: Principles and Practice*, London: Macmillan.

Dahl, Robert (1958) *A Preface to Economic Democracy*, Ann Arbor: University of Michigan Press.

Dalager, J. K. (1996) 'Voters, issues, and elections: are the candidates' messages getting through?', *Journal of Politics* 58(2): 486–515.

Department of Foreign Affairs and Trade (1997) *Charting Australia's Regional Future*, Canberra: Government of Australia.

Department of Foreign Affairs and Trade (1999) *Toward a Sustainable Future*, Canberra: Government of Australia.

Department of Foreign Affairs and Trade (2003) *Advancing the National Interest: Australia's Foreign Affairs and Trade White Paper*, Canberra: Government of Australia. Online. Available at: www.dfat.gov.au/ani/overview.html (accessed 12 May 2007).

Department for International Development (2000) *Realising Human Rights for Poor People*, London: HMSO.

Department for International Development (2004) *Essential Guide to Rules and Tools: The Blue Book*, London: HMSO.

Dickie, John (2004) *The New Mandarins: How British Foreign Policy Works*, London and New York: Tauris.

Dobell, Peter C. (1972) *Canada's Search for New Roles*, London: Oxford University Press for the Royal Institute of International Affairs.

Donnelly, Jack (2004) *Universal Human Rights in Theory and Practice*, Ithaca, NY and London: Cornell University Press.

Doyle, Michael W. (1995) 'Kant, liberal legacies, and foreign affairs', in Michael E. Brown, Sean M. Lynn-Jones and Steven Miller (eds) *Debating the Democratic Peace*, Cambridge, MA: MIT Press.

Egeland, Jan (1988) *Impotent Superpower – Potent Small State*, Oslo: Norwegian University Press.

English, John (2001) 'In the liberal tradition: Lloyd Axworthy and Canadian foreign policy', in Hampson, Fen Osler, Norman Hillmer and Maureen Appel Molot (2001) *Canada among Nations 2001: The Axworthy Legacy*, Oxford: Oxford University Press.

Ensign, Margee M. (1992) *Doing Good or Doing Well? Japan's Foreign Aid Program*, New York: Columbia University Press.

Evans, Peter (1979) *Dependent Development: The Alliance of Multinational, State, and Local Capital in Brazil*, Princeton, NJ: Princeton University Press.

Evatt, H. V. (1945) *Foreign Policy of Australia: Speeches*, Sydney: Angus and Robertson Ltd.

Federation of American Scientists, 'Israel: nuclear weapons', Washington, DC: Federation of American Scientists. Online. Available at: www.fas.org/nuke/guide/israel/nuke/index.html (accessed 24 March 2006).

Federation of American Scientists, 'Ukraine special weapons', Washington, DC: Federation of American Scientists. Online. Available at: www.fas.org/nuke/guide/ ukraine/ (accessed 24 March 2006).

Federation of American Scientists, 'Belarus special weapons', Washington, DC: Federation of American Scientists. Online. Available at: www.fas.org/nuke/guide/belarus/index.html (accessed 24 March 2006).

Federation of American Scientists, 'Kazakhstan special weapons', Washington, DC: Federation of American Scientists. Online. Available at: www.fas.org/nuke/ guide/kazakhstan/index.html (accessed 24 March 2006)

Flags of the World (2003) 'Flags of the World'. No location given: Flags of the World. Online. Available at: www.crwflags.com/fotw (accessed 11 May 2007).

Foerster, Andreas (1995) *Institutional Analysis of Development Administration: The Case of Japan's Bilateral Grant Aid and Technical Assistance*, Heidelberg: Springer Verlag.

Foreign and Commonwealth Office (1997) 'Foreign and Commonwealth Office mission statement', London: HMSO.

Foreign and Commonwealth Office (2003) 'UK international priorities: a strategy for the FCO', London: HMSO.

Foreign and Commonwealth Office (2005) 'Human rights annual report 2005', London: HMSO.

Foreign and Commonwealth Office (2006) 'Active diplomacy for a changing world: the UK's international priorities', London: HMSO.

Forsythe, David P. (1987) *Human Rights and US Foreign Policy: Congress Reconsidered*, Gainesville: University Presses of Florida.

Forsythe, David P. (2004) *Human Rights and Comparative Foreign Policy*, New York: United Nations University Press.

Franck, Thomas M. (1992) 'The emerging right to democratic governance', *American Journal of International Law* 86: 46–91.

Freeman, Linda (1985) 'The effects of the world crisis on Canada's involvement in Africa', *Studies in Political Economy* 17: 109.

Friedman, Thomas (1999) *The Lexus and the Olive Tree: Understanding Globalization*, New York: Farrar, Strauss, and Giroux.

Gartner, Scott Sigmund (1997) *Strategic Assessment and War*, New Haven, CT: Yale University Press.

Gartner, Scott Sigmund and Randolph M. Siverson (1996) 'War initiation and war outcome', *Journal of Conflict Resolution* 40(1): 1–15.

Gaubatz, Kurt Taylor (1991) 'Election cycles and war', Special Issue: Democracy and Foreign Policy: Community and Constraint, *Journal of Conflict Resolution* 35(2).

Gillies, David (1989) 'Do interest groups make a difference? Domestic influences on Canadian development aid policies', in Irving Brecher (ed.) *Human Rights, Development, and Foreign Policy: Canadian Perspectives*, Halifax, Nova Scotia: Institute for Research on Public Policy.

Gilles, David (1996) 'Export promotion and Canadian development assistance', in Cranford Pratt (ed.) *Canadian International Development Policies: An Appraisal*, Montreal and Kingston: McGill-Queen's University Press.

Gounder, Rukmani (1995) *Overseas Aid Motivations: The Economics of Australia's Bilateral Aid*, Aldershot: Avebury.

Government of Australia. Department of Foreign Affairs and Trade (2004) *Australia's National Framework for Human Rights, National Action Plan*. Online. Available at: www.dfat.gov.au/hr/nap/nap_2004.pdf/ (accessed 15 August 2007).

Government of Australia. Department of Foreign Affairs and Trade (2006) *Australian Aid: Promoting Growth and Stability* Online. Available at: www.ausaid.gov.au/publications/pdf/whitepaper.pdf (accessed 15 August 2007).

Government of Australia. Department of Foreign Affairs and Trade (2007) *National Action Plan – Human Rights – Global Issues*. Online. Available at: www.dfat.gov.au/hr/nap/natactp_plan.html (accessed 15 August 2007).

Government of Canada (1995) 'Canada in the world government statement', Ottawa: Foreign Affairs and International Trade Information Systems.

Gowa, Joanne (1995) 'Democratic states and international power politics', *International Organization* 49(3): 511–22.

Gowa, Joanne and Edward Mansfield (1993) 'Power politics and international trade', *American Political Science Review* 87(2): 408–20.

Greene, William H. (2003) *Econometric Analysis*, 5th edn, Upper Saddle River, NJ: Prentice Hall.

Grieco, Joseph M. (1988) 'Anarchy and the limits of cooperation: a realist critique of the newest liberal institutionalism', *International Organization* 42(3): 485–507.

Gurr, Ted Robert (1994) 'Peoples against states – ethnopolitical conflict and the changing world system – 1994 Presidential Address', *International Studies Quarterly* 38(3): 347–77.

Hampson, Fen Osler, Norman Hillmer and Maureen Appel Molot (2001) 'Introduction', in Fen Osler Hampson, Norman Hillmer, and Maureen Appel Molot (2001) *Canada among Nations 2001: The Axworthy Legacy*, Oxford: Oxford University Press.

Hanushek, Eric. A. and John E. Jackson (1977) *Statistical Methods for Social Scientists*, Orlando, FL: Harcourt Brace Jovanovich.

Harkin, Tom (1979) 'Human rights and foreign aid: forging an unbreakable link', in Peter S. Brown and Douglas McLean (eds) *Human Rights and U.S. Foreign Policy*, Lexington, MA: Lexington Books.

Healy, J. M. and A. G. Coverdale (1981) 'Foreign policy and British bilateral aid: a comment on McKinlay and Little', *British Journal of Political Science* 11(1): 123–27.

Hewett, Andrew (1996) 'Foreign aid: how's the Howard government doing?', Canberra: Oxfam Australia. Online. Available at: www.caa.org.au/horizons/h18/andrew.htm (accessed 9 July 2001).

Hill, Dilys M. (1989) 'Human rights and foreign policy: theoretical foundations', in Dilys M. Hill (ed.) *Human Rights and Foreign Policy: Principles and Practice*, London: Macmillan.

Historical Statistics of the United States on CD-ROM: Colonial Times to 1970, [computer file], Millennial edn, (forthcoming). New York: Cambridge University Press.

Hoebink, Paul and Olav Stokke (eds) (2005) *Perspectives on European Development Cooperation*, London and New York: Routledge.

Hofrenning, Daniel J. B. (1990) 'Human rights and foreign aid: a comparison of the Reagan and Carter administrations', *American Politics Quarterly* 18(4): 514–26.

Holsti, K. J. (1970) 'National role conceptions in the analysis of foreign policy' *International Studies Quarterly* 14: 233–309.

Holsti, Ole R. (1992) 'Public opinion and foreign policy: challenges to the Almond–Lippman consensus', *International Studies Quarterly* 36: 439–66.

Holsti, Ole R. (2004) *Public Opinion and Foreign Policy*, 2nd edn, Ann Arbor: University of Michigan Press.

House of Commons Foreign Affairs Committee (1998) *Annual Report on Human Rights*, London: HMSO.

Howard-Hassman, Rhoda E. (2003) *Compassionate Canadians: Civic Leaders Discuss Human Rights*, Toronto: University of Toronto Press.

Human Rights Council of Australia (1995) *The Rights Way to Development*, Canberra: HRCA.

Human Rights in United States and United Kingdom Foreign Policy: A Colloquium (1979) London: International Commission of Jurists.

Human Rights Watch (1994) 'Japan: Human Rights Developments.' Online. Available at: www.hrw.org/reports/1995/WR95/ASIA-06.htm#P414_144085 (accessed 15 August 2007).

Human Rights Watch (2007) 'Japan's peculiar silence on rights abuses'. Online. Available at: hrw.org/English/docs/2007/01/08/japan15098.htm (accessed 15 August 2007).

Huth, Paul (1988) *Extended Deterrence and the Prevention of War*, New Haven, CT: Yale University Press.

International Development Act 2002 (2002) London: HMSO.

International Monetary Fund (various years) *Direction of Trade Statistics, 1948–1990*, Washington, DC: International Monetary Fund.

Ireland, Michael J. and Scott Sigmund Gartner (2001) 'Time to fight: government type and conflict initiation in parliamentary systems', *Journal of Conflict Resolution* 45(5): 547–68.

Jaggers, Keith and Ted Robert Gurr, *Polity III: Regime Change and Political Authority, 1800–1994*, [Computer file], 2nd ICPSR version, Boulder, CO: Keith Jaggers/College Park, MD: Ted Robert Gurr [producers], 1995. Ann Arbor, MI: Inter-university Consortium for Political and Social Research [distributor], 1996.

Jardine, Matthew (1994) 'Recent books on Indonesia's occupation of East Timor and the

East Timorese struggle for self-determination', *Bulletin of Concerned Asian Scholars* 26(2): 119 -127.

Katada, Saori N. (1997) 'Two aid hegemons: Japanese–U.S. interaction and aid allocation to Latin America and the Caribbean', *World Development* 25: 931–45.

Keck, Margaret E. and Kathryn Sikkink (1998) *Activists beyond Borders: Advocacy Networks in International Politics*, Ithaca, NY and London: Cornell University Press.

Keenleyside, T. A. (1988) 'Development assistance', in Matthews, Robert O. and Cranford Pratt (eds) *Human Rights in Canadian Foreign Policy*, Kingston and Montreal: McGill-Queens University Press.

Keenleyside, T. A. (1996) 'Aiding rights: Canada and the advancement of human dignity', in Pratt, Cranford (ed.) *Canadian International Development Policies: An Appraisal*, Montreal and Kingston: McGill-Queen's University Press.

Keenleyside, T. A. and Patricia Taylor (1984) 'The impact of human rights violations on the conduct of Canadian bilateral relations: a contemporary dilemma', *Behind the Headlines* 42(Nov.): 1–27.

Keohane, Robert O. (1993) 'Institutional theory and the realist challenge after the Cold War', in David A. Baldwin (ed.) *Neorealism and Neoliberalism: The Contemporary Debate*, New York: Columbia University Press.

Kernell, Samuel (1993) *Going Public: New Strategies of Presidential Leadership*, Washington, DC: Congressional Quarterly Press.

Krasner, Stephen D. (1978) *Defending the National Interest: Raw Materials Investments and U.S. Foreign Policy*, Princeton, NJ: Princeton University Press.

Labour Party (1997) *Labour Party Manifesto*, London: Labour Party. Online. Available at: www.labour-party.org.uk/manifestos/1997/1997-labour-manifesto.shtml last accessed 12 May 2007).

Lancaster, Carol and Ann Van Dusen (2005) *Organizing US Foreign Aid: Confronting the Challenges of the Twenty-First Century*, Washington, DC: Brookings Institution.

Larsen, Henrik (1997) *Foreign Policy and Discourse Analysis: France, Britain, and Europe*, London and New York: Routledge.

Lieber, Robert J. (ed.) (1997) *Eagle Adrift: American Foreign Policy at the end of the Century*, New York: Longman.

Lipson, Charles (1993) 'International cooperation in economic and security affairs', in David A. Baldwin (ed.) *Neorealism and Neoliberalism: The Contemporary Debate*, New York: Columbia University Press.

Luard, Evan (1981) *Human Rights and Foreign Policy*, Oxford: Pergamon Press.

Lumsdaine, David Halloran (1993) *Moral Vision in International Politics: The Foreign Aid Regime, 1949–1989*, Princeton, NJ: Princeton University Press.

Mackie, J. A. C. (ed.) (1975) 'Introduction', in *Australia in the New World Order: Foreign Policy in the 1970s*, Melbourne: Thomas Nelson Ltd.

Maizels, Alfred and Michiko K. Nissanke (1984) 'Motivations for aid to developing countries', *World Development* 12(9): 879–900.

Manzer, Ronald (1988) 'Human rights in domestic politics and policy', in Matthews, Robert O. and Cranford Pratt (eds) *Human Rights in Canadian Foreign Policy*, Kingston: McGill-Queen's University Press.

Matthews, Robert O. and Cranford Pratt (1988) 'Introduction', in Matthews, Robert O. and Cranford Pratt (eds) *Human Rights in Canadian Foreign Policy*, Kingston: McGill-Queen's University Press.

McCormick, James M. and Neil Mitchell (1988) 'Is US Aid really linked to human rights abuses in Latin America', *American Journal of Political Science* 32(1): 231–39.

McKinlay, R. D. and R. Little (1978) 'A foreign policy model of the distribution of British bilateral aid, 1960–70', *British Journal of Political Science* 8(3): 313–31.

Mearsheimer, John (1990) 'Back to the future – instability in Europe after the Cold War', *International Security* 15(1): 5–56.

Mertus, Julie (2004) *Bait and Switch: Human Rights and US Foreign Policy*, London and New York: Routledge.

Millar, T. B. (1968) *Australia's Foreign Policy*, Sydney: Angus and Robertson Ltd.

Milner, W. T., S. C. Poe and D. Leblang (1999) 'Security rights, subsistence rights, and liberties: a theoretical survey of the empirical landscape', *Human Rights Quarterly* 21(2): 403–43.

Ministry of Overseas Development (1965) *Overseas Development: The Work of the New Ministry*, London: HMSO.

Miyashita, Akitoshi (1999) 'Gaiatsu and Japan's foreign aid: rethinking the reactive–proactive debate', *International Studies Quarterly* 43: 695–732.

Money, Jeannette (1999) *Fences and Neighbors: The Political Geography of Immigration Control*, Ithaca, NY: Cornell University Press.

Morrison, David (1996) 'The Choice of Bilateral Aid Recipients', in Pratt, Cranford (ed.) *Canadian International Development Policies: An Appraisal*, Montreal and Kingston: McGill-Queen's University Press.

Morrison, David (1998) *Aid and Ebb Tide: A History of CIDA and Canadian Development Assistance*, Waterloo, Ontario: Wilfred Laurier Press.

Morrison, David (2000) 'Canadian aid: a mixed record and an uncertain future', in Jim Freedman (ed.) *Transforming Development: Foreign Aid for a Changing World*, Toronto: University of Toronto Press, 15–37.

Morrissey, Oliver (2005) 'British aid policy in the "Short-Blair" years', in Hoebink, Paul, and Olav Stokke (eds) (2005) *Perspectives on European Development Cooperation*, London and New York: Routledge.

Morrissey, Oliver, Brian Smith and David Horesh (1992) *British Aid and International Trade*, Buckingham: Open University Press.

Morrow, James D., Randolph M. Siverson and Tressa E. Tabares (1998) 'The political determinants of international trade: the major powers, 1907–1990', *American Political Science Review* 92(3): 649–61.

Neumeyer, Eric (2004) *The Pattern of Aid Giving: The Impact of Good Governance on Development Assistance*, London and New York: Routledge.

Nossal, Kim Richard (1988) 'Cabin'd, cribb'd, confin'd: Canada's interest in human rights', in Matthews, Robert O. and Cranford Pratt (eds) *Human Rights in Canadian Foreign Policy*, Kingston: McGill-Queen's University Press.

Olson, Mancur (1965) *The Logic of Collective Action*, Cambridge, MA: Harvard University Press.

O'Neill, Tammie (ed.) (2006) *Human Rights and Poverty Reduction: Realities, Controversies and Strategies*, London: Overseas Development Institute.

Opoku-Dapaah, E. (2002) 'International aid: a study of Canadian opinions', *Canadian Journal of Development Studies* 23(4): 775–98.

Organization for Economic Cooperation and Development (various years) *Geographical Distribution of Financial Flows*, Paris: OECD.

Organization for Economic Cooperation and Development, Development Assistance Committee (1994a) *Development Cooperation Review Series: Canada*, Paris: OECD.

Organization for Economic Cooperation and Development, Development Assistance

Committee (1994b) *Development Cooperation Review Series: United Kingdom*, Paris: OECD.

Organization for Economic Cooperation and Development, Development Assistance Committee (1996) *Development Cooperation Review Series: Australia*, Paris: OECD.

Organization for Economic Cooperation and Development, Development Assistance Committee (1997) 'DAC policy statement: conflict, peace and development co-operation on the threshold of the 21st century', Paris: OECD. Online. Available at: www.oecd.org/pdf/M000015000/M00015054.pdf (accessed 7 August 2006).

Organization for Economic Cooperation and Development (2001) *Descriptions of Aid Categories*, Paris: OECD. Online. Available at: www.oecd.org//dac/ pdf/DAC7B.PDF (accessed 23 March 2001).

Organization for Economic Cooperation and Development (2001) *Assistance Guidelines*, Paris: OECD. Online. Available at: www.oecd.org//daf/ASIAcom/assistance/uz.htm (accessed 26 March 2001).

Organization for Economic Cooperation and Development (2003) *DAC Peer Review: Japan*, Paris: OECD. Online. Available at: www.oecd.org/document/10/0, 2340,en_2649_37413_22579914_1_1_1_37413,00.html (accessed 7 May 2007).

Organization for Economic Cooperation and Development (2004a) *DAC Peer Review: Australia*, Paris: OECD. Online. Available at: www.oecd.org/document/33/ 0,2340,en_2649_37413_34227425_1_1_1_37413,00.html (accessed 7 May 2007).

Organization for Economic Cooperation and Development (2004b) *DAC Peer Review: Norway*, Paris: OECD. Online. Available at: www.oecd.org/document/0/0,2340, en_2649_37413_33989696 1_1_1_37413,00.html (accessed 7 May 2007).

Organization for Economic Cooperation and Development (2004c) *DAC Peer Review: United States*, Paris: OECD. Online. Available at: www.oecd.org/document/27/ 0,2340,cn_2649_37413_37829787_1_1_1_37413,00.html (accessed 7 May 2007).

Organski, A. F. K. (1990) *The $36 Billion Dollar Bargain*, New York: Columbia University Press.

Orr, Robert M. (1990) *The Emergence of Japan's Foreign Aid Power*, New York and Oxford: Columbia University Press.

Orr, Robert M. (2003) *The Domestic Dimensions of Japanese Foreign Aid*, Kuala Lumpur: Centre for Japan Studies.

Oxfam Australia (2005) *Submission to the White Paper on Australia's Aid Program*. Online. Available at: www.oxfam.org.au/campaigns/submissions/aidprocess0905.pdf (accessed 15 August 2007).

Palmer, Glenn and Patrick M. Regan (1999) 'Power, domestic structure, and parties: untangling entangling democracies', paper presented at the 1999 Annual Meeting of the Peace Science Society.

Parliament of Australia (2001a) 'Report of the Joint Standing Committee on Foreign Affairs, Defense and Trade on the link between aid and human rights', Canberra: Government of Australia.

Parliament of Australia (2001b) *Foreign and Trade Issues in the Parliament*, Canberra: Government of Australia.

Poe, Steven C. (1990) 'Human rights and United States foreign aid – a review of quantitative studies and suggestions for future research', *Human Rights Quarterly* 12(4): 499–512.

Poe, Steven C. (1991) 'Human rights and the allocation of US military assistance', *Journal of Peace Research* 28(2): 205–16.

Poe, Steven C. (1992) 'Human rights and economic aid allocation under Ronald Reagan and Jimmy Carter', *American Journal of Political Science* 36(1): 147–67.

Poe, Steven C., C. Neal Tate and Linda Camp Keith (1999) 'Repression of the human right to personal integrity revisited: a global cross-national study covering the years 1976–1993', *International Studies Quarterly* 43(2): 291–313.

Pomper, Gerald M. (1993) *The Election of 1992: Reports and Interpretation*, Chatham, NJ: Chatham House Publishing.

Pratt, Cranford (1990) Middle Power Internationalism: The North–South Dimension, Kingston and Buffalo: McGill-Queen's University Press.

Pratt, Cranford (1996a) 'Humane internationalism and Canadian development assistance policies', in Pratt, Cranford (ed.) *Canadian International Development Assistance Policies: An Appraisal*, Montreal and Kingston: McGill-Queen's University Press.

Pratt, Cranford (1996b) 'Canadian development assistance: a profile', in Pratt, Cranford (ed.) *Canadian International Development Assistance Policies: An Appraisal*, Montreal and Kingston: McGill-Queen's University Press.

Pratt, Cranford (ed.) (1996c) *Canadian International Development Assistance Policies: An Appraisal*, Montreal and Kingston: McGill-Queens University Press.

Prins, Brandon C. and Chris Sprecher (1999) 'Institutional constraints, political opposition, and interstate dispute escalation: evidence from parliamentary systems, 1946–89', *Journal of Peace Research* 36(3): 271–87.

'Protocol for the assessment of nonviolent direct action' (PANDA) (2002) Cambridge, MA: Harvard University PONSACS Project. Online. Available at: www.wcfia.harvard.edu/ponsacs/panda.htm (accessed 8 July 2002).

Purdue University Political Terror Scale (1999) Purdue, IN: Purdue University Global Studies Program, Global Governance and Human Rights, Michael Stohl, Convenor. Online. Available at: www.ippu/purdue.edu/info/gsp/govern.htm (accessed 28 March 2006).

Raffer, Kunibert and H. W. Singer (1996) *The Foreign Aid Business: Economic Assistance and Development Cooperation*, Cheltenham: Edward Elgar.

Rawkins, Phillip (1996) 'An institutional analysis of CIDA'. in Pratt, Cranford (ed.) *Canadian International Development Assistance Policies: An Appraisal*, Montreal and Kingston: McGill-Queen's University Press.

Ray, James Lee (1998) *Global Politics*, Boston, MA: Houghton Mifflin.

Reed, William (2000) 'A unified statistical model of conflict onset and escalation', *American Journal of Political Science* 44(1): 84–93.

Reiter, Dan and Allan C. Stam (1998) 'Democracy, war initiation, and victory,' *American Political Science Review* 92: 377–89.

Riddell, Roger C. (1987) *Foreign Aid Reconsidered*, Baltimore, MD: Johns Hopkins University Press.

Russett, Bruce (1996) 'The fact of the democratic peace', in Michael E. Brown, Sean M. Lynn-Jones and Steven E. Miller (eds) *Debating the Democratic Peace*, Cambridge, MA: MIT Press.

Scharfe, Sharon (1996) *Complicity-Human Rights and Canadian Foreign Policy: The Case of East Timor*, Montreal and New York: Black Rose Books.

Shue, Henry (1996) *Basic Rights: Subsistence, Affluence and US Foreign Policy*, Princeton, NJ: Princeton University Press.

Sikkink, Kathryn (1991) *Ideas and Institutions: Developmentalism in Brazil and Argentina*, Ithaca, NY and London: Cornell University Press.

Sikkink, Kathryn (2004) *Mixed Signals: US Human Rights Policy and Latin America*, Ithaca, NY and London: Cornell University Press.

Singer, David J., and Melvin Small (1991*) Annual Alliance Membership Data, 1815–1965*, [Computer file], ICPSR version, Ann Arbor, MI: University of Michigan Mental Health Institute, Correlates of War Project [producer], Ann Arbor: Inter-university Consortium for Political and Social Research [distributor].

Singer, J. David and Melvin Small. Correlates Of War Project: International and Civil War Data, 1816–1992 [Computer file]. Ann Arbor: J. David Singer and Melvin Small [producers], 1993. Ann Arbor, MI: Inter-university Consortium for Political and Social Research [distributor].

Skilling, H. Gordon (1988) 'The Helsinki Process', in Matthews, Robert O. and Cranford Pratt (eds) *Human Rights in Canadian Foreign Policy*, Kingston: McGill-Queen's University Press.

Smith, Gary, Dave Cox and Scott Burchill (1996) *Australia in the World: An Introduction to Australian Foreign Policy*, Melbourne, Oxford and New York: Oxford University Press.

Spicer, Keith (1966) *A Samaritan State? External Aid in Canada's Foreign Policy*, Toronto: University of Toronto Press.

Stairs, Dennis (2005) *Confusing the Innocent with Numbers and Categories*, Calgary, Alberta: Canadian Defence and Foreign Affairs Institute, December.

Stohl, Michael (1973) *The Purdue Political Terror Scale*, Purdue, IN: Codebook.

Stokke, Martin (ed.) (1995) *Aid and Political Conditionality*, London and Portland, OR: F. Cass.

Stokke, Olav (ed.) (1989a) *Western Middle Powers and Global Poverty*, Uppsala: Scandinavian Institute of African Studies.

Stokke, Olav (1989b) 'The determinants of Norwegian aid policy', in Stokke, Olav (ed.) *Western Middle Powers and Global Poverty*, Uppsala: Scandinavian Institute of African Studies.

Stokke, Olav (2005) 'Norwegian Aid Policy: Continuity and Change in the 1990s and Beyond, in Hoebink, Paul and Olav Stokke (eds) (2005) *Perspectives on European Development Cooperation: Policy and Performance of Individual Donor Countries and the EU*, London and New York: Routledge.

Studenmund, A. H. (1992), *Using Econometrics: A Practical Guide*, New York: Harper-Collins.

Stumpf, Waldo, 'Birth and death of the South African nuclear weapons program', Washington, DC: Federation of American Scientists. Online. Available at: www.fas.org/nuke/guide/rsa/nuke/stumpf.htm (accessed 24 March 2006).

Theakston, Kevin (ed.) (2004) *British Foreign Secretaries since 1974*, London and New York: Routledge.

Therien, Jean-Phillipe (1996) 'Canadian aid: a comparative analysis', in Pratt, |Cranford (ed.) *Canadian International Development Assistance Policies: An Appraisal*, Montreal and Kingston: McGill-Queen's University Press.

Thorp, Willard L. (1971) *The Reality of Foreign Aid*, New York: Council on Foreign Relations.

Tomasevski, Katarina (1993) *Development Aid and Human Rights Revisited*, London: Pinter Publishers Ltd.

Tsebelis, George (1999) 'Veto Players and Law Production in Parliamentary Democracies: An Empirical Analysis', *American Political Science Review* 93 (3): 591–608.

Tsebelis, George and Jeannette Money (1999) *Bicameralism*, Cambridge: Cambridge University Press.

Tuman, John P., Jonathan Strand and Craig Emmert (2006) 'In the shadow of U.S. hegemony?: a study of Japanese ODA, 1979–2002', paper presented at the 2006 Annual Meeting of the International Studies Association, San Diego, CA, March.

Uhr, John (2005) *Terms of Trust: Arguments over Ethics in Australian Government*, Sydney: University of New South Wales Press.

United Nations (1997) *Relief Web*, New York: United Nations. Online. Available at: www.reliefweb.int/rw/dbc.nsf/doc100?OpenForm (accessed 7 May 2007).

Van Belle, Douglas A., Jean-Sebastien Rioux, and David M. Potter (2004) *Media, Bureaucracies, and Foreign Aid: A Comparative Analysis of the United States, the United Kingdom, Canada, France, and Japan*, New York and Basingstoke: Palgrave Macmillan.

Vincent, R. J. (1986) 'Introduction', in Vincent, R. J. (ed.) *Foreign Policy and Human Rights: Issues and Responses*, Cambridge: Cambridge University Press.

Wallace, William (1975) *The Foreign Policy Process in Britain*, London: Royal Institute of International Affairs.

Waltz, Kenneth (1959) *Man, the State, and War*, New York: Columbia University Press.

Waltz, Kenneth (1979) *Theory of International Politics*, Reading, MA: Addison Wesley.

Wilson, A. N. (2004) *London: A History*, New York: Modern Library.

Wilson, Woodrow (1917) Message to Congress asking for declaration of war, delivered 2 April.

Wright, Tony (ed.) (2000) *The British Political Process: An Introduction*, London and New York: Routledge.

Wright, Tony (2003) *British Politics: A Very Short Introduction*, Oxford: Oxford University Press.

Zaller, John (1992) *The Nature and Origins of Mass Opinion*, Cambridge: Cambridge University Press.

Index

eBooks – at www.eBookstore.tandf.co.uk

A library at your fingertips!

eBooks are electronic versions of printed books. You can store them on your PC/laptop or browse them online.

They have advantages for anyone needing rapid access to a wide variety of published, copyright information.

eBooks can help your research by enabling you to bookmark chapters, annotate text and use instant searches to find specific words or phrases. Several eBook files would fit on even a small laptop or PDA.

NEW: Save money by eSubscribing: cheap, online access to any eBook for as long as you need it.

Annual subscription packages

We now offer special low-cost bulk subscriptions to packages of eBooks in certain subject areas. These are available to libraries or to individuals.

For more information please contact webmaster.ebooks@tandf.co.uk

We're continually developing the eBook concept, so keep up to date by visiting the website.

www.eBookstore.tandf.co.uk